Design Literacy

Understanding Graphic Design

Steven Heller and Karen Pomeroy

ALLWORTH PRESS
NEW YORK

Published by Allworth Press
An imprint of Allworth Communications
10 East 23rd Street, New York, NY 10010

Cover and book design by James Victore, New York, NY

Page composition by Sharp Des!gns, Holt, MI

Blue Rabbit photograph reproduced on page 267 © Rick Dublin

ISBN: 1-880559-76-5 $32509\!$

Library of Congress Catalog Card Number: 96-79695

Printed in Canada

Contents

LANGUAGE

IDENTITY

INFORMATION

ICONOGRAPHY

STYLE

COMMERCE

Acknowledgments

This book was made possible by the support and encouragement of Tad Crawford, the publisher of Allworth Press, who has taken the lead in the publication of critical books on graphic design. Thanks also to Ted Gachot, editor at Allworth Press, for his invaluable contributions; to James Victore, designer of this book, for his splendid cover and interior design; to Charlie Sharp for his diligent page composition; and to Rick Dublin for use of his *Blue Rabbit* photograph in the "NYNEX" essay.

Many of the essays in this book appeared in different forms in various design magazines and journals. Much appreciation goes to the editors of these periodicals for providing an outlet that includes the range of material represented in this book. Thanks to Martin Fox, *Print* magazine, for his unflagging enthusiasm and tough editing; Julie Lasky, *Print* magazine, for her intellectual rigor; Rick Poynor, *Eye* magazine, for a journal that raised design from a craft to an art; Martin Neumeier, *Critique*, for a unique outlet of practical criticism; Chee Perlman, *I.D.*, for a smart herd of criticism and journalism; Margaret Richardson, *U&lc*, for producing a joyous quarterly; and Victor Margolin, *Design Issues*, for his continued enthusiastic support. To Ric Grefé, director of the American Institute of Graphic Arts, much gratitude for his support of the *AIGA Journal of Graphic Design*. And special thanks to Caroline Hightower, former director of the AIGA, for opening its doors fifteen years ago to serious commentary.

Finally, to Paul Rand, whose writing has been a source of inspiration and knowledge.

Introduction

There is now a realization that graphic design is not as ephemeral as the paper it is printed on. Certain advertisements, posters, packages, logos, books, and magazines endure as signposts of artistic, commercial, and technological achievement that often speak more about particular epochs or milieus than fine art. Many objects of graphic design are preserved and studied as more than mere historical wallpaper. Curiously, though, the makers of these objects, graphic designers, have tended to undervalue the historical significance of the artifacts found in their own backyards. Those who claim visual literacy are often ignorant when it comes to understanding and appreciating objects that are imprinted with the language of their own practice.

As an alternative to the omnibus compilations that reduce graphic design to just so much visual noise, *Design Literacy: Understanding Graphic Design* examines a variety of individual objects and focuses on their significance in the broader histories of graphic design and popular culture. Although graphic design can be defined in terms of critical masses of form and style that shift according to the dictates of the marketplace, an understanding of the singular work can be useful in determining how an individual designer makes graphic design operate. Graphic designers happily devour eye candy found in scores of design books, magazines, and annuals, but should also appreciate individual works of design as sources of historical information and contemporary inspiration.

Rather than typical case studies, which trace the stages of creation and production, the essays in *Design Literacy* address the inner workings of an eclectic collection of vintage and contemporary objects in numerous media. Each represents a unique development that relates to other manifestations of design culture. The object is not viewed as fetish, but as clue to the thinking of the designer and the working of the design. These object lessons are alternatives to such pedagogical conventions as the "great master" principle, which addresses the maker within a canon or pantheon; the "great movement" principle, which attributes certain characteristics to a school or ideology; or the "great style" principle, which categorizes design according to period, fashion, or trend. This is not to imply that these methods are invalid, but merely to show that understanding the object in context moves graphic design from a purely formal arena to a social and political one.

The majority of the objects examined here are created by known individuals, but anonymous work is also recognized. Most of the essays examine single objects or a group of related objects, but a few address larger genres when one work alone does not tell a complete enough story, as is the case with fascist posters or cigarette advertisements for women. Some of the objects have already been elevated to the design pantheon, such as A. M. Cassandre's Peignot typeface, Saul Bass's graphics for *Man with the Golden Arm*, or Milton Glaser's *Dylan* poster. Others are only marginally noticed, if noticed at all, in design history: for example Robbie Conal's *Men With No Lips* poster, Art Chantry's *Propaganda* poster, or the *East Village Other*. A few were selected because they are icons of their respective eras, others because they are superior designs that are routinely overlooked. We have tried to balance design objects that are acknowledged as important with those we personally believe should be so acknowledged.

With work that spans the twentieth century—from Lucian Bernhard's 1906 *Preister Match* poster to Paula Scher's 1996 New York Public Theater posters—this book might be seen as a collection of sidebars dotting a historical time line. Nevertheless, the material is not organized chronologically but thematically, according to the role the object has played in art and commerce. Within each section, however, the pieces are placed in more or less chronological order for purposes of context.

Sections include Persuasion: design in the service of control and influence; Language: design as a vocabulary; Identity: design as signature; Information: design as guidepost and pathway; Iconography: design as indelible symbol; Style: design as aesthetics and form; Media: design in mass communication; and Commerce: design as marketing tool. Admittedly, some of these subjects overlap and intersect, which is how design operates in the world. But within each section the objects were selected to provide a window on how the specific theme is served.

Wherever possible the objects' designers are quoted, but *Design Literacy* is by no means a verbatim account of their respective processes. The essays combine analysis and critique, aided by the makers' descriptions but not solely based on their insights. This book contains commentary that sometimes echoes the canon and at other times challenges it. We hope you will come away with the sense that although these objects may have been created for ephemeral purposes, each is deeply rooted in a popular culture where graphic design is a force to be reckoned with.

Many of these essays are adapted from articles, essays, and reviews by Steven Heller that were previously published in Print, Eye, U&lc, I.D., Critique, *and the* AIGA Journal of Graphic Design; *others were written expressly for this volume.*

Persuasion

DESIGN IN THE SERVICE OF CONTROL AND INFLUENCE

Simplicissimus Poster

THOMAS THEODORE HEINE

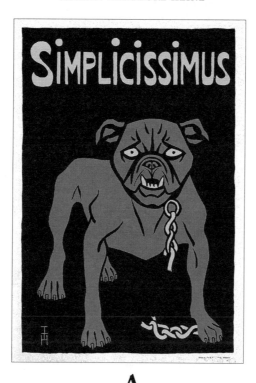

A red bulldog stares menacingly through stone-cold white eyes. A broken chain hangs from its neck. With sharp, spiky teeth it eagerly waits to attack unsuspecting fools, nitwits, and government buffoons.

Beware! This is not just some rabid canine, but the most unyielding watchdog ever conceived. Born not of flesh and blood, but of ink and brush, this bulldog was the embodiment of a nation's anger, the charged graphic emblem of *Simplicissimus,* one of the most biting, satirically critical magazines ever published. Its color was a flag, and its breed symbolized the snarling editorial policy of the weekly tabloid. Founded in 1896 in Munich, Germany, by a cadre of artists and writers that included Thomas Mann, *Simplicissimus* was fervently antibourgeois and unrepentantly *Volkish* (populist) in its rejection of materialism and modernization.

Simplicissimus, or *der Simpl,* as it was known, assailed German Kaiser Wilhelm II and his ministers, the Protestant clergy, military officers, government bureaucracy, urbanization, and industrialization while it lionized the peasant farmer and worker. The red bulldog symbolized the *Volk,* or common people, who were portrayed in the magazine's cartoons and caricatures as feisty opponents to the ruling class, even if in reality this was an exaggerated view.

The authorities used stern measures to muzzle the dog, but despite frequent censorship and periodic arrests, this illustrated tabloid rarely missed an appearance. When it was finally confiscated by the police, the black, red, and white poster on which the bulldog stood poised reminded friend and foe alike that *der Simpl* would not be chained up for long. Rows of these posters—designed in 1897 by Thomas Theodore Heine (1867–1948), a cartoonist and co-editor of *Simplicissimus*—were hung for months at a time and were replenished regularly with fresh ones. Bans, on the other hand, lasted only a week or two and usually attracted more new readers than they discouraged.

This was the power of *Simplicissimus,* the name borrowed from a fifteenth-century literary character, Simplicus Simplicissimus, who acted the fool around the aristocracy while tricking them into exposing their folly and corruption. This was Heine's reason for designing a somewhat comic bulldog mascot instead of a more frightening graphic icon.

The red bulldog was just one weapon in *der Simpl's* graphic arsenal. There were other mascots, though none as versatile. Whether it was the angry version from Heine's poster or other, more comical iterations (including one of the bulldog urinating on the leg of an official), anyone looking for relief from Wilhelmian oppression could find an ally, at least once a week on paper, under the sign of the bulldog.

Der Simpl vehemently critiqued the status quo until the advent of World War I when it was conscripted as a tool of German propaganda. Even in its patriotic form it was biting, proving that humor could be effectively used for the wrong causes. After the war, during the 1920s and early 1930s, it resumed its critical stance attacking Italian fascism and the emergence of first German Freikorps (paramilitary right-wing militias) and later Nazism. During this era the *Volk* were no longer portrayed as heroes. Working and peasant class romanticism was replaced by a foreboding and cynicism—a logical response to a devastating and horrific war. The Kaiser had abdicated prior to the war's end and was replaced by the Weimar Republic, the doomed democratic experiment that *der Simpl* reluctantly critiqued for its deficiencies and the incompetencies of its leadership. The red bulldog continued as the mascot, however, and *Simplicissimus* remained a social watchdog until 1933 when the Nazis came to power and made it into their lap dog.

Der Simpl is remembered for its golden age, from 1896 to 1914, when it published hundreds of strident political and social caricatures and cartoons attacking anything that suggested social and political folly. Few other journals had such a profound influence, not only on public opinion, but also on graphic style. The late 1890s was an era of artistic revolution, and *der Simpl* together with its cousin the cultural journal *Jugend* introduced to polemical graphics a variant of French art nouveau called Jugendstil. German Jugendstil was more rectilinear than curvilinear, rejecting the floreated decoration so popular in France. Emphasizing chiaroscuro values and bold economical brush strokes, *der Simpl's* artists departed from common academic verities; in turn they practiced a proto-expressionistic art.

Simplicissimus was one of the unrecognized tribunes of early modernism. The red bulldog exemplifies modern simplicity. Drawn in the manner of a woodcut, Heine used white paint to cut away extraneous lines, leaving only the most descriptive features and penetrating expression behind. Heine's was the prototypical modern logo. In subsequent iterations the red bulldog was further geometricized, suggesting the roots of the late 1970s-era corporate logo.

In its day Heine's *Simplicissimus* poster was a radical departure from typically fussy placards layered with excessive ornamentation and multiple colors. The red bulldog set against black was the antecedent of the German *Sachplakat* (or object poster) introduced by designer Lucian Bernhard eight years later in Berlin. Bernhard's posters were characterized by a single object set against a flat color with only a bold headline to identify the brand being advertised.

Heine's red bulldog poster was arguably inelegant. The sans-serif logo of the magazine *der Simpl* was more refined than the poster lettering. Heine's lettering was crudely hand drawn (on those versions of the poster where the ten pfenning price was included, it was downright messy). Yet the poster was a totality. The lettering suggested immediacy and complimented the bulldog's tense, frozen stance. This is perhaps one of Heine's most brilliant, persuasive, and iconographic works; what followed were mere cartoons.

Benito Mussolini fancied himself an art director. Although this is of minor importance to world history, his interest in visual propaganda had significant effect in Italy. In the early years of the fascist regime, beginning in 1921 when King Victor Emanuel II handed the reigns of government to Mussolini, fascism was viewed in Italy and abroad as the ideology of renewal. It signaled both the avant-garde and a return to the glories of classical Rome, and was a viable alternative to communism, which was perceived by many as the greater threat. Understanding that this movement meant different things to different people, Mussolini sought to forge unity, if not uniformity. The most obvious unifying force was the fascist paramilitary, or militia, initially organized as bands of thugs who violently propagated fascism. While the legions of parading black shirts were impressive in public, print and radio propaganda were vigorously employed to insure a lasting impact on the populace. Posters were effective tools. Il Duce's hard-jawed visage and streamlined fascist militiaman were ubiquitous icons on official street graphics.

Prior to World War II Italian fascist poster design was among the most exquisite of any nation. Italian graphic artists smartly adapted the *art moderne*, or art deco, style as a marketing tool for the new regime. Mussolini's rise to power was further aided by Italian futurist artists and poets, notably F. T. Marinetti, whose eccentric visual manifestos and poetic typography rhapsodized fascism's virtues. Futurism's raw aesthetic was repellent to many conservative fascist leaders, but aspects of the avant-garde art were valuable to the party's image. Futurists invented advertising methods that aggressively presented the party in a progressive light. Fortunato Depero, a futurist advertising designer, synthesized the raw expression into an accessible visual language combining aspects of cubism, expressionism, primitivism, and futurism into an unique decorative vocabulary. Depero was by far the most inventive graphic designer in Italy during the late 1920s and 1930s.

The Italian poster was more experimental than its German counterpart. The Nazis replaced modern art with turgid realism. But in the early years of the fascist regime, the Italians did embrace modernism, though Mussolini's personal tastes ran towards the monumental. The party allowed various approaches including a modicum of abstraction to enter their propaganda, making it easier for modernistic approaches to flourish.

Art moderne was both a compromise to youthful aesthetics and a viable tool for the conservative Fascist advertising directors who appreciated its romantic, heroic, and monumental characteristics. Airbrushed surfaces symbolized the machine-age progress that Mussolini sought to advance. *Art moderne*'s neoclassicism gave old symbols new veneers. Artists practicing *art moderne* smoothed away the cracks in Roman antiquities and brought the artifacts of Italy's glorious past up to date.

Not all propaganda was produced specifically for the party. Fascism was promoted as a way of life, and fascist iconography, particularly the ancient Roman axe, or fasces, that was adopted as the official party symbol, was omnipresent on posters and advertisements for coffee, banks, and travel services, among others. Italy's most skilled graphic designers, among them Federico Seneca, Erberto Carboni, and Oscar Signorini, transformed everyday products into personifications of the fascist spirit. The challenge most commonly faced by artists and designers was how to include the fasces in a work of art or design. In a typical manifestation, an upwardly thrusting fasces had a monolithic aura.

While adhering to a national graphic style, Italian artists were allowed to exploit the styles of their regions. Even the most modernistic images were somehow rooted in the Italian vernacular. In contrast to the strict uniformity of most German graphics, in Italy moderated individuality, consistent with the national character, was accepted until the late 1930s when the battle for world domination took precedence over domestic issues. While the party was improving the standard of living, "soft-sell" graphics lulled the citizenry into patriotism. But when Mussolini began his imperialistic pursuits in the mid 1930s "hard-sell" graphics became necessary. Propaganda was set for war with graphics that celebrated the glories of victory. By the beginning of World War II Italy's graphic style resembled that of her Nazi ally. And during the war, as Italian soldiers were dying, the propaganda machine pumped out graphics to convince the masses that all was not lost.

Neue Jugend

JOHN HEARTFIELD

The Malik Verlag was established in March 1917 in the critical period before the fall of Imperial Germany and the birth of the Weimar Republic. This politically active German socialist publisher of periodicals, portfolios, broadsheets, and books of fiction and nonfiction—whose first periodical was entitled *Neue Jugend*, or New Youth—is the trunk of the historical tree from which American alternative publishing of the 1960s was only a branch and from which elements of contemporary graphic design have surely grown. Its leading graphistes, George Grosz and John Heartfield (1891–1968) are known, studied, and appreciated today; but the Malik Verlag as an entity is virtually unknown, though it played a major role in German left-wing politics, literature, and the graphic style of the Weimar period.

In 1915 before Malik Verlag was conceived, John Heartfield's brother, the poet, Weiland Herzfeld was introduced to Georg Grosz and "fell in love" with his drawings. "Grosz felt that was an inappropriate response," wrote Herzfeld in *The Malik Verlag 1916–1947* (Goethe House, New York). "He told me: '. . . Herzfeld my works are worthless. Whatever you and I and any other incompetent people think of them is completely inconsequential. . . . If my drawings were of some value they would be paid for accordingly. . . .' His comments were the final impetus for the founding of the periodical *Neue Jugend* with Herzfeld as editor." The journal became an outlet for Grosz's political satires and "for all those who encountered opposition to their political ideas and lack of understanding by the public," continued Herzfeld. "We beg all European artists and intellectuals who are neither senile nor submissive to join us as contributors . . . ," states the call for contributors, which appealed to the cream of the German left. Many rose to the occasion with scabrous attacks against the ailing government.

Neue Jugend, then a quarto-sized monthly, was almost immediately banned in the autumn of 1916, and Weiland Herzfeld was coincidentally called to the Western Front. While he was away, in the spring of 1917, Heartfield resumed publishing *Neue Jugend* in its larger, newspaper format. Always the clever subversive, Heartfield had found a way to circumvent the ban by making the journal into a prospectus—an advertisement, essentially—for a portfolio of Georg Grosz drawings. Since this *Neue Jugend* was not strictly a publication the censors were befuddled.

During the war years all new journals and publishing houses needed a license, granted only when "pressing need" existed. While no such need existed for Heartfield and Herzfeld's left-wing publishing venture, they dreamed up a plan that would confuse the bureaucrats. Heartfield slyly stated in the application for the founding of the Malik Publishing House that German writer Else Lasker-Schüler's novella "Der Malik" (which translated from Turkish meant not only "prince," but also, fittingly, "robber chief,") had appeared in installments in *Neue Jugend.* "To complete its publication (keep in mind *Neue Jugend* had been banned), and for that reason only, a publishing house was needed," recalled Herzfeld. The authorities did not immediately catch on, granted the license, and the Malik Verlag proceeded instead to publish two Georg Grosz portfolios and two issues of a thinly disguised *Neue Jugend.*

The publication's design was an amalgam of variegated typefaces, elaborate surprints, and various geometric color blocks. Work on this journal marked an artistic turning point for Heartfield, who had destroyed all his more formal work and embraced anti-art as a means for social protest and propaganda. In 1915 Heartfield changed his name from Herzfeld to protest German militarism. He became a charter member of the Berlin dada group, whose members included Georg Grosz, Hannah Höch, Raoul Hausmann, Otto Dix, and Herzfeld. Heartfield originally adopted the title dada-monteur, eschewing the term *artist* in favor of *monteur,* which means "machinist," in an angry rejection of bourgeois art. He later changed to photomonteur because he believed that photography was the vanguard of a new art that would inevitably displace painting altogether.

The look of the new *Neue Jugend* was different, but the content continued in the style of the original monthly and, with its satire and pacifist stance, was just as outrageous in the eyes of the regime. Publication was summarily ceased in June 1917, but the journal existed just long enough for Heartfield to initiate the typographic revolution that would subsequently influence the New Typography. *Neue Jugend* was also a stepping stone for other German dada publications. The one-shot tabloid, *Jedermann sein eigner Fussball* ("everyman his own football," 1919), which included the first political photomontage created by Heartfield—a fan with the leaders of the new Weimar government superimposed—is a classic dada document. Two ongoing sister publications, *Die Pliete* (1919–1922) and *Der Gegner* (1919–1922), designed by Heartfield with drawings by Grosz, were the agitational arm of the German communist party, which, like the

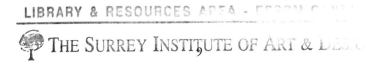

members of the dada group and Spartakus Bund, fought against the emerging right wing, the Nazis.

Heartfield is remembered today for his strident anti-Nazi photomontages for the *Arbeiter Illustierte Zeitung* (AIZ), but as art director for the Malik Verlag he was an innovative jacket and cover designer. His graphic imprimatur formed the visual personality of the publishing house and, moreover, was the model for kindred publishers active during the 1920s.

Under Heartfield's direction the Malik Verlag was a wellspring of avant-garde graphic design. They were influenced by Russian and Italian futurism, yet introduced Germans to typographic experiments that were later brought to fruition by Russian constructivists, Dutch de Stijl, and German dadaists.

Nie

TADEUSZ TREPKOWSKI

Tadeusz Trepkowski's (1914–1956) 1953 *Nie* (Polish for "no") was the first Polish poster to make an impact on American designers. The ruins of a devastated city framed within the silhouette of a falling bomb, in its graphic way, was as expressive of the horrors of World War II as the numbing photographs of carnage published in *Life* and other American magazines. Anyone who saw multiples of this poster hanging in rows on what remained of Warsaw's streets understood that *Nie* was more than an antiwar image, it was a testament to the redemptive power of art.

From the vantage point across the Atlantic, Poland had resisted the occupying Nazis only to be subsumed by the Soviets. From here, Poland was a prisoner behind the Iron Curtain, its arts dictated by the constraints of socialist realism. *Nie,* the first glimpse that many in the West had of powerful Polish poster graphics, was also the first sign that Polish art was alive. Later, thanks to conspicuous exposure in *Graphis* and the English language *Poland* magazine, Americans learned that the Polish poster was not only alive, but was flourishing in ways that far exceeded their own graphic arts.

It is ironic that a nation under the thumb of a repressive ideology could produce a graphic style of such high quality and integrity. To American designers, the Polish poster was the epitome of expressive and stylistic freedom. In the United States, graphic artists and designers had fundamental freedom, but even the most renowned were slaves to client whim and prejudice. American business imposed fashions designed to sell products in the competitive marketplace.

Few deviated from these conventions; experimentation was suspect. This isn't to say that American design was uninspired, but the Polish poster was poetry, seemingly unfettered by agendas of state.

Are artists inspired by the idea that visual language can subvert the tunnel vision of the state? The Polish posters that surfaced in the United States suggested that either the authorities were looking the other way, or artists, like Trepkowski, were brilliant subversives. The surreal images these artists created were the means to circumvent the strictures against free expression and, at the same time, invent new methods of discourse. Trepkowski's *Nie* poster was a humanist call to sanity, and most Polish posters were designed for cultural events that did not have to sell to consumer groups, please the chairmen of major corporations, or appeal to the special interests. They did, however, have to fool a regime that was suspicious of individual expression.

Black Power/White Power

TOMI UNGERER

From time to time circumstance fosters the climate for a radical cartoonist to emerge from the ranks—one who shocks the senses and at the same time redefines the form. When Alsatian-born Tomi Ungerer's (b. 1930) work premiered in the United States in the mid 1950s, it was a shock to complacency, not because his ragged line and farcical ideas showed a clear rejection of the sentimental and romantic realism published in most mainstream magazines and advertisements, but because his satire exposed folly that native-born cartoonists were afraid to touch, or even see. Writing in *Graphis*, Manuel Gasser said of Ungerer's audacity: "one cannot help noticing that he is a grown up child. Children have a habit of coming out with the truth, even when it is least opportune."

Truth underscores Ungerer's 1967 poster on race relations in America entitled *Black Power/White Power*. First conceived in 1963 as the cover of *Monocle*, a short-lived satiric journal published in New York, this topsy-turvy image of a white man eating a black man's leg as the black man does the same to the white, was an acerbic, if unpopular, critique of the dangers within the burgeoning civil rights movement. Like a child void of propriety and manners, Ungerer naïvely, though harshly, looked at both sides of the color line and found that white and black militants were threats to a movement that most liberals of the day were unwilling to criticize. The cartoon was a pox on both their houses. By the time Ungerer published the cartoon as a poster (reportedly over a quarter of million were produced) tension between militant and nonviolent segments of the movement had become frighteningly evident.

Ungerer never felt restrained from making strong political commentary even if it offended those purportedly on his own side. Self-censorship was never an issue, and the absence of taboos in his work resulted in drawings that eschewed the clichés and universal symbols that neutralized most graphic commentaries. Being an outsider, an immigrant and peripatetic wanderer, allowed him to see through the artifice of American politics and society, and underscored his vision.

Born in Strasbourg, Alsace, Ungerer grew up under French rule and German occupation. "It gave me my first lesson in relativity and cynicism—prison camps, propaganda, bombings . . . all to culminate in an apotheosis of warfare. My taste for the macabre certainly finds its roots here," he explained. Ungerer lacked any formal art training but found solace in his art. Before embarking on a career, though, he joined the camel corps of the French Army in Africa, from which he was discharged for ill health. At the age of twenty-four, however, he came to the Untied States to be a freelance illustrator. He ultimately produced various children's books for Harper and Row. His most significant, *Crictor*, published in 1957, was the first children's book to feature a boa constrictor (then taboo) as its main character.

During the 1950s, Ungerer did not have outlets for his personal work, so he filled many sketchbooks with surreal cartoons. His *Underground Sketchbook*, which took him many years to get published, was a repository for biting comic commentaries about sex, war, death, and love. He eventually turned his attention from the general human condition to realpolitik. He rejected any semblance of idealism, especially in terms of war: "Some wars are necessary evils," he once wrote, "but Vietnam was stupid." His drawings and self-published posters were savage indictments of that war's brutality. There is the feeling in looking at sketches and posters showing soldiers brutally forcing Vietnamese to metaphorically swallow the American way of life, that everyone was had by the lies and duplicity of government and its leaders. "Because America is a gutless country," he argued. "I do a political drawing because of a need I have. Out of anger." But posters with the conceptual intensity of *Black Power/White Power*, born of pure emotion, ultimately became historical essays on the mechanisms of life. "I am not really an artist, I am a thinker. I just use my drawings as a tool to make my thoughts accessible."

An artist this mercurial might be expected to have a limited cult following, but to his surprise Ungerer became the wunderkind of American editorial and advertising art. He was given hundreds of commissions, notably a series of billboards for the New York State Lottery with the headline "Expect the Unexpected," showing absurd and ironic vignettes as only Ungerer could make them. This headline and Ungerer's ideas were eventually adopted by the *Village Voice*, New York's leading alternative newspaper, for its own advertising campaign. But the methods of the commercial world eventually soured Ungerer, and in 1970 he severed his relations. "My intention was to get away from Madison Avenue and its gold-medal-sucking bogeymen. After thirteen years of hard work I had developed an allergy to the media," he said about turning exclusively to graphic and written commentary—the activity he had been subsidizing through commercial fees. Taking on the occasional commission, during the 1970s and 1980s he remained a prolific visual essayist on the *comédie humaine*.

Men With No Lips

ROBBIE CONAL

The notice Post No Bills was coined in mid-nineteenth-century England to prevent the hangers of illegal placards from littering London's otherwise dreary streets. By law, the Post No Bills notice had to appear approximately every four feet along a wall or hoarding for it to be considered a placard-free surface; but even the threat of fine or arrest didn't daunt the erstwhile posterist in the performance of his duty. Since then, Post No Bills has become an invitation to engage in the act of posting. Once the only method of displaying advertisements and proclamations for those without access to mass media, postering is still the cheapest and most defiant means of reaching the public.

Few have challenged posting ordinances more than Venice, California–based artist/activist, Robbie Conal (b. 1944). As the leader of a national band of agitators, he has flown coast to coast armed with rolls of incendiary paper to supply an army of poster snipers. In reality, this army is a loose network of urban poster guerrillas who in the wee hours of the morning plaster their respective cities and towns with messages that addressed a variety of social ills. Since the mid 1980s, Conal has produced, at his own expense, an average of three posters a year on subjects he believes mass media has failed to cover.

Conal's first foray into confrontational street art was an enigmatic though provocative poster titled *Men With No Lips,* an attack on former President Ronald Reagan's cabinet, whose tight-lipped responses to public inquiry obfuscated the dismantling of social welfare programs at home and the undermining of sovereign governments abroad. This poster, originally designed to fit standard traffic light switching boxes—the most ubiquitous unofficial poster surface in Los Angeles—was simultaneously hung on building walls, hoardings, and lampposts in New York and Chicago. A hybrid of fine art and agitprop, *Men With No Lips* was often mistaken for a rock band advertisement. Yet after a few sightings the intent of the message to tweak American's hearts and minds out of complacency became clear.

Conal admitted his decision to become a postermaker was part of a "plot to escape from the friendly confines of the art establishment," which he joined as a painter after majoring in psychedelic drugs in college during the late 1960s. He called his brand of agitprop "infotainment," and admitted that the last thing he wanted to do as a nonsanctioned public artist on social issues was to be deadly serious. "I knew that people on the street would ignore the humorless message on their way to work in the morning, and besides, I had a sardonic twist to my sensibility. So taking a little lesson from advertising, I thought I would just pique people's interest. I wasn't interested in telling them what to think as much as getting them to think along with me, and giving them a little chuckle, too," he explained.

Conal's social activism stems from being a "red-diaper baby" raised on the "upper left side" of New York City by parents who were labor organizers. "The apple doesn't fall too far from the tree," he said. Although he spent a few years trying to reconcile the often rocky relationship between art and politics, Conal eventually discovered a process of painting and postermaking whereby he could publicly express his indignation on issues such as Iran-Contra, women's reproductive rights, and censorship.

His second poster titled *Women With Teeth* was the opposite of *Men With No Lips*. "Considering myself something of a feminist, I figured I should give [women] equal time and image," he said. The series included portraits of Nancy Reagan, Margaret Thatcher, Jeanne Kirkpatrick, and Joan Rivers (whom Conal felt had traded in her alternative culture birthright for an establishment pedigree); these also sprang up around the nation thanks to the increasing number of volunteer snipers he and his friends had recruited. The response was gratifying. "There was a lot of silent resentment on the streets," he reasoned, "so when stuff started showing up in this subversive way, I think it was like a voice for a lot of people who had been silent. This grass-roots little yelp had become a chorus."

The theme of accountability runs through Conal's work. And so his third poster titled *Speak,* which featured Conal's expressionistic rendering of Iran-gate principal Colonel Oliver North, was a mammoth wanted poster. Conal regretted that he did not have enough money to print two others in the series, *Hear* and *See,* featuring portraits of President Ronald Reagan and his security aid, John Poindexter, but he did succeed at getting *Speak* hung in some of the most visible locations around the country, including site-specific Washington, D.C.

Grapus Posters

GRAPUS

The Paris student revolution of May 1968 was one of the most dramatic political events in a decade noted for its tumult. In a modern-day storming of the Bastille, a coalition of more than ten million students and workers mounted the barricades to protest Charles de Gaulle's aging conservative government. By the end of the year the nation was paralyzed by strikes and demonstrations. In contrast to the social protest concurrently hitting many nations, this whirlwind insurgency actually shook the system, provoking substantive though temporary concessions.

Intellectuals and workers were brought to the battlements by their shared interest in social reform and by their indignation at the repression—most aggressively represented by the paramilitary National Police who were brought in to squelch the protests through violence. Both groups were further induced by the daily barrage of critical posters designed by the Atelier Populaire to inform and mobilize the populace. This group of disparate painters, graphic artists, and art students produced hundreds of iconic, one-color, brush-and-ink posters that were pasted all over Paris and became an indelible symbol of the popular uprising. In keeping with the character of collectivism, these paper bullets were unsigned by any individual. Yet by the end of the brief struggle, three of the most vociferous practitioners did become known, if not individually at first, at least as the graphic arts collective called Grapus, which later devoted itself to making graphic design for the communist party, labor unions, and the public interest.

The original principals of Grapus were Pierre Bernard, Gérard Paris-Clavel, and François

Miehe. Each studied in Poland at a different time under master poster artist Henryk Tomaszewski, where an appreciation for anarchic design was nurtured. After leaving Poland, Bernard worked for the magazine *Jeune Afrique* and Paris-Clavel at a fashion studio. The trio came together in May 1968 at the École Nationale des Arts Decoratifs, where Miehe was a student and one of its political leaders. The revolution was just beginning. For three weeks they worked together in the Atelier Populaire No. 2, where each morning an assembly decided on the day's subjects. In the afternoon they designed the posters that by evening were printed and then sniped on the Paris walls.

By month's end the May Revolution was over for the Atelier Populaire. Hastily called national elections offered expedient solutions. "We were disappointed by the result of the elections," said Pierre Bernard, "but for ourselves this invitation to the political discussion was unforgettable." Such an electrifying month encouraged the trio to pursue the idea of influencing society through graphic arts. Despite France's venerable satiric arts tradition, French poster art was comprised of mundane product advertisements—even the best ones said nothing about society. Although nothing paralleled the Polish energy in the realms of politics or culture, Bernard was adamant. "We wanted to speak on the walls about cinema, theatre, poetry, history as had been done in Poland, and about politics as we had seen in the Cuban magazines," he said. "We needed a new type of client."

Among the most profound changes in government was the appointment of the author André Malraux as minister of culture. Malraux established a new school, the Institut de l'Environment, to consolidate architects, urban planners, and industrial and graphic designers in common cause. Bernard and Gérard were awarded two-year scholarships by the institute to research and analyze the propaganda images of the Popular Front (1936) and the Coup d'État de Gaulle (1958). They studied linguistics and the arts of persuasion, and learned the importance of semiology in relation to form. They graduated, ironically, right before the school was closed for being, as the government ruled, a breeding ground for Marxist agitation. Realizing that scholarly pursuit was not going to affect society anyway, Grapus was founded to take an activist role in design. Based on the teachings of the institute and on the practice of collectivism as a means to render and disseminate ideas, they strove "to make the best image for the best politics in a materialist way," said Bernard.

The name Grapus is a nonsense word for graphics, but also refers to *crapules staliniennes,* "Stalinist scum," what the Grapus founders were at one time called by fellow leftists for being too rebellious. In its infancy the members of Grapus tried to work for the communist party and labor unions while they earned money working for advertising agencies. "After some months," recalled Bernard, "the two activities could not co-exist. You cannot simultaneously have two heads, two hearts, and two lunches with two different persons." Hence they dedicated themselves solely to social concerns. Yet convincing these normally suspicious groups to place both their trust and limited funds with this fledgling studio was difficult. Moreover, the Grapus style, a distinctive marriage of graffiti and collage made into colorful abstractions, was spurned by the communists as not being "strictly significant." Rather than a tired socialist realism, Grapus was interested in "making posters with strong metaphors to speak about human beings with blood, muscle, and smile," said Bernard. "We quoted Picasso, Léger, and Eluard as examples to follow. And we were proud of [this] new ideology." Calligraphy was used because handwriting was a symbolic means for the viewer to participate in the process. The reason for this was, as Bernard explained, "to find the tone of truth—you cannot lie when you write with your hand." Although the party did not say no to Grapus's efforts, they certainly resisted.

Grapus decided to remain independent, not tied to any party or group. Although they agreed with the goals of communist and labor organizations, they also keenly understood the lessons of history regarding ideology and the function of art. Without total independence it would be impossible to argue their own goals of quality, emotion, and aesthetics. Each time they proposed a design, they had to fight for this color or that typographic choice. Grapus's approach to polemical art was stern but not pedantic, strong but refreshingly and surprisingly festive. Because of Grapus's nonconformity, "Sometimes they [the party] considered us as terrorists," said Bernard.

Grapus's philosophy was based on an interpretation of Marxism that was flexible enough to conform to changes in political climate, and that often put them at odds with more doctrinaire groups. Ultimately, they split with the communist trade union over methodology and tactics. "Today each of us can say, 'I have not changed,'" Bernard admitted, "but we cannot say that together."

WWhen Mikhail Gorbachev assumed power in 1985 the words *glasnost, perestroika,* and *demokratia* were not uttered. After a few years they became the most charged words of any language: glasnost, "new openness"; perestroika, "economic reform"; and demokratia, "popular rule." Ultimately, Premier Khruschev's admonition "We will bury you" was replaced by "Do you want fries with that?"

Glasnost posters were early manifestations of the flurry of social and political change that preceded the fall of the Soviet Union. Printed on flimsy paper, these posters expressed the frustrations and fears of a nation long under communist oppression. But the beginnings of change in Soviet graphics began much earlier than the Gorbachev years. The evolution in graphic design slowly gathered momentum towards the end of Khruschev's reign and continued through the early 1980s during the Brezhnev years.

When Gorbachev finally emerged as leader of the nation, Russia was still "the evil empire." Glasnost was not proclaimed overnight. But in terms of graphics the thaw had started. By 1985, when glasnost, perestroika, and demokratia were announced to the world, the initial evidence of this new graphic excitement emerged—or rather exploded—in the Baltic Republics of Latvia, Estonia, and Lithuania, where poster artists had already been exploring new methods of graphic presentation. Most of these new posters, which owe a debt to the Polish poster, were done for local cultural and performing arts events that had historically allowed artists more freedom.

In 1986 a new genre, the protest poster, was displayed at a Latvian political poster exhibition.

Laimonis Chenberg of Riga had designed a poster called *Perestroika?* showing two saucepans with different colored covers. The symbolism, though seemingly obscure, was rather pointed. Chenberg challenged authority by visually suggesting that if the government could not achieve the simplest task, that of matching the right cover to the right saucepan, could perestroika really succeed? For the first time in decades an artist publicly questioned official policy. "For the first time in a long time, the artist had the right, and he took it immediately, to communicate his own view of the world and its problems," wrote a contemporary critic. It further signaled a "new orientation in political poster art," and triggered a chain reaction that was felt even in Moscow.

Glasnost posters were "called to life by a revolution from above and supported by the powerful mass movement from below," wrote historian Anna Suvorova. Unmentionable social ills were being addressed, including compassion for the handicapped, drug and alcohol addiction, prostitution, and AIDS. Governmental abuses were subject to criticism, including the bloated bureaucracy and remnants of Stalinism. "All the posters created by perestroika/demokratia in the setting of glasnost have the same distinction: a peculiar 'distrust' of the word," continued Dr. Suvorova. Slogans that defined the social realist posters of the past were rejected due to a "visual scheme and a plastic flow"—the very same artistic attributes that were once deemed bourgeois baggage. Compared to revolutionary posters of 1917 the perestroika posters lacked some of the spontaneity, drive, and mobilizing emotion, but, claims Suvorova, made up for it with logic and irony. With perestroika the poster became intellectual and therefore demanded that the viewer perceive unfamiliar images and codes, such as aphorism and grotesquery, to show the problems inherent in Soviet society. One Russian observer noted, "The poster nowadays is contradictory; it's not always precise and understandable for everybody."

This was a time of painful reappraisal of ingrained Soviet values and a shattering of old stereotypes. It was also a period of great peril. Immediately before the fall of the USSR glasnost was pronounced dead, perestroika was called a myth, and the term demokratia was considerably downplayed in official circles. Although the environment was more conducive to the publication of some sanctioned controversial posters, the union poster publishing house, Plakat, in Moscow, was still managed by old party functionaries who imposed constraints and limited production based on prejudice and fear.

There were still taboos. Glasnost and perestroika posters were tolerated as long as they did not criticize the Premier. Gorbachev shut down and fired the editor of *Ogony*, one of the leading publications in the country, for criticizing his effectiveness. Many poster artists, most of whom were under age forty, did not trust the system.

"There is freedom of speech. But what's more important, if glasnost holds up, the Russians will continue to have freedom after they speak," wrote the comedian Yakov Smirnoff in a 1989 *New York Times* op-ed article. In the end, what happened shook the world. The short period during which glasnost posters were designed marked a crack in the Iron Curtain that grew larger until it shattered. Today these glasnost poster images are a monument to the power of polemical art to change the course of history.

I Shop Therefore I Am

BARBARA KRUGER

A shopping bag with the words *I shop therefore I am* might be mistaken for a promotion by some tony retail store. But seen in a museum as a nearly nine-foot-square photographic silkscreen on vinyl with a red enamel frame, this work assumes a different meaning. Is it advertising or art, design or propaganda?

Barbara Kruger (b. 1945) ignores these distinctions. She makes graphic work that expresses political and social folly through the traditional venues of both art and advertising: museums, art galleries, billboards, posters, book covers, matchbooks, shopping bags, and even covers for such mainstream magazines as *Newsweek, Ms.,* and *Esquire.* She rejects the terms design or advertising to describe her work stating, "I'm someone who works with pictures and words, and people can take that to mean anything they like." In 1990 the large-scale silkscreened version of *I Shop Therefore I Am* was exhibited in Cologne at the Kölnischer Kunstrerein; the printed shopping bag was given away free with the purchase of the show catalog.

I Shop Therefore I Am, like most of her work, was designed with economy. An enlarged black-and-white photograph of a single hand, tightly cropped, palm forward, fills the visual field. A red block almost perfectly proportional to a credit card appears to balance between the thumb and third finger in an act of optical trickery. The "card" is not actually held by the hand, but is instead mechanically positioned and appears to be pushed forward. The typeface, Futura Bold, reinforces the blunt declarative statement in what at once reads like advertising exhortation and philosophical pontification.

Kruger's art emerged in the milieu of 1970s feminism. Feminists argued that gender was not an innate condition, but rather a construct created by adaptation to societal norms and expectations. They contended that in a visual culture, the masculine eye objectifies and masters, casting women as objects of the male gaze. In his 1972 edition of *Ways of Seeing*, the British writer John Berger observed, "Men look at women. Women watch themselves being looked at." Kruger's early imagery combined stereotypical images of women borrowed from fashion magazines and advertising with text in a contrapuntal dialog. An untitled work from 1983 contrasts a photograph of a woman's manicured hands underwater pulling the stopper from a drain (an ad for dishwashing soap?) with the text "Now you see us, now you don't."

In 1984 Kruger expanded her targets with a series of posters attacking money and consumption as even more pervasive tools of masculine power. *I Shop Therefore I Am* is not only a parody of Descartes's *cogito ergo sum*, "I think therefore I am," but also an exposé of a culture so dominated by consumerism that it substitutes acquisition for thinking as the apotheosis of human existence. Shopping is no mere dalliance, but a crucial quest for an identity capable of being created, not just honed, through the acquisition of appropriate things.

In typical editorial or advertising design, words reinforce or support the visual message. Conversely, Kruger creates a vigorous dialogue between word and image, trapping the viewer somewhere in between. She instigates questions and encourages doubt. Kruger's strength lies in the tension and contrast: The images are anti-individual, stereotypical photographs appropriated from the cultural collective, old photographic albums, instruction manuals, and magazines; her statements use the personal textual pronouns, I, we, you, and speak to the spectator directly. The mixed messages make provocative alchemy.

Kruger draws inspiration from her earlier jobs. As an editorial designer at *Harper's Bazaar* she worked under art director Marvin Israel, who convinced her to assemble a professional art portfolio and introduced her to photography. Later she worked under art director Roger Schoening at *Mademoiselle*, and when the senior designer left six months after her arrival, twenty-two-year-old Kruger was given the job. Her rapid rise in the commercial art world was matched by an equal rise in disillusionment. After four years of full-time employment she took refuge in the darkroom doing work that allowed her to stay connected to the world as a freelance picture editor and designer. She continued commercial freelancing for almost eleven years.

Kruger's work has been compared to the polemical photomontages of German dadaist John Heartfield. She denies any conscious link; she didn't even know of Heartfield's political work for the Berlin-based communist newspaper *AIZ* until 1980, well after her own signature style was developed. "Critics always focus on the fine art/constructivism end of my work, rather than thinking that this was somebody who had a job, who had training in cropping photographs and who pasted words over them." She sees her work as a logical evolution from that framework, turning the word/image apposition into a socially meaningful device.

As Kruger has co-opted the tools of design and advertising, likewise the design field has borrowed from her. It should come as no surprise that the commercial world Kruger assails has reclaimed her methods. She doesn't seem to mind though, for when her style is stripped of its meaning and taken out of context—used only for its graphic vocabulary—it validates her critique of the system.

Cigarette Advertisements

Women have come a long way from the presuffrage era when it was unladylike to smoke. Taken up as a *cause célèbre,* women's right to cigarettes was a smokescreen in the struggle for more fundamental rights. On the way to achieving first-class citizenship, women became first-class tobacco consumers. And if women were going to smoke, reasoned the tobacco industry, then why not encourage them to smoke a lot? By 1910 advertisements hinted that smoking was a right—by the 1920s it was a duty.

No expense was spared by Lucky Strike in recruiting female customers. To promote the image of sophistication a series of 1930s magazine ads featured stylized paintings of women decked out in evening finery. In "OK Miss America! We thank you for your patronage" a woman wearing a revealing, low-cut satin gown is so above the fray that she isn't even holding a Lucky, but the implication is that she had just finished a satisfying smoke. In the haughty "I do" advertisement a sultry bride pauses for a relaxed smoke and gives her vow to the cigarette of choice. Cigarettes were marketed as fashion accessories, but these ads, which ran during the Great Depression, were not targeted exclusively to women of means. Using smoke and mirrors, cigarette advertising suggested the promise of a better life.

Advertising wizards also made cigarettes seductive to women by invoking the ideal. High culture was used in one sales pitch that borrowed Henry Wadsworth Longfellow's "First a Shadow Then a Sorrow," to announce Lucky Strike's diet plan. "Avoid that future shadow," the copy suggested, "by refraining from over indulgence. If you would maintain the modern figure of fashion." Under an idealized color painting of a young woman haunted by the shadow of a double chin, the copy read: "We do not represent that smoking Lucky Strike Cigarettes will bring modern figures or cause the reduction of flesh. We do declare that when tempted to do yourself too well, if you will 'Reach for a Lucky' instead, you will thus avoid over indulgence in things that cause excess weight and, by avoiding over indulgence maintain a modern, graceful form."

Cigarettes were a staple for Depression-weary and later war-torn Americans. Yet despite the claim of weight control, they offered no viable health inducements. Even tobacco manufacturers acknowledged that frequent product usage resulted in coughing, throat irritation, and raspy sounding voices. The last was, however, promoted as sexy. To deflect public attention away from what the industry viewed as minor physical ailments, cigarette advertising exploited certain perceived health benefits, including increased vigor and stamina. Camels asserted that "Smokers everywhere are turning to Camels for their delightful 'energizing effect' . . . Camels never get on your nerves. . . ." Lucky Strike took the homeopathic route with their motto "It's toasted." A typical ad read "Everyone knows that sunshine mellows—that's why the 'TOASTING' process includes the use of Ultra Violet Rays . . . Everyone knows that heat purifies and so 'TOASTING'— that extra secret process—removes harmful irritants that cause throat irritation and coughing." By the late 1930s Lucky Strike had added the following tag line to its motto, "sunshine mellows—heat purifies."

Men played a role in cigarette advertising for women. They ran the agencies, produced the images, and wrote the copy that created the commercially correct woman. But in men's club fashion they also made fun of their own ludicrous stereotypes. In "Shanghaied by a Silly Salt? . . . Light an Old Gold" the *Esquire* magazine pinup artist Petty's voluptuous gal is hit upon by a licentious old gent, but the copy positions Old Gold as her saving grace: "When a retired skipper proves he is anything but retiring by dropping anchor alongside of you . . . don't let him scuttle your whole evening. Offer him an Old Gold . . . he'll welcome it like a breeze in the doldrums . . . while you breeze gracefully away."

Movie stars and starlets frequently appeared as spokespersons. In a 1943 advertisement, Betty Grable, star of the movie *Pinup Girl*, is shown in a soldier's barracks, reinforcing the idea that Chesterfield is overseas "With the boys. . . ." In the same spirit, Joan Bennett, dressed in her Women's Volunteer Army uniform, lit up "His cigarette and mine," another in a series of Chesterfield testimonials. To soldiers, cigarettes were as valuable as rations; to the tobacco industry the war was a boon. Ads invoked the image of American boys, exploited the image of American girls, and portrayed cigarettes to be as American as apple pie. After the war men became active role models in ads targeted to women.

The cigarette ads created during the Great Depression and World War II targeted women with one purpose: to seduce by appealing to their patriotism and sense of fashion. While the stylistic manner of this seduction has changed since these ads were first printed, the method is still the same: appeal to weakness, bolster myth, and massage fantasy.

Joe Camel

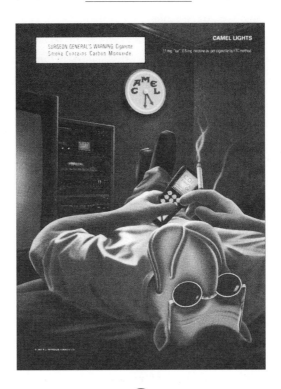

Since the late 1980s the RJR Nabisco Company has saturated American media with its Camel cigarette's "Smooth Character" campaign. The original Camel trademark, a gritty pen-and-ink rendering done in 1913 of Old Joe, a dromedary owned by the Barnum and Bailey Circus, has considerably more charm than the updated anthropomorphic playbeast seen today. But the issue is not about charm. The trade character who peers off massive billboards and thousands of deli counters is what one advertising critic refers to "as moron fodder that is so much a part of life that if we are not careful, we forget to be insulted by it." The less than subtle phallic appearance of Joe Camel is insulting to women, men, and camels alike, but aesthetics alone are not the issue, either. The public has become accustomed to most of the moron fodder perpetrated by advertising agencies "who bang their sticks in a bucket of swill," wrote George Orwell.

The cigarette smoker is society's current *bête noire*. So why not rail against the Marlboro man or the "real people" campaign for Benson and Hedges? The answer is that the "Smooth Character" ads more insidiously target teenagers. In a 1990 open letter to Louis V. Gerstner, RJR Nabisco's chief executive officer, Mark Green, who then was the New York City Commissioner of Consumer Affairs, wrote: "As the father of two young children, I am appalled at your . . . campaign, which risks addicting children to cigarettes."

The "Smooth Character" campaign is based on a French campaign for Camel that was initiated two years prior to being adapted for the American market by the celebrated art director

Mike Salisbury. Joe Camel does things most adolescent boys dream about—gets the girls, drives neat sports cars, and flies fighter bombers. The characters are rendered in an ambient airbrushed cartoon style and have anthropomorphic attributes similar to those of the popular Teenage Mutant Ninja Turtles. The human characteristics and expressions, while seemingly unthreatening, seductively hypnotize the younger viewer into believing Joe Camel is a pal. The Marlboro man speaks to a post-adolescent need for machismo, it is not aimed at kids in the same way. But this cocksure camel would be neutered if not for a brilliant, if sinister, marketing strategy that made it ubiquitous.

In his letter to RJR Nabisco, Mark Green explained the ways in which kids are targeted. "I came across your huge pull-out poster 'suitable for framing' in *Rolling Stone* magazine, along with language urging readers to send away for any of eight colorful posters." Each poster, he pointed out, shows the camel with representations of sexy women, "with symbols one needn't be Freud to understand." However, it was not until Green saw the perforated fold at the bottom of the poster, which allows readers to detach the Surgeon General's warning, that he realized the inherent danger. "True," Green wrote, "the *Rolling Stone* ad does say (in extremely small print) that a person sending in a coupon for posters is supposed to 'certify that I am a smoker twenty-one years of age or older.' On the other hand, who puts posters up on their walls—kids or adults? Who watches and talks about cartoon characters—kids or adults? Who is impressionable enough to associate smoking and success and sex—kids or adults?"

The billboards and point-of-purchase displays do not recognize age distinctions. Joe Camel peers like a schoolyard candy man from displays on counters next to Ninja Turtle premiums and Baseball bubble gum cards. "In our MTV era, many kids get more information from images than words," Green's letter continued. "It's very hard to square your ads with Rule No.3 in the Tobacco Industry's Principles Covering Cigarette Advertising and Sampling: 'Cigarette advertising shall not suggest that smoking is essential to social prominence, distinction, success, or sexual attraction.' These ads are potentially unconscionable because they appear to be targeted to unsophisticated minors who feel immortal and are uniquely subject to peer pressure—who may get addicted for life, a shortened life at that."

According to the cigarette industry's reports, approximately $2.6 billion is spent annually on advertising—or, as Green figured, $9 for every man, woman, and child. Advertising experts argue that despite this expenditure, which far exceeds the sum devoted to America's propaganda efforts during the first year of World War II, no one is really persuaded to start smoking. Statistics that show smoking on the decline in this country suggest that the majority of cigarette ads are rear-guard actions, simply trying to convince existing smokers to change brands rather than encourage new ones to begin. Yet "Smooth Character" is not just a passive ad campaign, but an aggressive assault designed to conscript as many customers as possible, regardless of age. Lyndon Johnson once said about the Vietnamese, "If you grab them by the balls, their hearts and minds will follow." The same principle applies to RJR Nabisco's marketing strategy. In bringing the "Smooth Character" campaign to the United States, RJR Nabisco may recapture its faltering market share, but even the most clever advertising ploy must ultimately fail when the product kills the conscriptees.

Media

DESIGN IN MASS COMMUNICATION

In 1896 not one but two revolutionary periodicals were introduced in Kaiser Wilhelm's Germany. *Jugend* codified a distinctly modern graphic style, and *Simplicissimus* translated it into graphic social commentary. Both signaled a rebellion of youth against court-sanctioned romanticism and dehumanizing industrialization. *Jugend,* published by Dr. Georg Hirth, gave a voice and a name to Jugendstil, or "youth style," and *Simplicissimus,* edited by Albert Langen and Thomas Theodore Heine (1867–1948), harnessed the graphic power of this new movement as a polemical tool.

Jugend, a Munich weekly published from 1896 to 1926, was the principal outlet for the dissemination of Jugendstil art and literature. Its fanciful cover illustrations and changing logotypes defined a style that was built on the rejection of the familiar and antiquated. Jugendstil dismantled entrenched artistic conventions, including classical approaches to rendering. It replaced realism with abstraction and rococo embellishment with curvilinear decoration. *Jugend* revealed a French influence (some of its artists emulated Henri Toulouse-Lautrec), but was nevertheless quite German in its adoption of gothic lettering and imagery. Page layout was often dictated by the complexity of the illustration, causing untold headaches for the printer whose job it was to rag the type to conform to the curvilinear designs.

Satire was the fuel that fired the profoundly influential *Simplicissimus,* also a Munich weekly published from 1896 to 1944. Co-edited by Th. Th. Heine, a poster artist and cartoonist, *Simplicissimus,* also known as *der Simpl,* was at once the progenitor of a new graphic style and a thorn in the side of the Kaiser (who saw to it that the artists were harassed and imprisoned more than once). Although *der Simpl's* covers were not as adventuresome as those of *Jugend,* it nonetheless pioneered a graphic style that influenced other pictorial journals throughout Europe. Most images were given full-page display, accompanied only by a caption and headline. *Der Simpl's* stable of contributors included modern cartoonist Bruno Paul (1874–1968), whose woodcut-like brush-and-ink drawings were said to have influenced the German expressionists, and Eduard Thony (1866–1950), who lampooned the *Junker*—or military aristocracy—with such beguiling subtlety that even his victims admired the work. Issues such as political corruption, religious hypocrisy, and militarist stupidity were assailed, while the virtues of the *Volk,* or peasant class, were extolled in beautifully proportioned, stylized vignettes and caricatures.

Jugendstil was a component of a short-lived but exuberant pan-European cultural episode that began in the late nineteenth century and ended before the outbreak of World War I. It was similarly practiced in Paris as art nouveau, in England as the arts and crafts movement, Scotland as the Glasgow school, Italy as Liberty, Austria as the secession, and Czechoslovakia as the Bohemian secession. Each nation imbued the style with its own social and political characteristics, but there was also a shared visual language rooted in a rejection of all things sentimental. Art nouveau inveighed against parochial nationalistic movements while promoting the international exchange of ideas. It refused to acknowledge any distinction between the "fine and lesser arts" and was both decorative and expressive.

Art nouveau was influenced by the simplicity of traditional Japanese design. Its practitioners swore allegiance to the natural object and cultivated an appreciation of symbolism. Theirs was a lexicon of sinuous, naturalistic, curvilinear forms. Jugendstil combined these organic impulses with a geometric edge. Pervasive in Jugendstil design was what one critic called "fantastical melancholy," communicated through Teutonic wit and folkloric symbology. Jugendstil took nourishment from William Morris's arts and crafts movement in England but did not reject all industrial things, which it instead sought to cover with decorative motifs. Jugendstil artists rejected traditional typography, choosing instead to render unique ornamental typefaces that worked harmoniously with an image. Brushed letterforms were used on posters and advertisements, while a few eccentric faces, notably those by Otto Eckmann, became emblems of the era.

Exponents of Jugendstil believed in the ideal that good design could change the world. While it had an impact, this was an unrealized goal that came to an abrupt end prior to World War I. Today Jugendstil is a stylistic reminder of rebellion against the status quo. The magazines *Jugend* and *Simplicissimus* were its clarions. Although it might seem tame in the postmodern epoch, Jugendstil possessed a quality that transcended the moment and continues to influence contemporary illustration and design.

The Composing Room of New York was no mere type shop. It was the vortex of progressive design activity from the late 1930s to the 1960s. No other type business promoted itself more aggressively, or so determinedly advanced the art and craft of type design, and in the process made such a significant contribution to practice and history. What began as a campaign to attract typesetting business from advertising agencies and book and magazine publishers evolved into one of the most ambitious educational programs that the field has ever known. It initiated type clinics, lecture series, single and group exhibitions, catalogs, and one of America's most influential graphic arts periodicals, *PM* (Production Manager), later called *AD* (Art Director), published bimonthly between 1934 and 1942.

The program, conceived and sustained for almost forty years by The Composing Room's cofounder, Dr. Robert Lincoln Leslie (1885–1986), was rooted in graphic arts traditions yet was motivated by his personal willingness to identify and promote significant new approaches even if they rejected tradition. What made The Composing Room so profoundly influential, in addition to being a recognized leader in quality hot-metal type and eventually photo typesetting, was a commitment to explore design approaches with a blind eye toward style or ideology. Despite his own preference for classical practice, "Doc" Leslie (he was a licensed physician) or "Uncle Bob," as he was affectionately called, gave young designers a platform on which to strut their stuff.

Leslie assumed that a well-informed professional—indeed an enlightened one—would be a more discerning customer and so in a corner of his shop he created a graphic arts salon. Regularly frequented by Ladislav Sutnar, Alvin Lustig, and Herbert Bayer, this salon put his type shop at the center of what would now be called "design discourse," but then was practical design talk. The Composing Room's unparalleled efforts to elevate the level of graphic arts and typography may have been driven by commercial priorities but nonetheless formed a solid foundation for the celebration and documentation of graphic design.

In 1934 Leslie founded *PM: An Intimate Journal for Production Managers, Art Directors, and Their Associates,* initially as a house organ. With its co-editor Percy Seitlin, a former newspaper man, this small-format (six-by-eight-inch) "journal" developed into the leading trade publication and outlet for traditional and progressive work, an American *Gebrauchsgrafik* or *Arts et Métiers Graphiques* (the latter published by the Deberny and Peignot Foundry in Paris, which also employed publications and exhibitions to further the French graphic arts). *PM* explored a variety of print media, covered industry news, and developed a strong slant towards modern typography and design. It was also the first journal to showcase the new European immigrants and included illustrated profiles on Herbert Bayer, Will Burtin, Joseph Binder, M. F. Agha, as well as native-grown moderns Lester Beall, Joseph Sinel, Gustav Jensen, and Paul Rand. In 1939 the name *PM* was sold to Ralph Ingersol, who started New York's only ad-less daily newspaper and called it *PM,* so the magazine changed its name to *AD,* which coincidentally reflected a creative realignment within the profession from production managers to art directors—marking a gradual shift from craft to art.

Each *AD* cover featured an original image and redesigned logo. E. McKnight Kauffer's was characteristically cubistic; Paul Rand's was playfully modern; Lucian Bernhard's was suitably gothic; and Matthew Leibowitz's prefigured new wave in its dada-inspired juxtaposition of discordant decorative old wood types. Although the articles were not critical analyses, they were nevertheless well written trade pieces peppered with interesting facts and anecdotes. A news column, titled "Composing Room Notes by R. L. L." provided an account of commercial arts from a vendor's perspective. For sixty-six issues *PM* and *AD* documented a nascent profession as it grew out of a journeyman's craft.

Three years after starting *PM,* Doc Leslie took over a small room in The Composing Room shop that, with the addition of a display case and bright lights, was transformed into the PM Gallery, the first exhibition space in New York dedicated to graphic design and its affinities. Percy Seitlin described the premiere exhibition: "A young man by the name of Herbert Matter had just arrived in this country from Switzerland with a bagful of ski posters and photographs of snow-covered mountains. Also came camera portraits and varied specimens of his typographic work. We decided to let him hang some of his things on the walls and give him a party. . . . The result was a crowd of almost bargain-basement dimensions, and thirsty too. Everyone was excited by the audacity and skill of Matter's work." The magazine and gallery were symbiotic. Often a feature in the one would lead to an exhibition in the other or vice versa. Doc Leslie believed "that there was an enthusiastic audience for a showcase featuring the work of artists-in-industry; and, furthermore, that the audience was larger than we had originally thought it ever could be."

In April–May 1942 the editors ran this note: "*AD* is such a small segment of this wartime world that it is almost with embarrassment, and certainly with humility, that we announce the suspension of its publication . . . for the duration," wrote editors Leslie and Seitlin. "The reasons are easy to understand: shortage of men and materials, shrinkage of the advertising business whose professional workers *AD* has served, and all-out digging in for Victory. . . ." The magazine did not resume publishing after the war but left a documentary record of an important period when American and European designers began to forge an international design language.

Direction

PAUL RAND

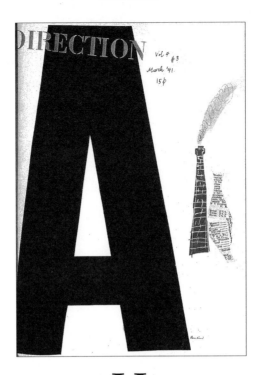

"He favors Le Corbusier's underlying philosophy . . . his avoidance of ornament, his dependence upon masses, proportions, and inherencies for success in the solution of a problem," exclaimed the October–November 1938 issue of *PM* magazine of Paul Rand (1914–1996), at twenty-four years old the leading American proponent of functional design. "Artistic tricks divert from the effect that an artist endeavors to produce, and even excellent elements, such as bullets, arrows, brackets, ornate initials, are, at best, superficial ornamentation unless logically and reasonably employed," Rand explained. But at that time these graphic accoutrements were considered soothing to most clients. So how did Rand succeed in expressing himself, and otherwise change conventional practice? The answer can be found in a series of covers designed for *Direction* magazine between 1939 and 1943.

Rand was reared in the commercial art bullpens of New York and understood the needs of American commerce. He never intended to be a radical, but from the outset of his career he had an instinctive understanding of modern painting, a passion for popular art, and a flair for wedding the two. He was harshly critical of the lack of quality in American design practice, and believed that even the most common aspects of everyday life could be enriched by an artist's touch.

Although he was enthused by the new currents in art and design, he refused to mimic or follow them blindly. Rand insisted that it was not only wrong but also "uneconomical from the aesthetic point of view" merely to borrow or separate from context without understanding the factors that brought an original into being. He further gave credence to Le Corbusier's dictum that it is necessary to understand history, "and he who understands history knows how to find continuity between that which was, that which is, and that which will be." *PM* concurred: "Rand is unhampered by traditions. . . . He has no stereotyped style because every task is something new and demands its own solution. Consequently, there is nothing labored or forced about his work."

Rand's artistic awakening came in the late 1920s at the New York Public Library where he explored the stacks and pored through volumes of *Commercial Art*, the British trade journal that published articles on the European avant-garde practitioners, including expatriate E. McKnight Kauffer. He had a second epiphany at a little magazine store adjacent to the Brooklyn Academy of Music, where in 1929 he bought his first issue of *Gebrauchsgrafik*, the most influential German advertising arts magazine ever published. It was in this periodical that Rand learned about the practice of, and the term, graphic design.

By 1938 Rand had produced enough noteworthy design that he caught the eye of Marguerite Tjader Harris, the daughter of a wealthy Connecticut munitions manufacturer. She was intent on having Rand design covers for *Direction*, an arts and culture magazine that she published on a shoestring, which featured articles by Le Corbusier, Jean Cocteau, and other avant-gardists. She offered Rand no recompense, but plenty of freedom and, ultimately, a couple of original Le Corbusier drawings. But Rand had another motive, "In a country that was used to decorative work, the common sense way to have what I was doing accepted was to do it for free," he explained.

More than any other project, the *Direction* covers exemplified the timelessness that Rand attributed to the most significant art and design. "When I designed a cover of *Direction*, I was really trying to compete with the Bauhaus. Not with Norman Rockwell," clarified Rand. "I was working in the spirit of Van Doesburg, Léger, and Picasso. It was not old fashioned. To be old fashioned is, in a way, a sin."

Each *Direction* cover illustrated a particular theme or point of view; the first, and his most politically astute, showed a map of Czechoslovakia torn in half, representing the nation's evisceration by the Nazis. Contrasted with an E. McKnight Kauffer *Direction* cover showing a realistic hand impaled by a Nazi dagger, Rand's abstract depiction was both subtle and eloquent. Rand avoided conventional propagandistic tools in favor of imagery he believed would serve as both art and message. His 1940 "Merry Christmas" cover was a visual pun that substituted barbed wire for gift wrap ribbon. Rand photographed real barbed wire against a white background lit to pick up the shadows. Little red circles made by a hole punch represented spilled blood. The barbed wire was a striking mnemonic symbol for oppression. "It pinpoints the distinction between abstract design without and abstract design with content," he insisted. "You can be a great manipulator of form, but if the solution is not apt, it's for the birds."

The surprising juxtaposition of visual elements and universal symbols was born of necessity. Messages had to be conveyed quickly and efficiently. Since there was no budget for materials he often used handwriting instead of type for many of the covers. He even pieced together the stenciled masthead (a precursor of the stenciled IBM logo, perhaps) from letters in type catalogs.

His images were often assembled from various elements. "Collages don't imitate reality," he stated. "The machine aesthetic dictated that you don't do things by hand anymore." Nevertheless, the *Direction* covers did not slavishly conform to such modern principles, and hand drawing was used on occasion.

Rand was the first to confess that these breakthrough covers were not entirely unique. "I never claimed that this was great original stuff," he confided. "Other guys in Europe were doing this kind of thing." But even though he admitted to paying homage both to Picasso and the surrealist art magazines *Verve* and *Minotaur*, Rand created a unique visual vocabulary—and a collection of memorable magazine covers—that was unlike anything being done in the United States at that time, or for a long time after.

Dell Mapbacks

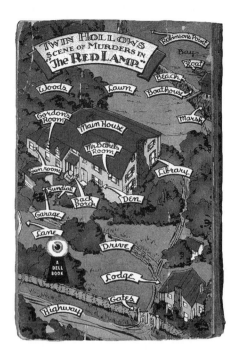

Paperback cover art was at its high—or low, depending on your point of view—from the 1940s to early 1950s when a dozen or so New York–based reprint publishers were in fierce competition. Of all of them the Dell Book "look" was the most distinctive. Dell's innovation was the colorful locator maps that positioned each book in the city, street, house, even room in which the plot developed. The series was referred to as Mapbacks, and for little less than a decade, before the maps were replaced with conventional blurbs, they were among the most popular line of mysteries, thrillers, and romances on the market.

The Dell Publishing Company was founded as a pulp house in 1922 by George Delacorte, Jr., a twenty-eight-year-old who built an amazingly profitable business by publishing pulps, mass market magazines, and comic books. Delacorte was an astute observer of popular trends. Noting the success of Pocket Books he decided to start Dell Books around 1941. By 1943 the first editions were released. To limit his liability and ensure efficient production, he entered into a partnership with Western Printing and Lithographing Company of Racine, Illinois, one of America's largest commercial printers, whose staff selected titles, created art, and printed Dell Books while Delacorte distributed them.

Dell Books competed successfully because their covers—initially promoting crime stories by Ellery Queen, Rex Stout, Michael Shyne, and Brett Halliday, among others—had sexual allure. Although many of the wartime paperbacks used romantic realism to present seductive scenes,

Dell used surrealism to suggest racy content. Sex was used, disavowed, and then used again as a marketing tool. The ebb and flow of sexual imagery was nevertheless arbitrary. Rather than using market surveys, the publishers decided on their own about how much was too much. To transcend the saucy and hard-boiled pulp aesthetic perpetuated in Delacorte's magazine division, Dell's Racine-based art director, William Strohmer, and his assistant, George Frederiksen (who also painted a number of the covers), turned to expressionistic art that used dramatic symbolism to suggest the theme or plot. The leading staff artist, Gerald Gregg, had adopted various Dali-esque conceits—fragmented body parts and floating objects—which he rendered in airbrush. His distinctive symbolic style was enhanced by the airbrush's smooth, continuous tones and the artist's preference for bright colors.

A lot of the lettering in the 1940s paperbacks resembled splash panels of comic books. Dell's lettering, exclusively hand drawn by Bernie Salbreiter, owes more to movie titles. In *Paperbacks, U.S.A.: A Graphic History, 1939–1959* (Blue Dolphin Enterprises, 1981), Piet Schreuders writes that in popular culture paperbacks fit somewhere between the comics and B-movies: "American paperbacks have had a close relationship with the Hollywood film . . . the *film noir* and the psychological thriller." Gregg's cover art for *Crime for a Lady*, a back view of a tiny trench-coated man whispering into an oversized woman's ear, is a comic book cliché reminiscent of B-movie posters from the thirties and forties.

Dell's covers were sometimes crude and often simple. The simplicity of their imagery may have had something to do with the fact that most Dell artists never read the manuscripts. They were given titles and an oral summary of the contents, a process that was bound to result in a reliance on clichés. Although the cover concepts were based on summaries, the back covers, Dell's exclusive "cartographic fantasies" required a close reading to determine what part of the plot would be depicted and then rendered (almost exclusively) by Dell's in-house map-maker, Ruth Belew. Dell used maps as a standard feature from 1943 to 1951. They were based on the scene-of-the-crime diagrams found in tabloid newspapers.

The style that distinguished Dell Books for less than a decade ended around 1951 when the art department moved from Racine to New York. Romantic realism was prevailing in illustration, especially for magazines, and Dell's New York art director, Walter Brooks, championed the sexy realism of Robert Stanley, one of Dell's leading realist artists. He modernized the overall look by adopting sans-serif lettering and replacing maps with blurbs. These changes did not hinder sales, but they ended a special era in posterlike paperback art.

Portfolio

ALEXEY BRODOVITCH

*P*ortfolio, published between 1949 and 1951, was the model of a twentieth-century graphic and industrial arts magazine. It elevated design and set the standard of magazine layout that few publications then or now could equal. "The format itself should be a graphic experience," editor Frank Zachary explained. The hefty nine-by-twelve-inch periodical designed by Alexey Brodovitch (1898–1971) incorporated special inserts, including shopping bags, wallpaper, and three-dimensional glasses. And publisher George Rosenthal, Jr., spared no expense in buying the best paper and the best of everything else.

"Then we decided to sell advertising," recalled Zachary. "Well, we hated the ads we got. So we said, 'Hell, we're not going to mar our beautiful magazine with crummy ads.' We were terribly idealistic." Void of such visual encumbrances, *Portfolio* was a hybrid, part book and part magazine. A subscription cost twelve dollars a year for four issues and a few thousand people subscribed. Rosenthal handled the finances, while Zachary developed the writers. He also collected all the photographs and illustrations for the stories.

Convention dictated that magazine covers be pictorial. But the first issue of *Portfolio* was like no other; it was type design, transparent process-color squares printed over the *Portfolio* logo which was dropped out of black. Like a main title for a motion picture, the cover introduced the cinematic interior. Brodovitch, the acclaimed art director for *Harper's Bazaar,* who introduced the new photography to fashion magazines, paced his layouts as though they were storyboards for films. The key to success was dynamic juxtapositions: big and small, bold and quiet, type and pictorial. Brodovitch splayed comps out on the floor, mixing and matching, moving pages and entire stories around as needed.

Zachary planned the issues with Brodovitch at his office at *Harper's Bazaar.* "We got along very well because I let him have his head," Zachary recalled. "But he was no prima donna. He worked in the most fantastic way. For example, I would come in, say, at seven o'clock in the evening with the idea of how many pages we had for an issue, and how many would be devoted to each story. I would come back [the next day], and Holy Christ, there was this magnificent layout. He used the photostat machine like a note pad. He would get stats of every photo, often different sizes of the same piece, in tiny increments that might vary from a quarter inch to an inch, or from an inch to two inches, and so on. You would see him surrounded by all these stats. But as he put them down, my God, all of a sudden a spread materialized beautifully proportioned, everything in scale, with just the right amount of white space, type and picture mass. I learned so many nuances of art directing just from watching him."

Portfolio premiered in late 1949 and lasted for only three issues. During this time, Zachary was also editor of *Jazzways*, a one-shot magazine on the folkways of jazz. The cover was designed by Paul Rand and among the interior photographers was Berenice Abbott. In addition Zachary and Rosenthal published paperback photo albums under the Zebra Books imprint. These were the first of their kind to present good photojournalistic portfolios for just twenty-five cents. The titles included *Murder Incorporated*, the first book on the Mafia; *Life and Death in Hollywood*, a pre–Kenneth Anger look at the foibles of the glitter capital; and *Naked City*, the first collection of pictures by famed New York street photographer Weegee. Each sold between 150,000 and 250,000 copies with all profits poured back into *Portfolio.*

The third and last issue of *Portfolio* was its most beautiful. To underscore Brodovitch's concept of this magazine as analog to film, the cover for #3 was the image of a film strip. But the dream of an ad-less magazine had turned into a nightmare. Financial problems did not weaken Zachary's resolve to publish (he even approached Henry Luce, publisher of *Time* and *Life*, to buy the magazine). But in 1951 the prime financial backer, George Rosenthal, Sr., decided to summarily kill *Portfolio* rather than incur further losses. Had it continued who knows what impact *Portfolio* would have on magazines of the era. More than fifty years have passed and this special magazine is a landmark of design history.

Industrial Design

ALVIN LUSTIG

Adesign icon doesn't come along every day. To be so considered it must not only transcend its function and stand the test of time, but also must represent the time in which it was produced. The cover of *Industrial Design*, Vol. 1, No. 1, February 1954, was not just the emblem of a new publishing venture, but a testament to one man's modernism; one of the last works created by Alvin Lustig (1915–1955), who suffered an untimely death from diabetes in 1955 at the age of forty.

Despite failing vision, Lustig was deeply involved in the design of the first two and nominally with the third issues of the magazine as art editor, art director, and art consultant, respectively. He saw his role as the framer of ideas that were visual in nature. Although he never had the chance to develop his basic design concepts further, he left behind a modern design icon, the cover, and a format that continued to define the magazine for years after.

Industrial Design was the brainchild of publisher Charles Whitney, who also published the successful *Interiors*. In 1953 he was convinced by his friend and advisor George Nelson that the time was right to introduce a specialized periodical devoted to practitioners of this burgeoning field. *Interiors* already featured its own industrial design column that had evolved into a discrete section, which Whitney realized had commercial potential as a spin-off. *Interiors* was also so beautifully designed that *Industrial Design* could have no less the visual panache of a coffee table book/magazine, replete with foldouts and slipsheets, not unlike the legendary design magazine *Portfolio*, published between 1949 and 1951. To accomplish this an eminent art director was sought. This was the age of great magazine art directors—including Alexey Brodovitch, Alexander Liberman, Otto Storch, Cipe Pineles, and Alan Hurlburt—and Whitney fervently believed that a magazine's design would be the deciding factor in its success. Hence Lustig was entrusted with considerable authority to design the magazine as he saw fit.

On the editorial side, however, Whitney decided to take a calculated risk by promoting two young *Interiors* associate editors to co-editors of *Industrial Design*. Jane Fisk (now Jane Thompson of the architectural firm Thompson and Wood in Cambridge) and Deborah Allen may have been inexperienced in the field of industrial design but nevertheless had a clear plan to introduce a distinctly journalistic sensibility into professional publishing that emphasized criticism and analysis rather than the puff pieces common to the genre. As it turned out, this became a point of philosophical contention between the designer and editors.

If they had a choice the editors would have preferred an art director who, as Thompson explained, "would have been in the trenches with us," a team player with journalistic instincts rather than a distant presence with a formalist sensibility. Because Lustig designed the initial dummy and subsequent two issues in his own studio and returned with the completed layouts to the editorial offices, he had made certain assumptions about the presentation of content that were often inconsistent with the editors' vision. "We did not want the words to be gray space, we wanted them to have meaning," recalled Thompson about wanting more spontaneous design responses to the material. But instead of being journalistically intuitive, Lustig imposed his formal preconceptions and designed the magazine as he would a book.

Blocks of text type were indeed used as gray matter to frame an abundance of precisely silhouetted photographs. But if there was a problem it was more in the editors' minds than Lustig's design. While it was not as journalistically paced as say, *Life* magazine, *Industrial Design* was respectfully, indeed elegantly neutral, allowing for a wide range of material to be presented without interference. Moreover, it was what Whitney wanted, so the editors reconciled themselves to building the magazine's editorial reputation through informative features written by authors not previously associated with trade publishing.

Thompson nevertheless hated the first cover with its tight grid and silhouetted photographs. Instead she wanted to disrupt the design purity with a few well composed coverlines. She further favored a conceptual method of intersecting photography and text, resulting in an editorial idea, not a pure design. Lustig thought coverlines would sully the design and intersecting ideas would be too contrived. Years later, Thompson grudgingly admitted that maybe Lustig's judgment was wiser: "He wanted to make a strong simple statement, which he believed (perhaps erroneously since *Industrial Design* did not have to compete on the newsstand) had to stand up against the covers of the elegant fashion magazines." Lustig's design set the standard for future covers, and his successor, Martin Rosensweig, continued to produce covers for a few years afterward that more rigidly adhered to the same formal practices.

Despite these creative tensions, the early issues of *Industrial Design* reveal a shift in the nature of professional publishing from a trade to cultural orientation that was in no small way underscored by Lustig's classically modern design.

Holiday

FRANK ZACHARY

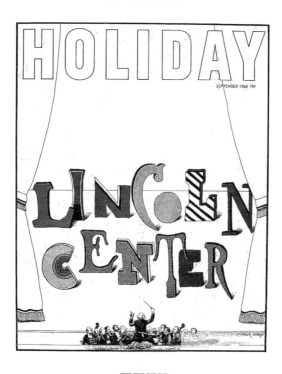

When it begin in the 1930s, *Holiday* magazine was clean and orderly, but its layout was made with a cookie cutter. In 1955 Frank Zachary (b. 1919), former editor of *Portfolio*, who had learned art direction from Alexey Brodovitch, changed all that. Zachary began as photo editor, but when he worked with pictures he made layouts that were not just picture spreads in the conventional sense, but cinematic presentations in the Brodovitch tradition. Noting a dramatic difference, *Holiday*'s editor, Ted Patrick, offered Zachary the job of art director. "Jesus Ted," responded Zachary to the offer, "I'm okay, but why don't you try to get Brodovitch? He's the real master." Zachary introduced Patrick to Brodovitch, but the two did not hit it off.

Zachary knew little about typography, but he did have experience laying out the pictures in Zebra Books—small thematic pictorial mass-market paperbacks—that taught him the importance of scale. He saw himself as a journalist, not a designer per se, more interested in using the photograph to tell the story than to prettify a page. "I learned the picture is the layout. If you have a great picture, you don't embellish it with big type. You make it tight and sweet," he said. Soon he developed a cadre of talented photographers who brought life to the magazine through thematic picture essays. Among them were Arnold Newman, Tom Hollyman, John Lewis Stage, Robert Phillips, Fred Maroon, and Slim Aarons, many of whom followed Zachary years later when he became editor-in-chief of *Town and Country*.

Photography was the heart of *Holiday*, illustration was its soul. Zachary rejected the prevailing sentimental illustrative approaches used in most American magazines; he eyed European artists, specifically from England and France, for their surrealistic comic vision. "Frank brought sophisticated illustration to American magazines," recalled a colleague. "Other art directors brought powerful or clever images, but Frank brought an unprecedented sophistication. Of course it came from Europe since in the early 1950s there weren't too many Americans practicing sophisticated pen work."

Through *Holiday*, the artists Ronald Searle, Andre François, Roland Topor, Domenico Gnoli, George Guisti, and Edward Gorey (one of the few native Americans) were given latitude to develop their own picture essays and portfolios. Zachary avoided the reigning stars—"that would be too easy," he argued—but rather discovered his own galaxy. In most cases the artists transformed themselves in this environment. "Frank gave me a lot of firsts," recalled Ronald Searle. "From around 1959 to 1969 he gave me all the space one could dream of, the chance to fill it with color, the freedom to travel, and what proved to be the last of the great venues for reportage. Off to Alaska! Cover all of Canada! Bring me ten pages on the dirty bits of Hamburg! No expense spared. The years of travel for Frank gave me experience that cannot be bought. There was only one problem, he always called me 'Arnold' instead of Ronald. Then he probably always called [photographer] Arnold Newman 'Ronald,' so it balanced out."

Zachary developed what he called "environmental portraiture," common in contemporary magazines but unique in the early 1950s. "I would say to a photographer, 'If a guy is a multimillionaire painter, I want to see a whole lot of his paintings in the background and on top of that I want to see his castle in the background, too.' A photographer just couldn't walk in and take a picture of a subject; he had to assemble the components of the subject's life," explains Zachary. An example of environmental portraiture is a photograph for a special issue of *Holiday* on New York City showing highways and parks czar and power-broker Robert Moses standing omnipotently on a red girder over the East River. The shot illustrates Zachary's willingness to expend a tremendous amount of effort to photograph one perfect image. That is what defined his remarkable art direction.

Vogue

ALEXANDER LIBERMAN

For Alexander Liberman (b. 1912), the Russian-born art director of *Vogue* and later editorial director of Condé Nast from 1942 to 1995, design was a means. Making elegant layouts was never an end. Nor was it his métier. "Elegance was [Alexey] Brodovitch's strong point," Liberman exclaimed in the authorized biography *Alex: The Life of Alexander Liberman* (Alfred A. Knopf, 1995), "The page looked very attractive. But in a way, it seemed to me that Brodovitch was serving the same purpose that [M. F.] Agha [art director of *Vogue*] had served, which was to make the magazine attractive to women—not interesting to women." Liberman wanted to break the design obsession, "so I defended a more journalistic approach—rougher lettering, no white space, crowded pages, messier layouts." Some of the more elegant layouts in *Vogue* throughout the 1950s (the ones that are celebrated in the Art Directors Club annuals) were either designed by his associate Pricilla Peck or produced in spite of himself because *Vogue*'s editor-in-chief, Edna Chase, was not interested in messy layouts. "He was tilting at windmills," argued biographers Dodie Kazanjian and Calvin Tompkins about his preference for tabloid-styled typography.

Liberman became a layout man in 1933 for *VU*, the illustrated French weekly, where he worked with photojournalists such as André Kertész, Robert Capa, and Brassaï. They had not yet become the great photographers or as Liberman said: "There was no cult of photography at that time." But with them he learned how to effectively lay out tension-packed visual essays. In 1940 Lucien Vogel, the creator of *VU*, had come to America to work with Condé Nast and urged the publisher to bring Liberman to America as well. Upon arriving he did layouts for *Vogue* (at fifty dollars a week), until one day Agha unceremoniously fired him. "That was on Friday," Liberman recalled. "On Monday Condé Nast asked to see me, not knowing I had been fired. I brought my gold medal [which he received for an exhibition design in the Paris World's Fair of 1937], and we talked." At the time Nast was fighting against the clichés of fashion presentation, such as obscure typography and strange handwritten titles. Nast admired the newly started *Life* magazine and wanted *Vogue* to be more modern, in fact, more like a newsmagazine. "So when he learned from Vogel that I had been involved with a newsmagazine he was very excited . . . ," continued Liberman. "He said 'a man like you must be on *Vogue*.' He asked Agha to come in and said 'I want Liberman on *Vogue*.' Since Condé was an absolute monarch, Agha never told him he had fired me."

Liberman's success was further guaranteed not just because Nast valued the young Liberman's judgment, but also because he was taken under the wing of the former editor of *Vanity Fair*, Frank Crowninshield, who, since the demise of his own magazine had been the fine arts consultant editor of *Vogue*. One day during Liberman's first month on the job he was playing with a Horst photograph of a girl in a bathing suit lying on her back balancing a beach ball on her feet. He substituted the *O* in Vogue for the ball, which had no fixed logo in those days. "Crowninshield happened to be walking through the art department . . . he stopped to look at Alex's design, which impressed him enormously," wrote Kazanjian and Tompkins. "'There's a genius in the art department,' he told Nast."

In those days fashion plates were photographed in their hats and "royal robes." The main *Vogue* pages were created in Paris and arrived in New York entirely laid out. When Liberman was appointed *Vogue's* art director in 1942 he rebelled against Parisian dominance. "I had always resented the fussy, feminine, condescending approach to women by women's magazines," he asserted. "I thought it was important to shake up this rather somnolent society. If we had to show hats, I tried to mix hats with contemporary life." He also introduced art into fashion photography, and had Cecil Beaton photograph a model in front of some Jackson Pollock paintings. He admired the lack of artifice in photographs by portraitists Nadar, Atget, and August Sander. "Fortunately, Irving Penn came into my life," Liberman boasted. "He worked as an assistant with me in the art department on design and layout until one day I said, 'Why don't you go and take the picture.'"

Clarity and strength of communication are what interested Liberman. He admitted that graphic design for its own sake was meaningless, and was never so "sensitized to type" that a sixteenth of a millimeter spacing mattered. He rejected fancy typefaces and in 1947 changed the logo of *Vogue* from an elegant Bodoni to Franklin Gothic, which he claims until then was only used in newspapers. "I thought it had strength and looked modern. All the captions and the titles were set in Franklin Gothic, which was then revolutionary in women's publications."

"[I]mperfection was the essence of what Liberman was looking for—the breakthrough from fantasy and artifice into the here-and-now," wrote Kazanjian and Tompkins. "It was the antidote to the 'visions of loveliness' that Mrs. Chase and generations of *Vogue* readers cherished—visions that Alex wanted to banish forever from the pages of *Vogue*, in part because he felt that they were demeaning to women. *Vogue* was not really about fashion, he always said; it was about women."

Like Brodovitch, Liberman focused his creative energy on photography; he encouraged many women photographers to enter a field largely dominated by men. Liberman urged *Vogue*'s editors to publish photographs of Dachau concentration camp by Lee Miller, a former model who learned photography from Man Ray. "Nobody realizes that *Vogue* published them," he related. "But for me this was practically a justification for being on *Vogue*." For Liberman the lessons of Lee Miller's and Cecil Beaton's war photography changed the style of fashion photography. News photography in general and the emergence of a daring paparazzi forced a rethinking at *Vogue* that exceeded the boundaries of visual presentation. "I've always felt that Vogue was one of the strong pioneers for democratization, for women's rights, and for breaking down false cultural values," asserted Liberman.

Like Brodovitch, Liberman shared the belief that cinematic pacing was the visual backbone of a magazine. However, Brodovitch saw photography as an art form while Liberman believed that "photographs . . . were documents—momentary glimpses of something that could be printing in ink on a magazine page and eventually discarded. That was their function and their fate," wrote Kazanjian and Tompkins. Liberman made layout sequences the way a film is cut, trying to communicate moods through narrative imagery. "I hate white space because white space is an old album tradition," he charged. "I need to be immersed in the subject matter."

Liberman's approach has been subjected to harsh criticism from other designers who argue that his contempt for design has lowered the standards of magazine layout. But his anti-design fervor was sincere, and his disgust for anything that was visually flabby and antediluvian influenced all the magazines he touched. The most significant change in *Vogue* from the 1960s to the 1980s was its shift from bold elegance to striking sensationalism. Reversed type and other strong typographic devices (such as torn edges and screaming headlines) borrowed from the sensationalist press were used to accentuate motion, catch the eye, and communicate the message. "Much bolder type is intended for faster communication," explained Liberman. "White space does not exist, but a certain power, a daring has emerged that wasn't there even when I first used Franklin Gothic. In retrospect it seems dainty."

Scope

WILL BURTIN

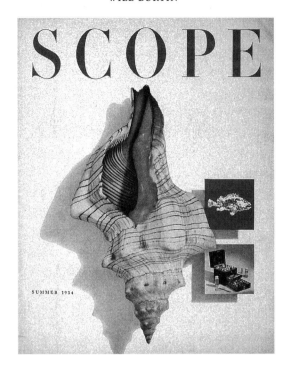

Bacteriology is about as interesting to graphic designers as typography is to bacteriologists. But for graphic designer Will Burtin (1908–1972), German-born son of a French chemist, learning to understand molecular biology, endocrinology, and bacteriology was like working with a classic cut of Didot or Bodoni. Making such complex data accessible to himself and others was as pleasurable as designing an elegant page of text. The role of the graphic designer, he wrote in *Print* (May 1955) was to increase the average man's understanding "between what the reading public knows and what it *should* know."

His professional life was, therefore, devoted to designing the kind of information that decorative designers reject as humdrum. Indeed such technical material might have remained forever ignored by aesthetics, relegated to dry textbooks, if Burtin had not become the champion of beautiful functionality. As design consultant for The Upjohn Company—one of America's largest producers of pharmaceuticals—from 1948 to 1971, he made functional design as attractive as any book or poster. Burtin refused to shy away from complexity, rather he interpreted it and then cast it in an accessible light. This was evident in the layouts and covers he designed while art editor for *Scope*, Upjohn's scientific house organ.

Burtin, who left Hitler's Germany in 1939 after being ordered to design posters for the Nazis, adopted Thomas Jefferson's dictum, "To learn how to keep learning is the mark of civilized man." He believed that designers had to know about more fields than just design, and among the ones he embraced, science was integral to every area of human activity. Science, the exploration and prediction of phenomena, is the holy grail of civilization, and for the sake of clarity scientists reduce time, space, and thought into abstract symbols. "The designer stands between these concepts, at the center, because of his unique role as communicator . . . interpreter, and inspirer," Burtin wrote in *Graphis* #4 (1949).

In this sense Burtin and Upjohn were the perfect match. His graphics for their advertisements, catalogs, and *Scope* were rooted in simplicity and directness with emphasis on the message. But Burtin imbued each piece with unique attributes that identified the work as his own. "Integration" was his mantra. It was also the defining trait of his graphic signature. "In designing booklets, posters, ads, exhibits, and displays, I noticed that the integration of job components towards a dramatic end-product asked for a measure of discipline difficult to define," he wrote. But he defined it as the marriage of order and instinct—learning everything there is about a particular subject and then allowing instinct to drive the design. In 1948 he designed an exhibition for the AD Gallery, entitled "Integration: New Discipline in Art," which demonstrated how he, and by extension others, clarify scientific information for general consumption. "Understanding of space and time relations is a main requirement in visual organization. In printed design images are superimposed on paper surfaces. The spaces inside and between letters, between lines of type, their relationship to illustration, are vital factors, which determine the eye's access to the basic information," he explained in terms that added a scientific dimension to graphic design.

Preoccupation with the graphic communication of scientific phenomenon and theory dominated Burtin's practice. As art director of *Fortune* from 1945 to 1949 he developed a vocabulary for conveying information through the design of charts, maps, graphs, and diagrams that made complex data discernible and understandable. Ladislav Sutnar noted in *Visual Design in Action* (Hastings House, 1961) that Burtin developed two basic approaches: The purist, where charts and diagrams were compressed into a two-dimensional projection, with color used to facilitate understanding; and the dramatized approach, the grouping of visual data with poster-like impact as in a chart describing how cosmic ray trajectories bombarded the earth. For this Burtin used airbrush to transform a photograph of the globe into a scientific diagram so concise and beautiful that it functioned both as art and information. This was the foundation on which he built even more intricate, yet no less accessible, graphics for *Scope*.

"Who said that science cannot achieve beauty," Burtin argued in *Print*. "What nonsense, that art cannot contain scientific truth! It is human limitation, deficiency of understanding, that make one or the other not do what they can do." Much like Leonardo da Vinci, Burtin asserted that art was the queen of sciences, a means of obtaining knowledge and communicating it to all generations. Being a designer was being a scientist. Design was about clarity, not sterility, and *Scope* was the embodiment of this goal. Originally designed by Lester Beall, *Scope* already had a modern format; its type was elegant and the graphics were sprinkled with signposts that guided the viewer through a hierarchy of information. Burtin took this to an even greater level of virtuosity. Edited for physicians, *Scope* was intended to improve the understanding of modern therapeutics, establish goodwill, and help sell Upjohn's products, yet Burtin gave it entry points that allowed access to the average reader, as well. It is no wonder that Burtin's mastery at translating tough scientific concepts—the ability to transform technical language into visual symbols—afforded readers a clear grasp of the material.

For the professional reader, arcane medical articles were not cluttered with dreary text boxes and drab flow charts. "The choice of format was . . . of great importance, not only to give the new journal the distinction we wished it to have but to appeal appropriately to the physician," explained Burtin in *Print*. The house organs already in existence ran the gamut in design from the most conservative to the most modern, and from those that used design sparingly to those that were highly and almost flamboyantly ornamental. Since conservatism was inappropriate for a journal devoted to a rapidly progressing science, contemporaneousness of design seemed mandatory but frivolousness seemed out of place. Burtin's designs were conceptually acute and couched in an idiom that was scientific in its clarity. His use of photographs of microscopic imagery gave the work an abstract quality, that suggested modern art. And in the modern spirit, design was not used for its decorative effect but as an integral part of the scientific presentations. Even the covers of *Scope* were designed not only to be attractive, but also to suggest the content. Inspired by contemporary art, the visually poetic collages and montages echoed formal elements of modern plastic art. In so doing Burtin developed a visual method that influenced how the pharmaceutical industry approached advertising and promotion for years to follow.

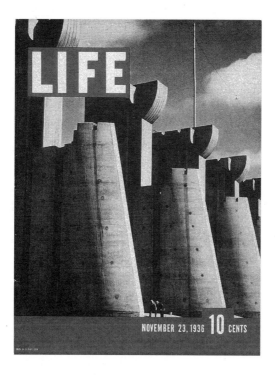

LIFE

NOVEMBER 23, 1936 10 CENTS

Life magazine was born during a period of sweeping social and political change, and quickly became the eyes and conscience of its continually expanding readership. Few magazines captured the world through such a powerful lens. No other picture magazine—certainly neither *Look* nor *Colliers*—could guide (or mold) the average American's perceptions of the world, nation, and neighborhood. *Life's* photo essays alternately celebrated individual courage, attacked tyranny, praised technology and science, and focused on the trivial, superficial, and ephemeral sides of life. Publisher Henry R. Luce described photography as "a new language, difficult, as yet unmastered, but incredibly powerful"—the most important machine age communications medium because it offered an objective window on the world. Yet *Life's* pictures were mastered and managed by photo editors who saw the importance of manipulating gesture and nuance. Before television no other medium reached as many individuals at once; and for decades no magazine stamped the collective consciousness with as many indelible images.

For all its influence, however, *Life* was not an original idea. Even its title belonged to a fifty-seven-year-old New York humor magazine whose publisher greedily held on to it until declining sales forced him to sell its name for $92,000 in 1936. The buyer was thirty-eight-year-old Henry R. Luce, cofounder of *Time* and *Fortune*. By the early thirties the idea of starting an American picture magazine was definitely in the air. Publishers like Condé Nast and the Cowles Brothers (who published the first issue of *Look* a month after *Life's* premiere) were contemplating their own. Luce aspired to develop a suitable theater for photographs long before he founded *Life*. *Fortune* was the inadvertent rehearsal. With *Fortune* Luce wanted to make the "most beautiful magazine in the world," but not a photography magazine per se. Nevertheless a key component of *Fortune*'s visual personality was striking still-life and journalistic photographs by Margaret Bourke White, Erich Salamon, and Edward Steichen.

The first complete, though unprinted, total dummy of what would become *Life* was produced in February 1936; it was designed to be a sixteen-page picture supplement for *Time*. The contents included features on skating champion Sonja Henie, Mexican politics, Czech president Eduard Benes, young Katharine Hepburn, the queen of England, and a variety of other views. This was the first clear definition of what would become *Life*.

The dummy was not greeted with praise. Paul Hollister, a top advertising executive at Macy's and self-described graphics expert, was disappointed with the design of the dummy. When he received a copy he had the temerity to write Luce a harsh critique: "It is inconceivable that even an avowed dress-rehearsal just for 'fun' should have turned out so far short . . . Great God—that a magazine should make even a tentative peek looking like this. . . . The dangerous thing is you have good raw material; it must not be butchered." Instead of earning Luce's rancor, Hollister's candor earned him the job of revamping the dummy. "My task," he later related "was to make a better pattern of each page, conforming to a total 'basic format' character: to 'sell' each page for itself, each picture within that pattern; to suggest changes of pace; to clean up margins and gutters; to eliminate sloppy disturbances and tricks from the page." After spending the ten days of his vacation cutting and pasting, he delivered an accordion-folded dummy that when spread out revealed the entire format at a glance. Luce did not respond for two weeks, but when he did he invited Hollister to lunch and reportedly said in front of his executives: "Good! Now we have an editorial prospectus! Now we have a basic format. . . . Now what do we do?" Hollister's reply was a profoundly condescending characterization of art directors:

What you do is get an art director and put him at a drawing board. Put tire tape over his mouth, because whatever he has to state should drain off through his fingers onto paper. Never let an art director talk.

On a table at his left put your basic format dummy for reference. On a table at his right feed him batches of photographs, with a note saying you want one, two, four, eight—any number of pictures you need, for each batch, and any suggestions you have for playing up any particular angles of the picture story.

So he makes layouts from the pictures.

If they are right, you pat him on the head. If they have strayed from the mood of the basic format, you take a small hammer, which you have chained to the wall for the purpose, rap him smartly over the skull, point severely to the basic format dummy—cry "No, no, no! Naughty!" He then repents and makes the layout right, or you get yourself a new art director.

At Hollister's urging Howard Richmond, Macy's chief designer, became the first art director of *Life*. With Richmond on the layout board, the second dummy was published for the week ending September 25, 1936. The content and design were closer to what would become *Life's* trademark design until the 1960s: a loose grid noted for varied and often unattractive gothic typography. There appeared to be a conscious rejection of design nuances in favor of a jumbled tabloid look. And yet the layout seemed to be appropriate for the stark black-and-white photography on disturbing subjects, such as "Hitler Speaks," about the pageantry of a Nuremberg Rally; "Cotton Pickin'," about the squalid conditions of Southern black laborers; and "Seen in Catalonia," about the horrors of the Spanish Civil War. Reviews came in quickly, and many were harsh even within the *Time* ranks. One executive wrote a memo to Luce saying that if the potential for a picture magazine existed this dummy was not it. "I found that I knew no further facts nor had I added to my visualized sense of the scene. . . . I think any reader would finish the dummy in half an hour or less" Other critiques came from commentator Dorothy Thompson who called the magazine "unmodern," and said that she expected something that would burst upon the eye "with the sort of inevitableness which has always been your [Luce's] genius."

Luce was not deterred. Richmond was given the job to design in a matter of days what became one of the most emblematic magazine covers in the world. Yet it was a freelance artist/illustrator, Edward Wilson, who suggested that the cover always be a black-and-white photo, a full bleed on all sides. Richmond added the sans serif logo dropped out of a red rectangle positioned in the upper left corner of the cover. After much discussion among *Time's* executives it was decided that a stationary logo was better than a movable one and it became the most identifiable design element of *Life*. Richmond also recalled taking a photostat and putting it on red paper with the paper extending over the picture. Luce liked it. The red was agreed to because Luce believed that if it worked for *Time*, it would be lucky for *Life*.

The first issue of *Life*, not unlike the rehearsal dummy, was a photo album rather than a well-paced collection of sophisticated photo essays in the tradition of the Berlin or Munich illustrated weeklies. This changed within the next two years as *Life's* picture editors and photographers became more confident about their missions. But although the stories and editing became tighter, the quality of the design betrayed a conscious effort not to rise above basic functionalism. It could be argued that the matter-of-fact format allowed the photographs the room to breathe. That the no-style design style was actually consistent with *Life's* style of photography, which rejected artifice (i.e., photographers like Edward Weston or André Kertész were never to be found in *Life*). But it could also be argued that *Life's* graphic neutrality was an impediment to its being a truly superb magazine.

Life's influence on America was greater than anyone, even Luce, ever imagined. *Life's* mix of truly remarkable photo essays (particularly leading up to and during World War II) by masters of photojournalism and terse writing style proved to be a winning combination. *Life's* editors understood the importance of packaging a picture story with the right balance of words. *Life's* caption and headline style—with its emphasis on clear, simple facts—guided the reader's interpretations of the evidence supplied in the photographs so that there was scant ambiguity. *Life* was more than a mere window, but a clearinghouse for information that only pictures could convey.

Herald Tribune

PETER PALAZZO

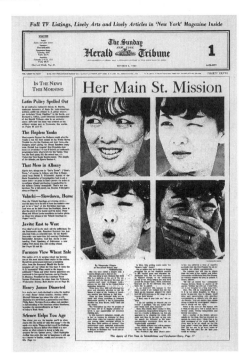

Good newspaper design was rare in 1963. Most dailies were composed by a makeup desk, not an art director or designer. At the end of the day or night after the "lock-up," as it was called, a more or less logically ordered newspaper was printed and delivered. The *New York Herald Tribune* was the exception to that rule.

Founded in 1924, the *Trib* was as drab as the "Old Gray Lady," the *New York Times*. Then, in 1963 it was miraculously transformed into something modern. It sported a livelier front page— not a typical presentation of news stories set in monotonous straight vertical columns, but a menu of appetizing world, national, and local events. It ran a unique summary of the paper's contents on the front page: A column of flush left/ragged right type with Bodoni subheads that introduced as many as eight separate items stretching down the left side of the page. Slightly wider columns and gutters throughout the paper made it more legible when contrasted to the tightly packed, eight-column *New York Times*. The headline typefaces were more consistent than in other newspapers. The photographs were noticeably larger, too. And most importantly, there were many clearer entry points into stories.

The *Trib's* makeover gave it a visual cohesiveness that allowed smooth navigation through the mass of information. It was a counterpoint to the screaming headlines and seemingly arbitrary layouts of the tabloids. The design was actually so "friendly," that readers initially complained that they couldn't take it seriously. But that didn't last long.

The new *Trib* was the work of Peter Palazzo (b. 1932), an advertising and publications designer who shoved American newspapers into the late twentieth century by enhancing news presentation through journalistic design. Not a single design element was superfluous, each was a signpost that guided the reader through the traffic of a daily newspaper. Prefiguring today's information glut, the *Trib* announced that design would have to play a meaningful role in the communication of ideas.

The daily *Herald Tribune* was revolutionary, but the rebirth of the Sunday paper was even more remarkable. The *Trib's Book World* and *New York* magazine were the prototypes of the modern newspaper supplement. Although the Sunday *New York Times* was stuffed with various sections and supplements, its makeup lacked a defining character. Conversely, Palazzo's *Book World* was typographically elegant—even to the untutored eye. He rejected the *Times's* bland visual diet of famous works of art and stock author's photographs in favor of imaginative illustrations by contemporary illustrators. These portraits, caricatures, and conceptual spots were entry points providing access to the sometimes dense literary criticism. They also synthesized, galvanized, and made accessible complex ideas. Although the black-and-white line made them reminiscent of nineteenth-century book illustrations (e.g., Tenniel's for *Alice in Wonderland*), they were not nostalgic interpretations of bygone themes.

The original *New York* magazine published as the Sunday supplement of the *Trib* was another milestone. There had been magazine supplements in most Sunday newspapers dating back to the early 1900s. But *New York's* seamless marriage of editorial and visual ideas was unprecedented. *New York* gave birth to both the "new journalism" (first-person reportage) and a new graphic journalism (smartly packaged information and visual essays). Typified by generous white space (unusual in newspapers), elegantly unobtrusive Caslon typography, gritty photography, and conceptual illustration, *New York* was a "slick" magazine on newsprint. Its covers defined a new fashion: many of the images were ordinary yet felt extraordinary through cropping and scale. The covers were single images often of a typical New York scene, rather than illustrating a story inside. A typical cover, a close-up of an everyday parking meter, was simple, memorable, and so New York. The celebration of the mundane object was consistent with trends in pop art.

Palazzo also transformed the "fronts" of all the other Sunday news sections so that they were designed like magazines. Photographs and illustrations were large, but rooted in good news judgment. Each section had a distinct look, while conforming to the whole. Palazzo orchestrated a presentation that neither fought with nor trivialized the news.

Unfortunately the new *Trib* did not last long. In 1963 a crippling newspaper strike forced an unhappy merger between three papers, the *Trib*, the *New York World*, and the *Journal American*, resulting in the *World Journal Tribune*. Although rooted in the design principles of the *Trib*, the trifurcated daily failed to garner a sizable audience and did not survive for long. In its wake, the *New York Times* began its makeover, and other newspapers followed suit. Yet in the beginning the *New York Herald Tribune* stood alone but influenced many.

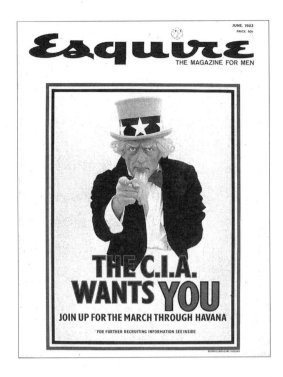

In revoking *Esquire*'s second-class mailing privileges the Postmaster General of the United States charged that the magazine was obscene and that its content was not "information of a public character." Although this sounds like the kind of detour around the First Amendment that Senator Jesse Helms might try, this action was actually taken in 1943 against a ten-year-old magazine whose reputation for taboo breaking was at that time more accidental than deliberate. Publisher David Smart never intended for *Esquire* to be revolutionary when he founded it in 1933, but rather to serve as a deluxe men's companion of literature, fashion, art, and women. It was the latter, specifically the sultry "pinups" painted by Alberto Vargas, creator of the Vargas Girl, that prompted the official action. *Esquire* immediately appealed its case to the Supreme Court, which in 1946 ruled that the Postmaster General had no discretion to withhold any privileges simply because it failed to live up to some vague standards of public morality. Justice William O. Douglas wrote that such an act would be "a power of censorship abhorrent to our traditions."

This wasn't the last time *Esquire* ignited public controversy or challenged public taste. Indeed for many of its almost six decades *Esquire* has been an American publishing institution without equal in the realms of art and literature, and sometimes politics. It has been alternately a trendsetter and bellwether. It has at times rocked the foundations of propriety, challenged cultural traditions, and has itself been shaken under the pressures of public opinion.

Henry Wolf (b. 1925) was hired as graphics editor of *Esquire* in 1952, five months after he joined the promotion art department as a junior designer. He was twenty-six, one of the youngest design stewards at any national magazine. Not only his age but also his elevation from the chorus line, or art bullpen, to a leading role on the masthead was the stuff of publishing industry legend. Arnold Gingrich, *Esquire's* founding editor—who set the tone of the magazine in the 1930s with an entertaining mixture of high literature and a touch of salaciousness—had returned to the company after resolving a major disagreement with publisher David Smart that had forced the former's temporary retirement. Since Gingrich left in the early 1940s, *Esquire* had taken a nose-dive, becoming ostensibly a girlie magazine with some mediocre fiction and fashion sections. When he returned, *Esquire's* layout was tawdry, replete with crass novelty lettering and sentimental cosmopolitan-styled illustration. He sought to cure its most superficial ills with a bright new talent.

Wolf took a year or two to get the magazine the way he liked it. The first big changeovers included conceptual photographic covers (shot by Dan Wynn and Ben Somoroff), streamlining of the rather horsy *Esquire* masthead (by Ed Benguait, who was in the art bullpen) into a distinctive logotype, introduction of simple interior typography, and development of a stable of expressive illustrators (including Tom Allen, Robert Weaver, Tomi Ungerer, Rudy de Harak, R. O. Blechman, and others). "Still," he lamented, "I couldn't get rid of the girlie gatefold for some time because Gingrich didn't want to lose that part of his audience."

Gingrich's tastes molded *Esquire* and influenced the young Wolf. "I do a magazine I'd like to get in the mail," stated the dapper man-about-town in an interview with Edward R. Murrow. "I like fishing, I like cars, I like some girls." He also appreciated what his editors and art director liked, and so gave Wolf as many as eight pages in each issue to present whatever he wanted. In the late 1950s *Esquire* was not just a collection of random stories and features, but an entity with a massive "editorial sandwich" as well. While some vestiges of the past remained, such as the girlie pics and gag cartoons, during Wolf's tenure the editorial mix had changed considerably. Wolf's interests in high and low culture was manifest in exciting photo shoots by some of America's most promising image makers. Indeed all writers and artists wanted to be showcased in *Esquire*. Ben Shahn and Richard Lindner did illustrations for one-hundred-and-fifty and seventy-five dollars.

Wolf left in 1958 and was replaced by his assistant, a young cartoonist and writer, Robert Benton (b. 1932), who later became an Academy Award–winning director (*Kramer vs. Kramer*). Benton was art director during a period of "fun anarchy." Gingrich was loosening control, and two editors, Harold Hayes and Clay Felker, were in a face-off for the editorship. For most of Benton's tenure no one was really in charge, allowing him freedoms that otherwise might have been impossible. Benton is credited by many of those with whom he worked for evolving editorial illustration to its next conceptual stage. Robert Andrew Parker, for instance, walked in from off the street with a series of "Imaginary War" paintings that Benton rushed into print. Milton Glaser recalls that "Benton was inventive and funny, and gave a very special stamp to the magazine during his period. It differed from Henry's *Esquire* not in terms of design but on the literary side. He had great ideas for stories that he and [writer] David Newman [later his movie collaborator] were always generating. To a large extent they formed the backbone of *Esquire*'s character at that time." Benton and Newman's most lasting contribution was Esquire's "Dubious Achievement Awards." Each year the "Dubies" laid waste pompous, hypercritical, and scandalous public figures with biting wit and needle-sharp truth, sometimes just bordering on libel.

Around 1963 Harold Hayes won the hard fought editorship of *Esquire*. About the same time Benton left to begin his movie career. David November was brought in as graphics editor to, as one observer puts it, "do the mechanicals for Harold." In practice, Hayes, a rather astute editor, was doing the art direction—and doing it poorly. The magazine was beginning one of its slides when Sam Antupit (b. 1932) was introduced to Hayes. Antupit had previously been Wolf's assistant at *Harper's Bazaar* and *Show*, and was working at Push Pin Studios when outgoing editor Clay Felker, whom he knew casually, asked if he would like to be art director of *Esquire*. Antupit took the job with the proviso that he have full control of the visual content of *Esquire*. The only caveat to which Antupit did not object was that George Lois (b. 1931)—whose agency Papert Koneig Lois was doing innovative advertising at the time—would conceive and design the covers. "It didn't bother me," admitted Antupit "because there was so much to do anyway. And Harold made a really good political point: . . . every editor felt that his or her articles were the best in the magazine and that they should be featured on the cover. Hayes said that it was up to him to decide which was the most important and not anybody else. But he couldn't do that without alienating his editors. So here was the perfect thing. An outsider read all the manuscripts and picked the one he wanted to illustrate on the cover. Sometimes he didn't pick Harold's lead. The Andy Warhol soup can thing was not the main featured article, but it was one of the best covers George ever did."

George Lois's *Esquire* covers produced from 1962 to 1971 are icons of graphic art, publishing, and American history. Many collaborations with photographer Carl Fischer took an average of three days to produce and are considered among the most memorable propaganda imagery in any medium. Harnessing the technique of photo manipulation, Lois and Fischer's covers equal the acerbity and acuity of pioneer German photomontagist John Heartfield. The trenchant coverlines were written by Hayes and Lois together. "Half the sentence would be said by one, and then the other would interrupt and finish it," recalled Antupit.

But Antupit did not sit on the sidelines. His first act was to reformat *Esquire*. He standardized all the column widths and made room for illustration. His goal was to let a reader open the magazine anywhere and know that it was *Esquire*. The type was understated by today's standards, but playful. He consistently used many new illustrators (including one student per issue) because, he said, "the same few old hands were used to excess by most national magazines, thus creating a visual sameness." But there was a fine line between the *Esquire* look and that of other magazines. One of Antupit's proudest accomplishments was a story on the building of the Verrazano Narrows Bridge (linking Brooklyn to Staten Island) with dramatic photographs by Bruce Davidson. The photo essay was so strong that Gay Talese was assigned to write an accompanying text. Despite their power, Antupit said, "It started out being twelve pages, but that was too much. To have all photography without text was no longer *Esquire*. It was *Life* or *Look*."

During the late 1960s *Esquire* covered the social and political revolutions of the era. While many of its covers announced stories about political folly and changing mores, its sardonic parodies, Dubious Achievement Awards, campus supplements, and other features underscored a commitment to a generation of "New Left" constituents. For a while, under Harold Hayes, *Esquire* even seemed to shed its male focus for a more ecumenical stance. But contrary to appearances Hayes was no radical. As Antupit said, "Harold would get a lot of his ideas from *Time* magazine. Here we're all going to openings and talking with writers and getting cut by the leading edge, and Harold's reading *Time*. . . . He was never a flaming activist." But he had an "absolute genius" for putting the wrong writer with the right idea. "Sending Genet and Beckett to the Democratic Convention was brilliant. I think Harold just wanted us to keep everybody off balance," said Antupit.

Seventeen

CIPE PINELES

The announcement for "An Evening with One of the Best," a lecture series in the late 1980s sponsored by the Art Directors Club of New York, promised to be an illuminating conversation with six veteran advertising art directors and graphic designers. The title of the evening was not false advertising, but the event was more than a little tainted. The participants were all men. Once upon a time, few would have raised an eyebrow at this, but when these evenings were held in the late 1980s, women had already become the majority gender, if not in advertising, then in graphic design. One woman who should have definitely been invited to participate was Cipe Pineles (1910–1995). As art director of *Glamour*, *Overseas Woman*, *Seventeen*, and *Charm*, the Viennese-born Pineles had as much, if not more, influence on publication design and illustration in America as any member of the Art Directors Club.

In 1948 Pineles became the first female member of the New York Art Directors Club (founded in 1921) and was eventually the first woman inducted into the Art Directors Hall of Fame. That she broke the sex barrier was indeed the reason for receiving a two-column obituary (with a photograph) in the *New York Times*, an honor usually reserved for individuals who have made lasting lifetime achievements. Although Pineles would have vehemently denied that this was an accomplishment on which to hang a legacy, it certainly was significant at a time when men—young and old—jealously guarded the gates to the exclusive sanctum. Pineles was proposed for membership in the late 1930s but was repeatedly turned down until, the story goes, her first husband, William Golden (she was also married to Will Burtin) refused to join, saying that he wanted no part of a men's club. Pineles was admitted the next day.

As a Pratt graduate, Pineles started looking for work in the early 1930s, landing a job with Contempora, a consortium of internationally renown designers, artists, and architects, where she designed modish fabric designs and displays. In 1933 she was hired as an assistant to Dr. M. F. Agha, art director of *Vanity Fair* and *Vogue,* where, as a novice at publication design, she received an invaluable education from this brilliant taskmaster. "We used to make many versions of the same feature. If we did, let's say, twenty pages on beauty with twenty different photographers we made scores of different layouts in order to extract every bit of drama or humor we could out of that material. Agha drove us to that because he was never happy with just one solution. And he was right too. We learned that magazine design should never play second fiddle to advertising," Pineles explained. Five years later she was appointed art director at *Glamour,* a poor relation to *Vogue,* targeted at women who couldn't afford the high cost of dress-up. Pineles was told that while money was no object at *Vogue,* at *Glamour* she'd have to do whatever she could on a meager budget. She made the proverbial silk purse, but was so indignant over Condé Nast's demeaning posture over this magazine that she left *Glamour* in 1944 to become art director of *Overseas Woman,* an army magazine for American servicewomen stationed abroad. From there she moved to *Seventeen,* a magazine that defined the teenage market for girls.

"That was the best job I had because the editor was attuned to the audience, and no matter what anybody else did, she and I knew that for seventeen-year-olds the subjects had to be done in a special way," Pineles recalled. She personalized her art direction in the sense that if she showed a cape, she chose the model, the accessories, and the atmosphere in which the garment was presented. Often, she also conceived the issue's theme. "Subject to the collaborative process with editors, art assistants, and artists, my personality was pervasive but not obtrusive."

As art director she transformed American illustration from a saccharine service to an expressive art. "I avoided illustration that was weighed down by cliché or convention, and encouraged that which was unique to the editorial context," Pineles said. She launched the illustration careers of the likes of Seymour Chwast and Robert Andrew Parker (whose work was then showing in art galleries) and commissioned illustration from painters Ben Shahn, Jacob Lawrence, Kuniyoshi, Raphael Soyer, and Robert Gwathmey. She was convinced that the magazine's audience of teenage girls was intelligent enough to appreciate sophisticated art and so she gave her artists unprecedented freedom. The convention in the late 1940s and 1950s was for art directors to give the illustrator rather detailed instructions of what passage or sentence to illustrate. Rather than force her artists to mimic the text, Pineles allowed them to paint what they felt. "If it was good enough for their gallery then it was good enough for me," she explained. The artists also made her design differently. "My sense of magazine pacing was altered because I had to separate one artist from another by distinctly different stories. And I was forced to use different typography than I had been used to so as not to compete with the illustration."

Her photographic sense was equally unconventional. Pineles found fashion to be a fascinating subject, and was interested in the effect it had on the way people felt about themselves. But she despised the haughtiness of *Vogue*'s fashion photography and urged *Seventeen*'s photographers to focus on real life situations. "Make the models look normal," she charged.

Type was as important as image. Pineles developed sound typographic principals on which *Seventeen* was based. "Changing the typeface for the headlines or the body type were outside manifestations. Although they would make the reader think that the magazine had changed, but actually, in order to make substantial alterations the contents had to be tackled from the outset," she explained. Nothing was formulaic. Type was designed according to the same expressive mandates as illustration, and her layouts had a timeless quality.

As an art director, Pineles described herself as personally responsible for interpreting in visual terms the contents of a publication, from appointing photographers and artists to certain features, to deciding to use many typefaces or just one. "But most important is the talent to harness it and create momentum so that the reader will keep turning the pages."

Eros and Avant Garde

HERB LUBALIN

Few graphic designers embody the aesthetics of their times as totally as Herb Lubalin (1918–1981). From the late 1950s to the early 1970s he was American typography. He built a bridge between modernism and eclecticism, joining rational and emotional methodologies in the service of commerce. His conceptual typography made letters speak and words emote. He was a pioneer of photo typography and promoted the practice of smashing and overlapping letters. He liberated white space from the orthodox moderns by refusing to follow the edict that "less is more." He experimented in the marketplace, not the academy, and once his radical approaches to type and page design surfaced in design annuals and shows they were thoroughly accepted and ultimately turned into fashion.

"We've been conditioned to read the way Gutenberg set his type, and for five hundred years people have been reading widely-spaced words on horizontal lines Gutenberg spaced far apart. . . . We read words, not characters, and pushing letters closer or tightening space between lines doesn't destroy legibility; it merely changes reading habits," Lubalin once wrote. He based his own approach upon the ideas of earlier twentieth-century type/image-makers, such as Kurt Schwitters and Lazar El Lissitsky, and then further married type and image into a single composition. Lubalin's work was very much of his time, and his understanding of the impact of the new technologies on contemporary perception was visionary. In 1959 he argued before an assembly of typographers that television had begun to have an influence on the way that type was read, and likened this kinetic quality to the speed with which type shoots by on advertising on the sides of buses. He reasoned that in this environment smashing letter forms together and including images in a rebus-like manner made type easier to decipher.

Lubalin had a tremendous impact on the practice of American and European graphic design for a generation. His hothouses were *Eros* and *Avant Garde*, which he art directed and designed. The former was America's first unexpurgated celebration of erotica, the quintessence of magazine pacing and composition at the time (despite its high design merits, its publisher, Ralph Ginzburg, was convicted and imprisoned for pandering through the U.S. Mail). The latter was a slightly more acceptable expression of the social and cultural flux within American society as influenced by the antiwar movement, civil rights, and the alternative New Left and youth cultures. A hybrid that crossed a magazine with a literary journal, *Avant Garde* lived up to its name. It was square (the size of a record album) in shape not in content, and featured illustration and photographs that busted the verities of 1950s sentimental and romantic commercial art. Both publications were alternatives to mainstream design conventions, but not in the raucous and anarchic sense, like the underground and psychedelic graphics of the same era.

Although Lubalin was soft-spoken, almost painfully shy when addressing people, he spoke loudly through design. His headlines for articles and advertisements were signs that forced the reader to halt, read, and experience. Story titles were tweaked and manipulated to give Lubalin just the right amount of words or letters to make an effective composition. The graphic strength of "No More War" (originally an advertisement for *Avant Garde*'s antiwar poster competition), which featured block letters forming the pattern of an American flag with a bold black exclamation point at the end, became an icon of the Vietnam war epoch. Lubalin rarely missed the opportunity to make his own variant of concrete poetry. Making words into sculptural forms was one of his typical mannerisms.

Some of the smashing and overlapping was contrived, and the conceit ultimately became self-conscious. But since Lubalin was its inventor, even the excesses must be viewed in the light of one who was testing the limits of form. For example, the Avant Garde typeface has been misused by a generation of designers who could not master Lubalin's distinctive ligatures. Lubalin played with and modernized these historic letter forms, but releasing the family of ligatures to the public as the key characteristic of the font was a mistake. In most other hands, Avant Garde became a silly novelty face; in Lubalin's, it was a signature.

Lubalin pushed design sometimes beyond the ken of his contemporaries. With few exceptions his experiments were conducted under marketplace conditions, which at once provided certain safeguards and made taking liberties all the more difficult. Lubalin's was not design for design, but design for communication.

Push Pin Graphic

SEYMOUR CHWAST, MILTON GLASER, REYNOLD RUFFINS, EDWARD SOREL

In 1953 when the first *Push Pin Almanack* was published it would have been impossible to predict that its four principle contributors, Seymour Chwast (b. 1931), Milton Glaser (b. 1929), Reynold Ruffins (b. 1930), and Edward Sorel (b. 1929), would develop a graphic style that challenged the prevailing ethic of functionalism imported from Europe (during the Bauhaus immigration), practiced by some leading American corporate and advertising designers, and manifest in work by exponents of the Swiss International Style. Yet when that first four-inch-by-nine-inch compilation of facts, ephemera, and trivia illustrated with woodcuts and pen-and-ink drawings was mailed out as a promotion for these freelancers, other New York designers and art directors began to take serious notice. Indeed the *Push Pin Almanack* brought in so much work from book, advertising, and film-strip clients that the four Cooper Union classmates decided to leave their day jobs and start Push Pin Studios, the major proponent of illustrative design in America.

The *Almanack,* originally conceived by Chwast and Sorel as a bimonthly promotional piece, was consistent with emerging historicist design trends. Victorian, fat letter type had previously been revived for use in advertising during the 1930s, fell out of favor in the 1940s, and was revived again in the 1950s when Otto Storch, art director of *McCall's* began using Victorian woodtype and ornament for editorial layouts. Indeed a taste for things old fashioned was returning, apparently as a reaction to what was perceived as cold, humorless modernism. "It was called the

Push Pin Almanack," Chwast said in a 1990 interview, "because it was a quaint name—and quaintness was popular in those days."

The contents were usually tidbits excerpted from books and periodicals and illustrated in styles that evoked the past. Each issue related to seasonal themes and included a few articles written especially for the *Almanack* on graphic design topics. Although it might be compared to Will Bradley's early 1900s *Chap Book* and other printer's keepsakes, the *Push Pin Almanack* was a special publication in the early 1950s, since most commercial artists who advertised their services to the trade were doing it in very straightforward, unimaginative ways. The *Push Pin Almanack* was a paradigm of conceptual acuity.

Six issues of the *Almanack* were published before the studio was started and two after. The printing of three thousand copies and the typesetting were basically done for free (or at cost) in exchange for designing and publishing the supplier's ad in the *Almanack*. Other operating expenses were paid for through the sale of small space ads sold after the first issue.

The narrow *Almanack* format was, however, creatively limiting. Wanting more freedom to explore different themes and graphic approaches, the *Almanack* was transformed into the *Push Pin Monthly Graphic*, which began as a broadside, printed in black and white on one sheet (usually newsprint). While the elegant and emblematic logo was designed by Glaser in a variant of German Fraktur, each studio member conceived at least one of his own issues, as well as combining their talents when the theme called for it. Themes were not exclusively design-oriented. There were issues on railroading, dada, and *War and Peace.* The subjects reflected the variegated interests of their makers. Chwast remembers conceiving an issue chronicling his first trip to Italy, which included photographs and drawings, and Glaser developed an issue on Italian sculpture. In these issues the Push Pin members further developed their interest in historical styles in a contemporary context.

The response to the *Graphic* went beyond immediate commercial success. It was historically significant in that it exerted an extraordinary influence on individual designers, and so the entire field. To this day, designers who were beginning their careers in the late 1950s and early 1960s recall how excited they were when a new issue arrived in the mail. For Push Pin included designers with varying talents sharing a distinctive methodology—a passion for what today would be called mass popular culture—who had an ability to translate their particular vocabulary of forms into mass communication (and selling) tools. They did so through a marriage—long rejected by the modernists—of drawing and typography. The *Push Pin Monthly Graphic* (and the subsequent *Push Pin Graphic,* renamed because they could never keep to the monthly publishing schedule) proved that designer/illustrators were not simply pairs of hands doing the bidding of a client divorced from the total context, but were creatives capable of developing ideas in totality. And Push Pin's work was not simply derivatively decorative, but originally witty.

Beginning as a newsprint tabloid, the *Push Pin Graphic* eventually came in a variety of sizes and shapes, evolving into discrete books and booklets on a variety of subjects, usually six times per year. The most memorable issues were on art deco automobiles (what Chwast referred to as "Roxy" style), "The Kings and Queens of Europe," "Rhymes by Edward Lear," "The Push Pin

Book of Dreams," "Good and Bad," "The Kiss," "Rock and Roll," a collection of wooden targets (Paul Davis's first significant work as a junior member of Push Pin), and Chwast's tour de force, "The South," a series of classic (and often racist) Southern stereotypes as backdrops for photographs of slain civil rights leaders. To heighten the polemic a die-cut bullet hole pierces through the heads of the civil rights workers until in the last picture, the bullet hole shatters the calm of an image representing the Old South, which is inset against a backdrop of the civil rights march on Washington. This poignant and caustic commentary was one of the few *Push Pin Graphic*'s with such an overt political message.

By the mid 1970s, the contributions made by Push Pin Studios had become part of the mainstream and the *Push Pin Graphic* had lost some of its innovative spark. To rejuvenate himself and expand into different realms of design, Glaser left Push Pin in 1975 and founded his own design firm. Chwast kept the Push Pin name and in 1976 decided to revamp the *Graphic* into a standard, nine-by-twelve-inch magazine format printed in full color. Chwast's goal was to make it commercially viable by rigorously selling advertising and subscriptions. He printed eleven thousand copies of each issue and eventually garnered around three thousand subscribers at the rate of fifteen dollars yearly (mostly designers in the United States and abroad who were not on the complimentary mailing list). Interest was high, but as a commercial property, the *Graphic* was losing money at a prodigious rate. Nevertheless, as a magazine it continued for four years and twenty-two issues.

Despite a seeming abundance of advertisements from graphic arts suppliers (mostly designed by Chwast and given in return for their services), financial pressures ultimately took their toll. "The All New Crime Favorites" issue was the last *Push Pin Graphic*, and perhaps not coincidentally it was the least interesting of all the issues. In all, eighty-six issues were published from 1953 to 1980, and ran the gamut from silly to profound. In its early incarnation the *Push Pin Graphic* had an incalculable influence on the conceptualization of graphic design and provided other firms and studios a model, and indeed a medium, to show their conceptual skills. But taken as a whole, the eighty-six issues show the evolution of a significant graphic style (and its makers) that not only eclecticized American graphic design, but also changed the style and content of American illustration.

Evergreen and Ramparts

KEN DEARDORF AND DUGALD STERMER

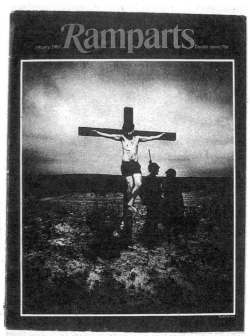

Few American magazines can claim to be agents of change. Most, even the once ubiquitous *Life* magazine, are reporters or chroniclers of their time and place. Others like *Vogue, Bazaar,* and even *Rolling Stone* have supported, cultivated, and propagated fashions, styles, and trends, but did not invent them. Most magazines are lightning rods, not lightning.

Among a generation weaned on the world war and raised on the sour milk of McCarthyism, the late 1950s and early 1960s was a period of intense cultural and political re-evaluation. In the 1960s the new bohemians began to push the boundaries of propriety through sexual and cultural expression in two magazines. *Ramparts* on the West Coast and *Evergreen* on the East, were the clarions of new aesthetics, politics, and morality. *Ramparts* was the voice of the political left and *Evergreen* was the voice of the cultural left. The former re-introduced muckraking to American journalism, the latter introduced banned authors' controversial texts. The former exposed CIA involvement in American colleges and universities, the latter revealed the erotic side of the American subculture.

In terms of design these were not 1960s versions of 1920s constructivist, futurist, or dada manifestoes—the more raucous underground newspapers of the late 1960s are a more accurate visual analog. Yet in content these magazines were no less radical than the political and cultural progressive journals of the 1920s. *Ramparts* and *Evergreen* conformed to appropriate design verities, with legibility the most important. "I never wanted a magazine where the design overpowered the content," asserted Fred Jordan, *Evergreen*'s managing editor from 1957 to 1971. Similarly, Dugald Stermer (b. 1936), *Ramparts*'s art director from 1964 to 1970, explained that a classical design format, rather than an anarchic approach, "lent more credibility to what must have seemed then like the hysterical paranoid ravings of loonies." The significance of *Ramparts* and *Evergreen* to the history of design is not as form givers but as conduits for various graphic forms in the service of politics and culture.

Evergreen Review was founded in 1957 as a quarterly literary magazine that published writers and poets whom its parent company, Grove Press, was already publishing in books. In 1952 Grove Press was a small, insignificant New York publishing house which was bought by Barney Rossett, a sympathizer of alternative politics and aficionado of radical literature whose tastes were influenced by progressive European writers. Grove was the first to publish Henry Miller's *Tropic of Cancer,* William Burrough's *Naked Lunch,* and Samuel Beckett's *Waiting for Godot* in America. Each book challenged America's puritanical values and intellectual standards; for in those days descriptions of the sexual act were veiled, and four-letter words were forbidden by the major publishing institutions. Rossett busted taboos and thwarted convention.

Evergreen began in a quarto format, at first publishing Grove's authors and expanding outward. Fred Jordan administered to the unillustrated layout of the quarterly and a few years later the bimonthly. In the late 1950s he used art photographs, including pictures by Robert Frank, as the primary illustration, and eventually he introduced ribald cartoons by one of Grove's author/artists, Tomi Ungerer, the black humorist from Alsace-Lorraine who became the golden boy of American illustration in the 1960s. In 1964, with issue #32, Rossett relaunched the magazine as a monthly, called it simply *Evergreen* (from a tree that grows in the grove), and filled it with stories and art designed to provoke the establishment. *Evergreen* was the vortex of cultural flux. "We printed subway and wall posters showing covers of the magazine with the tagline, 'Join the Underground.'" recalled Jordan.

That same year, 1964, Dugald Stermer was hired as art director for *Ramparts.* Founded in 1962, *Ramparts* was published by Edward Keating, a lawyer who had sunk a private fortune into a magazine that he described as having an anticlerical, liberal Catholic bias. Those early issues of *Ramparts,* which Stermer says was named for the "Ramparts We Watched," looked like a college literary magazine, with its unrelated typefaces, amateurish illustrations, and unsophisticated layouts. *Ramparts* was not a threat to the body politic. Keating was not an America basher, but rather a concerned citizen who saw aspects of America turning sour.

Ramparts was the "soft wing" of the left. This began to change in 1964 when Warren Hinckle III, then *Ramparts*'s brash promotion director, and Howard Gossage, a veteran San Francisco advertising man (who was also on the *Ramparts* advisory board), gradually took control away from Keating. Hinckle was named editor and Bob Scheer, a budding young investigative journalist, was hired as foreign editor. The former, who was not allied with any political movement or ideology, was a muckraker in the Hearst tradition and viewed sacred cows as moving targets; the latter, who maintained a healthy skepticism of all "isms," uncovered and sourced the earliest stories about CIA involvement in the Vietnam War and on American college campuses just prior to the emergence of a national antiwar movement. With Hinckle's taste for muck and Scheer's remarkable news instinct, *Ramparts* began to publish hot national stories ignored by most national media.

One of *Ramparts* most inflammatory stories was the confessions of a Green Beret who quit over the secret war in Vietnam. In fact, *Ramparts* drew stories from other disaffected government and military personnel whose consciences were bothering them, but who at that time—a few years before the Pentagon Papers story broke in the *New York Times*—could not sell their stories to the newspapers. The mainstream press was skeptical of such antigovernment attacks and more or less followed an "America Right or Wrong" stance. Stermer recalls that the goal of *Ramparts* was to "just raise hell."

Evergreen and *Ramparts* were two sides of the same coin. They were competitors only in that they appealed to the same audience, but enjoyed a rather a large crossover of readers and subscribers. Both magazines were sold on newsstands in the largest metropolitan areas, and given such visibility there was a mandate to look inviting.

Ramparts's design was based on classical, central axis book design. Stermer used Times Roman, with dingbats and Oxford rules to accent pages. At the time using book design for a magazine format was unique, and subsequently influenced the formats of *Rolling Stone* (which in fact copied Stermer's grid for its first issues) and *New York* magazine. Being an illustrator, Stermer had a healthy respect for conceptual illustration and commissioned quality work by known artists despite the magazine's pauper-like fees. He lured Edward Sorel into *Ramparts* by offering him a monthly visual column—Sorel's Bestiary, where the likenesses of famous people were portrayed as satiric animals in acute attacks on sacred cows. He commissioned Push Pin Studios, including founders Seymour Chwast and Milton Glaser. Robert Grossman did one of his best Johnson caricatures for *Ramparts*. Paul Davis did a number of covers, including one of South Vietnamese doyenne Madame Nhu as a cheerleader for Michigan State, where it was asserted in a *Ramparts* investigative report that the CIA was recruiting operatives for clandestine work in Vietnam. Stermer also hired Ben Shahn out of virtual retirement to do a portrait of the early antiwar senator William Fulbright. In the 1960s Shahn was under attack by the art establishment for being a propagandist. Stermer also commissioned Norman Rockwell to paint a portrait of Bertrand Russell. As art director Stermer also had a say in the editorial direction, which allowed him leeway in developing stories and features, including a memorable photo essay on the American town that endured the most Vietnam casualties.

Likewise, Ken Deardorf (b. 1935), *Evergreen*'s art director of longest duration from 1967 to 1972, designed an airy, economical format that relied on art and photography to define the magazine's visual personality. Deardorf did not have the same editorial power as did Stermer to assign articles and graphic features, but given a commodious working relationship with his editors, he was master of *Evergreen*'s visual persona. While it did not overtly resemble *Ramparts*, Deardorf admits he owes a debt to *Ramparts*'s elegance and simplicity.

Deardorf was not an illustrator, but like Stermer, he had a healthy respect for conceptual illustration. *Evergreen* used many of the same artists, including Robert Grossman, Edward Sorel,

Seymour Chwast, and Paul Davis, who created one of the most highly charged visual icons of the 1960s—the Che Guevara cover. Deardorf had a policy of trying out at least one new artist per issue. One such newcomer was Brad Holland who did some of his earliest editorial work for *Evergreen,* including an illustration for the premiere publication of "Viva Vargas" by Woody Allen, the story on which the film *Bananas* was based.

Ramparts's investigative stance required strong political covers, such as the John Heartfield-like photomontages by Carl Fischer, who at the same time was collaborating with George Lois on *Esquire* covers. *Evergreen* did more erotic than political covers. Rossett, the sole arbiter of covers, was convinced that the cover, not the content, sold the magazine. Given that much of Rossett's groundbreaking legal precedents were through the publication and litigation of sexually sensitive material, and that he believed that sex was a key political issue, it is logical that much of the visual material in *Evergreen* was indeed sexual. Fred Jordan adds that the left in the mid to late 1960s was not yet in tune with the nascent women's movement or above sexual exploitation. It wasn't until the end of the 1960s that the feminist movement began to exercise some control over left-wing publishing. At *Evergreen* Jordan cites the resignation in the late 1960s of two important male contributors over sexploitation; and Stermer admits, even though *Ramparts* was not overtly exploitive and ran some stories about the feminist movement, they had a blind spot, too. "The feminists had no reason to trust us," he admitted.

Rossett was no stranger to government censorship and litigation, and *Evergreen* was enjoined and seized, more than once, owing to its sexual content. One case involved the Nassau County district attorney's injunction against a 1964 issue citing pornographic content. According to the complaint, a confidential informant employed at the bindery "observed black and white photographs in the magazine which showed the nude human form, possibly male and female, but reputed by fellow workers to be two females; and that the forms portrayed various poses and positions indicating sexual relations. My informant further stated having read portions of the printed material . . . [that it consisted] of four lettered obscene language." In fact, the pictures were shot through a can of Vaseline and were barely visible to the reader much less the informant, who was a part-time employee of the bindery and whose husband was a retired police officer.

Ramparts was no stranger to legal hassles, either. The most threatening was the time Dugald Stermer arranged a 1967 cover shoot with Carl Fischer that showed his and three other *Ramparts* staffers' hands holding their burning draft cards—a symbolic gesture of nonviolent resistance against the war that broke at least two federal laws. The statute that was broken was known as the Disrespect Law, referred also to the burning of money or the flag. Since the disrespect was towards the symbol itself, Stermer determined that it didn't matter whether the cards were real or facsimiles, and so decided to burn the real thing. Not surprisingly an act of such defiance, commonly perpetrated in street demonstrations and now codified on the cover of a national magazine, forced the government to impanel a federal grand jury to investigate a possible indictment. While Stermer and Scheer initially wanted to fight the case as a freedom of the press issue, their counsel, Washington lawyer and football team owner Edward Bennett Williams refused to let his clients risk imprisonment and persuaded them to plead not guilty should an indictment be handed down. In the end, however, Williams pulled strings with his friend Lyndon Johnson, one of the bitterest of *Ramparts*'s enemies, to squash the investigation. In the end, the cover was a powerful emblem of Vietnam protest.

Ramparts and *Evergreen* have not published for almost three decades, but to look back at them now is not an exercise in nostalgia. They should not be seen merely as documents of the 1960s, but as monuments of activist publishing, where the writing, art, and design were brought together to make a revolution.

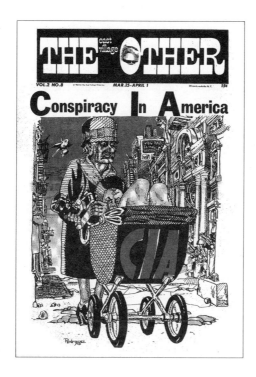

Robert Hughes once described the weekly paste-up night at the *East Village Other* (*EVO*) as "a dada experience." The year was 1970, and none of those who were toiling into the wee hours of the morning at one of America's first sixties-era underground papers (founded in 1965) knew what he was talking about. "Dada was the German anti-art political-art movement of the 1920s," he explained in a nasal Australian accent. "And this is the closest thing I've come to seeing it recreated today."

Hughes, the new art critic for *Time* magazine, was as welcome as any other weekly observer. Paste-up night at *EVO* was open to anybody who came up to the dimly lit second floor loft above Bill Graham's Fillmore East, a former Loews Theater on Second Avenue and Sixth Street just next door to Ratner's famous dairy restaurant. In the 1920s and 1930s the Lower East Side neighborhood was the heart of New York's Yiddish Theater. Since 1967 (the Summer of Love) it was the "East Village," the hippie capital of the East Coast.

Starting at 8:00 P.M. and lasting until dawn, the volunteer layout staff, under the watchful eye of *EVO*'s seventeen-year-old, self-appointed art director Stephen Cohen took the jumble of counterculture journalism and anti-establishment diatribe that was the paper's editorial meat and threw it helter-skelter onto layouts that bore a curious resemblance to the digital typography done in *Ray Gun* during the 1990s. Anyone could join in whether they had graphic design experience or not, yet many of the gadfly layout artists were usually too stoned to finish.

Corrections for their pages were often waxed at the office and cut-in during the long subway ride to the printer in Brooklyn.

The paste-up night was a 1960s tribal ritual. The plentiful joints and acid tabs were advance payments for a good night's work. The art director routinely emerged from the editor's office around 8:30 P.M. with a shoebox full of the stuff, as well as with the night's layout assignments, which included at least three pages of "intimate" classifieds. The layout crew would help themselves to the grass and manuscripts, find their tables, select their decorative ruling tapes, benday and transfer-type sheets, and settle down to design pages.

The *East Village Other* premiered in 1965 and quickly evolved from a neo-beat community organ into an alternative culture clarion. It was among the first to publish the masters of underground comix, including R. Crumb, Spain, Kim Dietch, and others. Intentionally or not, it borrowed graphic techniques from dada and surrealism. The cover of one early issue was a photomontage (in the manner of German satirist John Heartfield) of a serpent emerging from the battle fatigues of America's commanding general in Vietnam, William Westmoreland. For irrepressible irreverence, for dogged anti-establishmentarianism nothing could match the *East Village Other*. As a testament, it was declared contraband by the United States armed forces.

As for its graphic design, *EVO* was resolutely formless. While it had an anchored editorial page, the features and regular columns were unfettered by aesthetic or functional rules. The layout staff of between five and ten people on any given Thursday were all erstwhile amateurs without a clue how to create consistent design even if they wanted to. This had been true since its inception, but occasionally a professional would wander in, someone who knew the ways of the grid and central axis composition, who would attempt to insert a "correct" page into the anarchic mélange. But rather than bring order to the chaos, in the end, all approaches were thrown into the stew that was *EVO*.

In the final years of *EVO* during the early 1970s, the biggest influence on the layout sessions was the work of a veteran animator, Fred Mugubgub, who drew obsessively intricate designs for the covers (including the masthead) and some inside pages. He usually indicated that they be printed as a split fountain (the gradual mixing of two colors from top and bottom of the page) going from unreadable yellow to garish orange to bright red. Mugubgub's quirky, detailed, comic style for Seven-Up and Bit-O-Honey television spots had changed the look of animated commercials in the early 1960s, but he left Madison Avenue to pursue an unrealized film career. Along the way he had altered the style of *EVO*.

By 1972 the *East Village Other*'s circulation, which in its heyday hovered around seventy-five thousand, had plummeted to five or six thousand. It was kept afloat only by the sex advertisements and classifieds. Indeed this was consistent with the general demise of the underground press. The issues of *EVO* printed on cheap newsprint are difficult to find these days—they were either discarded or have turned to dust. The few that remain, however, represent a remarkable period of counter culture publishing, naïf design, and youthful exuberance that marked a truly democratic period (prefiguring zines and the World Wide Web) when cheap communications were available to many.

Rolling Stone

FRED WOODWARD

W hen he was thirty years old Mick Jagger predicted that nothing could be more embarrassing than singing "Satisfaction" at age fifty. Today the elder rocker eats those words. "Satisfaction" has become such a classic that it remains in the Stone's concert repertoire. Likewise, in the 1960s few would have imagined that *Rolling Stone* magazine would still be publishing after all the other counterculture rock magazines had folded. But having endured rock music's various fads, *Rolling Stone* is editorially vigorous and smartly designed. Like the Rolling Stones, *Rolling Stone* is an institution that sets standards.

Rolling Stone has changed through the years, though not as a slave to fashion. In each of its incarnations, during the tenures of art directors John Williams (1967–1968), Robert Kingsbury (1968–1974), Mike Salisbury (1973–1974), Tony Lane (1974–1976), Roger Black (1976–1978), Mary Shanahan (1978–1982), Derek Unglass (1982–1987), and Fred Woodward (1987–present), the magazine has steered its own course through design fashions and trends. When it premiered in 1967, psychedelia prevailed in *Rolling Stone's* home town of San Francisco, but the only concession to this popular style was the hand-drawn logo designed by psychedelic poster artist Rick Griffin (which was replaced in 1976). The rest of the magazine appeared in classical dress, down to the Oxford rules framing each page. When compared to the anarchic layout of most other underground newspapers *Rolling Stone* was not alternative, it was progressive.

When the magazine approached middle age in the late 1980s, Fred Woodward (b. 1953) decided to reprise many of the classic design characteristics that had been allowed to atrophy over time, such as Nicolas Cochin type, Oxford rules, and woodtypes. This was not nostalgia. *Rolling Stone*'s design direction does not retreat into the past for safe and easy answers, but rather builds upon imaginative typography and iconic photography. What distinguishes *Rolling Stone* from most other magazines is that its layouts are based on *ideas*—playful, historical, and unconventional—not knee-jerk responses to the latest computer font or trick.

Wit and play are hallmarks of *Rolling Stone*'s pages, especially in a layout like "Big Shot." While it helps to have a great photograph, not every designer would have taken advantage of the opportunity to use the big inner tube as a mnemonic element. The type is not particularly elegant—it's kind of horsy, but in the right proportions to all the other elements on the page. Moreover, the dot on the *i* is just silly enough to be brilliant—by echoing the tube it anchors the type. This is not serendipity, but planned play.

Two decades ago *Rolling Stone*'s key competitors were *Circus*, *Creem*, and *Rock*; they more or less covered the same subjects from different perspectives. The others approached rock and roll as fashion. So did *Rolling Stone,* to a degree, but it was also a forum for news, reviews, and commentary. *Rolling Stone*'s format underscored the writing. The others emphasized pictures. As the others died, *Rolling Stone* matured into middle age, though it would be erroneous to say that its format is aimed only at a late thirty- or forty-something audience. In the argot of today, it is age-unspecified.

Nevertheless, not every rock and roll aficionado wants news and analysis when squibs and gossip will do. Not every music fan cares about design elegance, in fact some say it's an anachronism. Some anachronism. *Rolling Stone* remains true to Alexey Brodovitch's vision of magazine design and his "astonish me!" principle that layouts should be well modulated for maximum impact and readability. *Rolling Stone*'s graphic persona at once rebelled against and defined a late 1960s design aesthetic, and, over time, evolved into something classic. *Rolling Stone* has aged well because its editors appear to understand what its readers want, and its designers realize that serving them needn't be about flagrantly busting convention. Unlike most magazines, *Rolling Stone* has known when to reinvent itself, and while representing a field that is mired in fashion, it has avoided its traps.

Parody is a form of derision that ridicules a work or its style by adapting and deliberately distorting its features. "Certainly parodies have been committed since the dawn of man's existence (7:38 A.M., daylight savings time)," Richard R. Lingeman explained in the *New York Times*. "According to one scholar . . . the earliest identifiable parody was by a Sumerian named Aktuk, who parodied the famed *Epic of Gilgamesh*." Visual parody has roots in antiquity as well, notably in Greek pottery by anonymous artisans. It was also common in major artworks during the Italian Renaissance. Pellegrino Tibaldi's frescoes on the Palazzo Poggi in Bologna, for example, are playfully mocking of Michelangelo's style. Today, Tibaldi's frescoes are intact and highly respected not as jibes at the Renaissance master, but as artworks on their own terms. Countless other commentators and jesters have, however, not been as revered for their parodies. History tells of many who suffered dearly for satirizing a monarch, dictator, or prelate. Lingeman reports that the rebellious Aktuk "was sentenced to twenty years as a galley slave—a cruel punishment at the time since there was very little water in that part of the world."

The job title "Lawsuits," listed in *MAD* magazine's masthead, is no joke. In the late 1950s and early 1960s, when *MAD* was publishing acerbic parodies of American consumer culture, many corporations and products were pilloried in mock ads that were not merely harmless or silly jests, but focused attention on such hot issues as rising medical costs, alcohol and tobacco dependency, homelessness, and environmental crime. Parodies of popular advertisements so realistic as to fool the casual reader might have been secretly enjoyed by Madison Avenue's bad boys, but many of their high-billing clients did not find anything funny about parodies that overshadowed their original ads. "Madison Avenue was savvy enough to know it would result in bad publicity," reported Maria Reidelbach, author of a history of *MAD*. The magazine was, however, never sued for its parodies of print ads, but it was sued for its song parodies that paired famous tunes to ridiculous lyrics. "The suit charged that the parodies were 'counterparts' to the originals since they could be sung to the tunes of the original," continued Reidelbach. Although two New York State courts agreed with *MAD* that the spoofs were indeed parody, and that "parody and satire are deserving of substantial freedom—both as entertainment and as a form of social and literary criticism," *MAD*'s publisher, William Gaines, realized it was prudent to have a lawyer on permanent retainer to block and tackle any potential litigants.

Such are the vagaries of parody, that *MAD* took precautions to prevent charges of trademark infringement by routinely altering the names of products (i.e., Crest toothpaste became Crust) while keeping the identifiable characteristics of a product or institution through mimicry of a package, logo, or ad format. One of *MAD*'s classics is a 1961 parody of the drug company Parke Davis's once ubiquitous Great Moments in Medicine campaign. Each ad featured a detailed painting of a warm-hearted healer tending to the sick and infirm. *MAD* lampooned the campaign by showing a doctor (holding back a smirk) presenting his inflated bill to the horrified patient and family members around the sick bed. The caption read "Presenting the Bill, reproduced here, is one of a series of original oil paintings, Practicing Medicine for Fun and Profit . . ." The tag line read: "Park-David . . . pioneers in bigger medical bills."

MAD's spirit was later adopted by Topps Bubble Gum for their extraordinarily successful, yet decidedly sophomoric Wacky Packs, a send-up (aimed at preteens) of well-known supermarket products, featuring pernicious puns on famous brand names. "Rather than a negative parody," argued Wayne Small, a marketing analyst, "Wacky Packs actually reinforced brand names in the minds of children." Nevertheless, under the threat of numerous legal actions Topps made a number of out-of-court settlements with offended corporations. Indeed, consistent with the Reagan administration's support of big business, during the 1980s the courts enforced stricter rules against defaming corporate (as opposed to individual) reputations.

Parody is a tricky and dangerous art for two primary reasons. First, because it involves fidelity to the original work. Second, because as an instrument of criticism and entertainment parody can infringe on intellectual property. Since parody is "a form of derision," even benign parodies are bound to get somebody's head out of joint. Moreover, the law is somewhat vague in its definition of what constitutes a violation of intellectual property rights, and what action is taken depends on the perception and inclination of the victim. Serious parody, no matter how biting, is more acceptable than that which is irresponsible or libelous. Parodying well-known images or icons not to satirize the host form directly, but to make additional commentary is common among graphic designers. As a graphic design tool parody makes sense only when the relationship, or visual pun, between the original and the new work is comprehensible. A successful parody is one that exploits the original style and character of a work for the purpose of making humorous and insightful commentary. A good parody makes sense; a bad one, none.

SPY

STEPHEN DOYLE

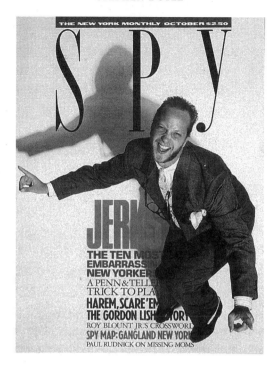

I am not a maniac about knowing who cut what face or if it's true to the original drawing," said Stephen Doyle (b. 1956), the cofounder of Drenttel Doyle Partners in New York, who in 1986 also designed the format of the original *SPY* magazine and supervised its first four issues. "I am a maniac about legibility and whether something is interesting enough to be set into type in the first place. With all the expense involved in typesetting one better be damn sure that a manuscript is worthwhile." Doyle described himself as a "translator" who believes in the power of typography to induce readers to read.

This may seem disingenuous coming from the designer who has promoted typographic anarchy in *SPY,* the New York–based satiric journal of culture and politics that defined the 1980s while it pilloried its leading players. But if Doyle encouraged the use of four-point text type and bled copy blocks off the page, it was consistent with a faithfulness to content. When articles in *SPY* were composed in multiple text faces of varying weights—some on excruciatingly tight column widths—Doyle was simply responding to the demands of the magazine. "*SPY* had many different voices," Doyle explained, "so we kept flipping type styles to reflect that. The editors liked sidebars so we used them everywhere and even gave the sidebars their own sidebars. We let the type be the messenger for the manuscript. So the type misbehaved because the manuscripts misbehaved. It was as though we let the writers design the magazine."

Doyle's design respected the content and rejected decoration for its own sake. In *SPY* every visual element had a purpose. "*SPY* was like a magazine in therapy," Doyle continued. "It was so much about the process of making magazines that we let it all show." *SPY*'s frenetic pace was a reflection of media-blitzed America, but Doyle based its visual persona on a variety of personal precepts, too. "I have a theory," he said, explaining why much of the type is set small enough to require a microscope. "People will read what they want to no matter how big or small the type. And while I don't believe in obscuring a message, through scale changes, one can nevertheless have a little fun with it." Doyle took a lot of heat for his Lilliputian preferences, but never repudiated himself. For *SPY*'s first anniversary party Doyle even designed an invitation with the necessary information set in two-point Granjon italic in the form of an exclamation point—he included a magnifying glass. "I wouldn't have done that with a lot of copy," he admitted, "But some things just call out for it."

A few years after it premiered the *SPY* style was mimicked by other magazines, usually in instances where the subjects didn't merit it. Doyle reacted by turning down the volume. Doyle's typography is not really about misbehaving. As he has pointed out, the inspiration for the original *SPY* was not the urban environment or decontructionist architecture, but a 1540 polyglot Bible where each language is set in a different typeface.

Culture Tabloids

FIRST ANNIVERSARY ISSUE

NY **Talk**

GETS THE DIRT OUT!

APRIL 1986

ONE DOLLAR

Tabloids developed their malodorous reputation because of the gutter journalism practiced by their earliest proponents in Britain and the United States. It wasn't until after 1900 that the term *tabloid*, which originally connoted a newspaper half the size of a standard broadsheet (about the size of today's *New York Times*), became synonymous with the lurid and scandalous. In 1919 two cousins, Joseph Medill Patterson and Robert Rutherford McCormick, began publishing the New York *Daily News*. Its reduced, tabloid size was immediately successful, being easier to hold and read on New York's sardine-packed subways. The *Daily News* was assured even greater circulation by its unbridled preoccupation with sex and violence, conveyed by screaming headlines and full front-page halftones. It became the largest selling tabloid in America and spawned many competitors. One of these was Bernarr Macfadden's *Daily Graphic*, which entered into an unprecedented circulation war, giving its readers the most reprehensible displays of gutter publishing ever practiced. Despite, or because of this, tabloid mania flourished in the 1920s until loud outcries from the protectors of the public's morals tempered, somewhat, the rumor, sex, and gore.

Recently, there has been a more benign reason for publishing a tabloid: economy. Printers could offer publishers twice the product for half the price. For this reason a tabloid explosion began in the mid 1960s, coinciding with the free-speech movement and subsequent rise of youth culture. Low-budget underground or counter-culture papers appeared around the country and abroad. Anarchic drug, sex, and political weeklies, like the San Francisco *Oracle*, the Los Angeles

Free Press, and the *East Village Other*, were in the vanguard of this movement. They were cheaply produced, inexpensively sold (average twenty-five cents), and widely read. They were records and totems of their times.

The tabloids' design was governed by a marked lack of money and technology, and administered by naïfs, who, armed with press-type, benday and patterned Letraset screens, ruling tapes, Addressograph phototype, freebie photographs, and raunchy comix, produced raw but expressive nongraphic design. Despite the differences in approach, the instinctive underground layout practiced then and the mannered culture tabloid design of today are remarkably similar.

Underground papers began declining in the late 1960s. A new genre of alternative "sex-culture" papers (many published by the underground papers themselves to make money) stole a fickle audience that preferred nudity to profundity. The underground tabloids finally died in the mid 1970s with the end of Vietnam War, the resignation of Richard Nixon, and as the "me" decade was taking hold. At the same time, a national paper shortage resulted in the decrease of the standard tabloid size and an increase in production costs. Moreover, many of those involved in underground publishing either were irrevocably burned-out, or simply grew up and became interested in more conventional lives and livelihoods.

Those designers who used the underground press as a kind of graduate school—including Roger Black of *Rolling Stone* and Ronn Campisi of *Fusion*—wed the street-smart design and exuberance they learned with conventional design practices while working for more establishment journals. Hence, during the mid 1970s a second wave of counter-culture tabloids emerged, such as the *Real Paper, Boston Phoenix,* and *Chicago Reader*, among others, which were neither raw nor anarchic, but rather found solace in convention. Indeed, the only editorial difference from regional consumer magazines like *New York*, was that the tabloids appealed to a slightly younger, but nevertheless upwardly mobile readership. In terms of their design and editorial bent, these publications were upbeat, yet somewhat staid blends of New York's *Village Voice*, the *New York Review of Books,* and *Rolling Stone.* Their purpose was to educate, inform, and otherwise provide readers with reviews and calendar features.

Slightly before the second wave crested, the granddaddy of new tabloids, *Andy Warhol's Interview,* appeared. In the early 1970s a few avant-garde artists gave vent to their ego needs by publishing artsy, gossip-filled magazines. That Warhol's was the only one to survive was a tribute to a basically sound idea: interviews with movie stars, glitterati, and eccentric personalities otherwise ignored by the establishment press, and a forum for fashion-conscious writers. The first issues were quarterfold formats, with lackluster design and no exceptional visual personality. But *Interview* quickly developed a constituency and, during the latter 1970s, a distinctive look when Richard Bernstein was commissioned to do regular full-color cover portraits. *Interview* developed into an odd but enjoyable amalgam of *W, Vogue,* and *Harper's Bazaar,* spiced with a dash of *People.* Its gossipy tone appealed to culture vultures, those maturated groupies who thrived on *avant-gardism. Interview* became a safe haven for the Jekylls and Hydes of society called Yuppies, who were squeaky clean by day and down and dirty at night. *Interview's* interior is minimally designed, like a hip *New York Review of Books,* to allow for maximum photographic impact, and so as not to compete with its advertising. Nevertheless, it has influenced the appearance of many subsequent culture tabs.

By the late 1970s, boomers born in the late 1950s and early 1960s were clamoring for their own cultural voices. On the West Coast, punk was the predominant attitude and style. Its proponents in Los Angeles spawned a neo-underground tabloid called *Slash*, a raucous blend of type, image, and neo-underground comix (cartoonist Gary Panter was the leading practitioner), and perfected what has been called the "ransom note" style of cut-and-paste design (somewhat related to futurist experiments in the teens). In San Francisco, a bizarre publishing diversion, *Wet: The Magazine of Gourmet Bathing*, ingeniously wed the 1970s sexual preoccupation with fashion-conscious nihilism cut, of course, with tongue-in-check, ribald wit. *Wet's* art director practiced an ad hoc, gridless approach to layout (at least for the first year, after which *Wet* changed design and editorial format and dropped bathing from its title). *Wet* signaled a post-underground obsession with esoterica.

On the East Coast, *Fetish*, a similarly arcane culture tab, was published and designed by David Sterling and Jane Kosstrin. But *Fetish* was a linchpin of sorts. Its content was not sex or drug oriented, but was a somewhat rarefied exploration of "the man/object matrix in contemporary culture" (translation: articles on art, architecture, and design against an avant-garde backdrop). Although its design was once described as a marriage of underground and Condé Nast fashion-magazine sensibilities, it made a purposeful departure from ad hoc gridless design, to a controlled, yet playful, anarchy (or "new wave" design). Also on the East Coast, new wave/punk music and its offshoots gave rise to tabloids like the *New York Rocker* and the *East Village Eye* (apparently a reference to the *East Village Other's* eye logo). Both had a random and skewed approach to layout that resembled their underground forerunners, but without the naive integrity.

Although it seemed that the underground aesthetic was not entirely dead and the torch had only changed hands, the truth was that alternative culture had changed. Politics was no longer operative, rather interest in material culture was dominant. The antiestablishmentism, so naively practiced by the underground, was codified by a new group of design-literate practitioners. Outrageousness became an end in itself, manifest in the design clichés of the period—a *Mad Max, Road Warrior*, post-Holocaust vision of life wed to a skewed 1930s modernism. It quickly emerged as a distinctly identifiable style, easy prey for style merchants, the entrepreneurs who learned from the 1960s that even the most sincere youth culture can be a profitable commodity. Punk was co-opted and commercially packaged as new wave. A domino effect began, in which a plethora of new wave products—from clothes to watches to records—created a need for eye-catching advertising, which in turn created demand upon publishers for outlets.

In Los Angeles, the surge in chic, trendy, and not altogether uninspired new wave–styled publicity for boutiques, restaurants, and galleries fostered the tabloid *Stuff*, ostensibly an elegant supermarket handout whose only editorial content (save for a few insignificant text pages) was its paid advertising. Indeed, some of the ads were designed with more zest, imagination, and panache than a lot of conventional graphic design. On the East Coast, similarly focused "square" tabloid/magazines, including *Details, Paper,* and the full-sized tabloid, *New York Talk,* were merely editorial environments for advertising. As a rule these East Coast periodicals ran "soft" feature stories, picture spreads, and random items covering their cultural milieu. Although each masthead listed a considerable number of contributing writers, it is not unfair to say that the writing would not overtax the average reader. At best it would entertain and at worst, separate one page of ads from the next. Still, these publications should not be totally dismissed as fluff.

A famous photograph taken by Berenice Abbott in the early 1930s shows a packed newsstand in midtown Manhattan with more than one hundred different magazines for sale (most for about a nickel, as compared to today's average three-dollar cover price). Despite the varied photographs, illustrations, and titles on their covers, many of the publications look alike. Graphic style is a visual indication of a cultural period. Many of the magazines in Abbott's photograph are in the deco mold—then the dominant style. Although style represents a period, it does not always state content. In every period there are manifestations that define the dominant attitude and those that copy it. That many of today's culture tabs look the same is simply a signpost of a design-conscious and technologically advanced period. Some of the publications discussed here will be forgotten, like the hundreds of me-too undergrounds published during the late 1960s and early 1970s. Others will make a lasting contribution to (rather than merely being a reflection of) the visual culture and the culture as a whole.

The Face

NEVILLE BRODY

Neville Brody (b. 1957) was weaned on the dada-inspired nihilism of British punk in the 1970s. But *The Face*, his first important magazine design, was no neo-punk tabloid, but a slick, youth culture magazine that combined a 1920s avant-garde sensibility with contemporary style. The magazine focused on music, film, nightlife, art, dance, and the lifestyle of Britain's hip culture. Brody was twenty-four when he joined *The Face*, bringing his rebellious punk sensibility to a larger, consumer-oriented venue. In Nick Logan, editor and publisher, Brody found a sympathetic collaborator. Logan never undertook any market research, preferring to trust his instincts. He gave Brody great freedom to invent the visual structure of the magazine, even to the extent of moving the masthead logo all over the cover (including sideways). Budget limitations and tight deadlines (Brody would design forty pages in as many hours) were offset by on-the-spot decisions on design and editorial content that afforded risk-taking that would be impossible in a larger publishing house.

In 1976 Brody entered the Royal College of Printing expressly to learn enough about visual communication to use it for his own ends. Although he rejected fine art as elitist, his early work centered on images, and when he used typography it was in a similar, illustrative way. A decided contrarian (if a teacher approved of his work, he redid it), Brody found a catalyst and a philosophical home in the anticommercialism of the punk movement. Just out of school, he joined designers like Barney Bubbles, Malcolm Garrett, and Peter Saville in designing record sleeves. He first worked for the design studio Rocking Russian, then for Stiff and Fetish Records, two of the most popular independent record labels in Britain. Set up by Jake Riviera, a friend of Bubbles, Stiff Records was a freewheeling environment where outrageousness not only applied to sleeve design, but also to marketing schemes. Stiff once printed a sleeve with the wrong band on the cover hoping fans would then buy the corrected version. Brody relished the creative freedom but became disenchanted with the commercial manipulation.

Brody's first few issues of *The Face* were image oriented. "I hated type," he once confessed. In fact, in school he dismissed type as incredibly boring. This admission belies the fact that under Brody's art direction, *The Face* was a wellspring of typographic quirkiness. Brody presented text in a straightforward manner but surrounded it with compelling imagery, headlines, lead decks, and subheads. He soon realized he could extract as much emotive energy from the typography as from the imagery. Inspired by the work of Russian constructivist Alexander Rodchenko, Brody began to use heavy rules and hand-drawn, sans-serif typefaces, and to craft letterforms that functioned like emblems and crests. Typefaces were custom designed for headlines; letters were truncated, squashed, lopped off and blurred; fonts were mixed within a word; icons replaced letters within words, and headlines combined with symbols and functioned like corporate logos. "I had no respect for the traditions of typography, because I had no understanding of them." Brody explained.

As his confidence grew, Brody used the magazine as a virtual stage allowing himself more freedom to question the very core of visual expression. He reframed the magazine as an ongoing dialog with the readership where idiosyncratic graphic signposts and icons, which may have initially appeared incomprehensible to the reader, gained meaning through consistent application over a series of issues. Brody, uninhibited by the edge of the page, treated the magazine as a continuum where what happened on page five connected to what happened on page fifty-five. He re-examined the use of page numbers, considering symbols instead. Regarding the contents page of a magazine he said, "You decide to have a contents page to act as a key—it's an advert for the magazine, a second cover, equivalent to the back of a book jacket where you read the blurb."

In 1984 the contents page logo in issue #50 was a banner-like emblem with mixed-font typographic forms. The letterforms were sideways, but were drawn in such a way that when looking at them straightforwardly the *T*s became pluses, the *E* became an *M* and *C* doubled as a lower case *N,* introducing multiple interpretation. From issue #51 through #55 Brody incrementally deconstructed the graphic elements within the logoform as well as the exterior shape itself, until only abstract glyphs in a strong rectangular shape were left. In deconstructing the contents page logo over several issues he tested the limits of readability and the strength of continuity.

The Face was unorthodox, but not anarchic. "Everything in *The Face* was reasoned; every single mark on the page was either an emotive response or a logical extension of the ideas," said Brody. It was the interweaving of two narratives, one visual and one textual on a gridded plane. Brody's headlines became objects, like in the February 1985 issue a custom-designed *M* for the opening spread of an article on Madonna becomes in the March issue the *W* to lead into an article on Andy Warhol. It was not a joke, or a response to a budget cutback, but a visual analog of the way Warhol appropriated imagery. The grid was a simple system to complement the complexity and innovation Brody brought to it, yet definitive enough to convey unity.

Brody envisioned a magazine that would inspire other designers to ask more questions, not provide a crib sheet for quick graphic solutions. "Essentially, I think I failed. My ideas were weakened into style. The very thing I used in order to get the ideas across—a strong personal style—was the thing that defeated reception of the ideas," Brody lamented in 1990, years after leaving the magazine. *The Face* ultimately did become a style guide. In 1986 he moved on to *Arena,* also edited by Logan, who, disregarding market failures of larger publishing houses, like *Cosmo Man* for Condé Nast, decided it was time for a magazine that targeted a male audience. *Arena* was a more sophisticated version of *The Face,* a consumer-oriented quarterly publication featuring upscale people-watching fashion, sports, and travel in addition to the mainstay lifestyle articles that had worked for *The Face.*

Frustrated with the appropriation of his work, Brody decided to stop designing "the new thing." After the first two issues of *Arena,* which resembled *The Face,* he returned to classic modernist methods. He used Helvetica and chose typefaces like Garamond Light Condensed and Kabel Bold for headlines and cover lines. Photographic quality was paramount. This was a postmodern homage to the Swiss school, yet it was not Swiss, but rather "Swiss Tech," the marriage of Swiss-influenced typography and futurist composition. But critics and imitators were not far behind, and graphic style in Britain edged toward this neo-modernism.

By 1988 Brody's career reached a turning point. The publication of *The Graphic Language of Neville Brody,* written by Brody and his collaborator Jon Wozencroft, coincided with an exhibition of his work at London's Victoria and Albert Museum. Both were misinterpreted as self-congratulatory hoopla. Almost immediately afterwards, Brody, suffering from a severe case of overexposure, stopped getting British work, which triggered a financial crisis. At the age of thirty the man who had been called the first graphic design superstar needed to regroup. He found new clients in Japan and Europe. He immersed himself in digital technology. Testing entrepreneurship, he became a partner in FontWorks, the British arm of FontShop, the international font-distributor started by Erik Spiekermann. In 1991 he launched the experimental type magazine *Fuse* with Wozencroft as editor. A quasipromotional tool for FontShop, each issue of *Fuse* presented a set of typefaces in a digital format organized around a theme, background material on the fonts and their designers, printed style sheets, and an editorial essay.

In *Fuse* #10, Brody introduced Freeform, a collection of abstract shapes. It was designed with the articulation of a typeface, it had a certain rhythm, coloring, and repetition, but it abandoned the consensual meaning of the alphabet in favor of pure emotional impact. Freeform was criticized for its illegibility and dependence on a personal visual language. Brody explained, "It's moving from representational to expressive typography. I think the parallel with what happened in painting is absolutely precise. . . . Putting desktop technology in the hands of the nondesigner liberates the designer from the necessity of representation in the same way that the camera liberated the artist."

From *The Face,* whose typographic idiosyncrasies prefigured the modern digital revolution, to

Fuse, which attempts to describe the intersection of the linguistic and the pictorial, Brody has been unwavering in his quest for a new visual sensibility based on ideas. Always more comfortable with questions than answers he asked, "In the West, the Roman and Greek alphabets provide the basis of the consciously designed letterform, but you can carry this further back to the ancient Egyptians' use of hieroglyphs or even to ritualistic markings in caves. At what point does true typography begin?"

Emigre

RUDY VANDERLANS AND ZUZANA LICKO

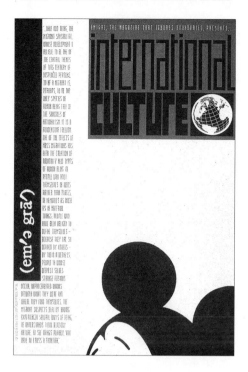

Deconstructivist typography, an idea more or less inspired by linguistic theory, had a complicated birth and many midwives. During the 1970s Basel designer Wolfgang Weingart developed a system of typographic reordering as an alternative to the dominant *Neue Grafik* or international style. On the surface his radical approach was chaotic, yet underneath it was built on a structure of hierarchical logic. Many of Weingart's exponents were schooled in academic modernism and found that this new method released them from old strictures. The modern method was becoming unresponsive as shifts in technology, economy, and politics began to unhinge the canonical absolutes.

The spread of electronic media and computer technology began to suggest, if not define, new ways to present information. With new interactive media, graphic design could no longer be one dimensional. As traditional methods of designing books and magazines were challenged, visionary American designers like April Greiman and Dan Friedman found new ways of busting the grid. Harnessing the primitive characteristics of electronic media and making strengths out of technological weakness resulted in new methods that, over time, evolved into a language. The use of multiple layers of discordant typefaces integrated with imagery became, on the one hand, a commentary on the information deluge, and, on the other, a signpost that underscored new perceptual pathways. A similar discordant eruption in typography took place in the late 1890s, the Victorian era—the chaotic, nascent period of commercial design when job printers purposely mixed different typefaces together in the service of fashion and function.

In 1983, a year before the introduction of the Macintosh computer, Rudy VanderLans (b. 1955) and Zuzana Licko (b. 1961), the former Dutch and the latter Czech, founded an alternative culture magazine they called *Emigre*. What started as a cousin of the 1960s underground newspaper developed into the clarion of digital typography and design. The first Macintosh and its primitive default faces inspired *Emigre*'s founders to focus on design. VanderLans called it "a cultural force," rather than a passive observer. Emigre Graphics (later Emigre Fonts), the type business, became a pioneer in typeface design, and *Emigre*, the magazine, propagated the faith. Emigre Fonts introduced some of the earliest and quirkiest dot-matrix and, as the technology improved, high-resolution digital typefaces. *Emigre* magazine showcased the leading proponents and exponents of a new typography that wed youthful rebellion, evolutionary imperatives, and intellectual curiosity into type and page designs that challenged the canonical rules. These designers sought to reach audiences that were either disinterested in, or turned off by orthodox modern approaches, and they developed visual codes that forced re-evaluation of conventional type design.

As *Emigre* challenged the status quo it earned the ire of certain proponents of classic modernism. Massimo Vignelli referred to the new typography as "garbage," and in "The Cult of the Ugly" (*Eye*, No. 3, Vol. 9) I (Steven Heller) called it a "blip in the continuum of graphic design history." This antipathy was not entirely a knee-jerk reaction to the new, but it did reveal an inevitable generational schism. On the surface trends and fashions were being scrutinized, while underneath lurked discomfort with change.

Once released from the safe haven of the laboratory the tension between young and old ignited. Progress in art and design is certain, but the baton is rarely passed smoothly. Action and reaction in design are as natural as the changing tides, and just as necessary. Arguments force practitioners of all ages to assess and defend. Stasis, the hobgoblin of creativity, is invariably disrupted. The approaches promoted by *Emigre* encouraged a reevaluation of old methods and aesthetics in the light of a new technological era. They became touchstones for progress but, paradoxically, also provided templates for mimicry.

It is axiomatic that when a progressive method becomes popular its edges are smoothed. By the time the avant-garde enters the mass consciousness many of its successful experiments have already been diluted, reduced to little more than style. In fine art the acceptance of radical approaches into the mainstream may mean victory for their proponents, but ultimately the most progressive forms are neutered to appeal to a larger audience. The outsider in graphic design is even more of a contradiction. The commercial nature of design necessitates that what's outside be brought inside or become irrelevant. Regardless of how determined *Emigre* was to forge new directions, they were incapable of preventing appropriation.

The cultural feeding frenzy that overtook the *Emigre* "style" was predictable. What *Emigre* initiated was co-opted by scores of mainstream, cultish manifestations—from magazines to MTV. The ethos further outgrew its experimental stage and became the "cool" or "hip" way to communicate. But this should not diminish *Emigre*'s impact or significance.

Emigre was not just the standard bearer, but the bearer of standards for experimental digital typography—and it continues to be. As other serious type designers initially adapted traditional methods to the digital medium, *Emigre* pushed the boundaries. VanderLans and Licko, while launching a business, took the necessary, courageous leaps that pioneers must take. Although the mechanics of type had changed frequently, the fundamental nature of type remained constant throughout the shift from hot metal to photo, even to early computer type. VanderLans and Licko were not satisfied to follow tradition, and ultimately they created a tradition of its own.

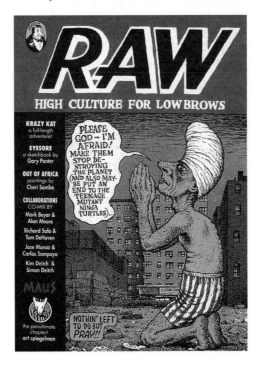

Françoişe Mouly (b. 1955) and Art Spiegelman
(b. 1948) were married in 1982. Within a few months they gave birth to a publishing business
which they named Raw Books and Graphics. It was consigned to a corner of their loft in
Manhattan's SoHo district, where it quickly grew into a healthy concern. Mouly, a native of
Paris, had been an architecture student at the Ecole des Beaux-Arts and worked as a colorist for
Marvel Comics in New York; Spiegelman, a native New Yorker, was an underground comic strip
editor and artist with a unique analytical approach to comic page construction. The comics
brought them together; and because they agreed that viable outlets did not exist in America for
the kind of experimental work that interested them, they decided to fill the void left by the
demise of underground comix in the mid 1970s by starting a publishing venture that would
somehow provide a forum for new and radical forms. This entrepreneurial commitment thrust
them into the roles of publisher and editor, and more reluctantly into being the virtual foster
parents to a group of artists whose unconventional styles and approaches were given little
encouragement in mainstream publishing circles. Within a few years *RAW* magazine, the flagship
of Raw Books and Graphics, had enlivened a moribund field.

The reasons for starting Raw Books and Graphics were compelling. "There was no place
worth appearing in," Spiegelman said. "There were magazines interested in me, but they wanted
me to bend myself out of shape to do comics that would be fitting for them." Mouly had already
single-handedly published *The SoHo Map and Guide,* an ambitious first project that sold

advertising space to SoHo merchants. Now she wanted to learn printing, so they bought a used multilith press and rebuilt it in their loft.

"The real genesis of *RAW*," admitted Spiegelman, "was Françoise's goading it into existence, because it had a certain logic after she began getting involved in publishing. That meant setting up a makeshift distribution system so that things she printed could get around, which she did. And then her being ready to take on something more ambitious. For a while it seemed that might be books rather than the magazine, but the advantage after we did the first issue of *RAW* (which we swore we would never do again) was that we'd already set up something we could build on. A book is always another book and requires a whole new constituency to be gathered each time. The magazine gave us a core of readers." *The SoHo Map and Guide* provided enough capital to publish a first issue, and the makeshift distribution Mouly had set up eventually paid them enough to keep going without further infusions of outside capital.

In a way, *RAW* evolved from Spiegelman's anthology *Breakdowns*, at least in adapting the book's expansive dimensions (eleven by fourteen inches), which enabled him to print his strips at almost their original size. There were other reasons for the new magazine's format, too. "*RAW* started at a time when there were a number of large-size cultural tabloids, such as *Wet*, *Fetish*, *Skyline*, and *Interview*," recalled Spiegelman. "The only thing they had in common was the fact that they were 'New Wave,' with a large size and a new sensibility. So whether it was fashion, architecture, art, or politics, they sat next to each other on the newsstand. Whatever vestigial marketing sense I had said that if we did comics as a large-size thing, they could sit next to the architecture magazines and nobody would say 'where should the comic book go?'"

From the outset, Spiegelman and Mouly wanted a three-letter title in the tradition of *MAD*. They went through many ideas before settling on *RAW*, which for them meant "having vital juices intact" rather than untamed or aggressive. To this they added a new, enigmatic subtitle with each issue, among them, "The Graphix Magazine for Damned Intellectuals," "The Graphix Magazine of Abstract Depressionism," "The Graphic Aspirin for War Fever," and "The Graphix Magazine that Overestimates the Taste of the American Public." By comic book standards, *RAW*'s premiere issue was tame: every element was purposefully designed. But in the beginning *RAW*'s design was a disquieting mix of what seemed like trendy new wave detailing, and, by modernist graphic design standards, a comic book heavy-handedness. Every page had an obtrusive running head, an inelegant rule with a panel in which the artist's name appeared, and a page number dropped out of a circle. Although this became *RAW*'s signature design element, when it was first introduced it appeared a distracting conceit. Each contents page was an artwork in its own right, with overprints, drop-outs, and other design details that echoed the punk graphic aesthetic of the time.

RAW #1 was printed on heavy white paper and included a small comic book by Spiegelman called "Two-Fisted Painters" (one of his many strips devoted to exploring and satirizing the comic form). The front cover had a color panel pasted on it to give Spiegelman's stark black-and-white illustration another dimension and to compensate for the lack of full-color printing. "A lot of attention was paid to its objectness," said Spiegelman, who was creative consultant for Topps

Bubble Gum Company during that period, and has always harbored a fetish for novelty that he translated into the magazine. Though many of the strips were visually raw compared to those of slick mainstream comics, their surreal and heady unpredictability forced the reader to take notice. By *RAW* #5, which Spiegelman and Mouly agree was the most challenging issue, the various mixtures of typography, art, and novelty were so well integrated that *RAW*'s style was decidedly its own. *RAW* had become a genre.

"It was never meant to be a long-lived project," sighed Spiegelman, revealing his characteristic angst. "It was meant to be a demonstration of how something could be in a better world, and ended up having its own logic and momentum; it began, more or less, steering us rather than us steering it. And I think that's still true." That momentum was generated in part by the *RAW* artists, who were being given a venue in which to grow and were not eager to give it up. "Once everything was set up," continued Spiegelman, "it was just as easy to feed it as to kill it."

RAW certainly did fulfill a need. It became a veritable mecca for quirky and visionary artists and storytellers from all over the world. From the initial five thousand print run, subsequent runs increased incrementally to almost twenty thousand by *RAW* #8, the last of the large-format issues. Among the relative newcomers were Gary Panter, who already had a cult following for his *Jimbo* strip, which appeared in a West Coast punk magazine called *Slash*; Charles Burns, who had only ever published spot illustrations before sending his meticulously drawn translations of 1950s horror and love clichés to *RAW* for consideration; Jerry Moriarty, who was teaching at the School of Visual Arts in New York and barely getting published before *RAW* picked up his "Jack Survives," a surrealistic view of the banal; and Mark Beyer, with his *art brut* tales about depression and death. Other homegrown discoveries included Drew Friedman, Ben Katchor, and Mark Newgarden.

Spiegelman and Mouly also published the cream of the European comic strip artists, including the brilliantly designed strips of Joost Swarte from Holland and Ever Meulen from Belgium; the explosive graphic fantasies of Pascal Doury and the *noir* storytelling of Jacques Tardi, both from France; and the seductive comicalities of the Spaniard Javier Mariscal. In his effort to separate *RAW* from underground comix, Spiegelman featured the masters of the genre and published new stories by Robert Crumb, Kim Deitch, Justin Green, and Bill Griffith. He wanted to provide a forum for illustrators, too, but most of those he invited failed to produce. The notable exception was Sue Coe, who provided some of the most strident polemical visual commentary in *RAW*, as well as two *RAW* One-Shot books, *How to Commit Suicide in South Africa*, a visual indictment of the effects of apartheid, and *X*, a paean to Malcolm X.

In the time since Raw Books and Graphics was conceived, more *RAW*-inspired magazines were published. *RAW* itself has been seriously analyzed for pushing the limits of the form, and for reviving the nascent intelligence of the American comic strip. This cottage publishing entity that Spiegelman and Mouly invested their hearts into has, arguably, done more to awaken Americans to the integrity of the comic strip than all the efforts of comics writers, artists, and producers since comic strips began in the American newspapers almost one hundred years ago.

Beach Culture

DAVID CARSON

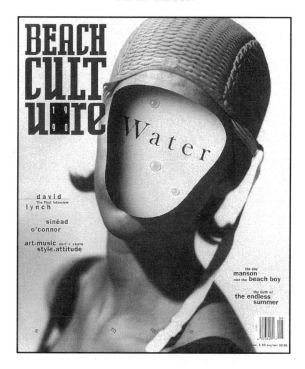

Good magazine design is not simply a process of imposing tried and true formulas, but one of creating formats that complement an editorial viewpoint. Yet much magazine design is tried and true because publishers want to be safe. Advertisers prefer it that way.

On rare occasions magazine designers rise above the design clichés imposed by marketing experts, and when an intrepid designer does take the plunge notice must be taken. Every so often a magazine captures the Zeitgeist. In the mid 1970s *Wet: The Magazine of Gourmet Bathing*, with its premiere cover showing two photographs, taken ten years apart, of a mother and her daughters sitting naked in a bathtub, marked a shift from "underground press" politics to cult fetishism. In the early 1980s *Emigre*, with its alternative cross-cultural coverage and raucous type design, suggested a new wave was about to crest. In 1990 *Beach Culture*, a journal of West Coast watersports, became the cult magazine of the moment when it surfaced in design competitions and annuals nationwide. Its primary audience was surfers, but it became the benchmark of 1990s design. Its sole designer, David Carson (b. 1956), transformed the magazine into a showcase for radical typography and design tomfoolery.

Beach Culture was full of design indulgences and technological trickery, but it also included striking photography and illustration by talented artists, such as Geof Kern, Marshall Arisman, Milton Glaser, Matt Mahurin, and Henrik Drescher. As a chaotic pastiche of typographic excess it was often unreadable, but conventional readability was not necessarily a virtue given its context. *Beach Culture* catered to an audience that was able to navigate the visuals and text. No one ever said a surfing magazine should look mainstream. But neither was there a demand that it be cutting edge. Certainly most other surfing magazines were void of distinguished design. Since surfing is such a specialized activity and writing about it is arcane, one would hardly have expected a surf magazine to be typographically innovative or risqué.

Beach Culture was born out of a two-hundred-page annual advertorial called *Surf Style* that included puff pieces about the products advertised therein. Carson embraced the publisher's idea to make *Surf Style* into a real magazine. This former design intern at Surfer publications, former art director of *Skateboard* magazine and *Musician,* had studied typography with designer Jean Robert in Switzerland and learned about the power of vernacular forms and how type could be made expressive through abstraction. After the premiere issue of *Beach Culture* many advertisers dropped out, confused by its odd mix of beach and culture, yet enough of them remained to continue publishing. Carson seized the opportunity; following in the footsteps of contemporary design progressives, such as Wolfgang Weingart, Rudy VanderLans, Rick Valicenti, and Neville Brody, he began his own expedition into new—and often illegible—realms of visual presentation. Carson's spin on typographic anarchy was different than his predecessors. He not only infused his pages with wit and irony, but also accepted that a magazine page is ephemera.

In one issue he ran a story in three conventional columns of type, but rather than reading the traditional way, vertically down, it read horizontally across with each sentence jumping from one column to the next. "Usually, I take my design cue from the story or art," said Carson, "but this time I just did it to have fun. Once the reader caught on I'm sure they had fun too." On another page Carson designed the page numbers to be larger than the main headline, a joke in itself, but when the editor changed the order of the pages, he kept the original number on the page because, he explained, "I just happened to like it there." In the final issue (of a total of six) the page numbers were eliminated and jump-lines simply said "continued." These hi-jinks forced the reader to find his or her own way.

Initially, Carson used the newest Emigre typefaces. "I wanted to use whatever was totally new and untried," he explained. However, he became more dependent on existing typefaces and published a "Special No Emigre Font Issue" (a reference that went over the heads of most surfers). "Emigre faces were becoming like clip art, too identifiable, too dated," he explained. "*Beach Culture* was trying to be fresh, and I was using typefaces that were appearing everywhere because they were hip and cool; it was just too easy."

Carson went further to make design that was difficult for his readers *and* writers. "In the beginning there were some writers who were real upset that their stories were too hard to read, but I found after a few issues that the very same writers who complained about crazy design were also upset if their article was not given that kind of treatment." Giving an article his special attention signaled that it was important. By the final issue, Carson had taken this premise to the extreme by obliterating most headlines. Letterforms were overlapped, overprinted, smashed, and otherwise covered by black, mortised, random bands abstracted to the point of incomprehensibility. Carson was designing for the code-busters to make sense of it all.

Colors

TIBOR KALMAN

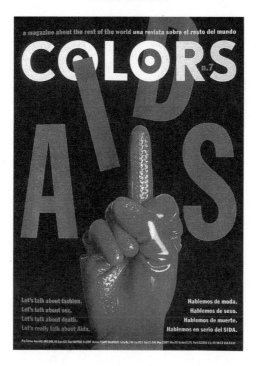

Critics argue that Benetton's highly visible, captionless double-truck ads and billboards featuring, among other images, a dying AIDS patient, war-weary refugees, and an Angolan rebel soldier nonchalantly holding a human bone, are sensationalist ploys to manipulate public perception. And for what? To sell sweaters? Yet Benetton claims that its motive in publishing such imagery is not just to garner the most publicity for the least possible PR dollar (although this certainly has been the effect), but to use their position as a successful business to communicate strong, if unpopular, messages about society and the world.

Productless advertisements are not new. During World War II, American corporations showed support for the war effort through institutional advertising that wed patriotism to corporate identity. Since the 1960s, Mobil Oil has propagated corporate citizenship through editorial ads on op-ed pages. In the 1980s Esprit, Kenneth Cole, and Ben and Jerry's devoted advertising and packaging space to promote social and environmental causes. But in the 1990s Benetton went a step further with a compelling campaign created by advertising director Olivero Toscani that attached the Benetton logo to a series of sensitive issues. What began as "The United Colors of Benetton," a product-based series of ads showing multicultural kids and promoting ethnic and racial harmony, evolved into captionless double-truck journalistic photographs of the kind mentioned above, which ultimately begot Benetton's own magazine, *Colors.*

Colors is not a fashion or style magazine in the "downtown," experimental, post-punk tradition; nor is it an institutional or corporate house organ. Rather its editorial focus is dedicated to presenting a harshly realistic, though often humorous, world view. Tibor Kalman (b.1949), editor-in-chief of *Colors* from 1990 to 1995, characterized the magazine as a cross between *National Geographic, Life,* and *The Face.*

The primary reason for starting *Colors,* noted Kalman, was that Toscani was unhappy with the magazines in which he advertised; "He would get insane when *Vogue* and *Vanity Fair* had the audacity to turn down Benetton ads because they crossed the line from being safely elegant to strongly editorial." Toscani wanted a magazine that would build upon what he was already attempting to do through advertisements, and Kalman, who had been working with him on researching the photographs, wanted a magazine that would do nothing less than "change the world." Hence the bilingual (English and Italian) *Colors* was "The first magazine for the global village," said Kalman, "aimed at an audience of flexible minds, young people between fourteen and twenty, or curious people of any age."

Colors is ostensibly a visual magazine because no matter how good a translation of text is, some meaning or nuance is always lost. An image needs no translation. The magazine further intended to be "nomadic and focus on subcultures and tribes," and its design has been just as "nomadic." Under Kalman's tutelage *Colors* did not adhere to a single format. Each issue had a different graphic configuration (although the same gothic typefaces were repeated); the first three had radically different sizes and shapes. "It was not tied to any one environment." Kalman explained. And since he believed that most magazines trade on despair, he wanted *Colors* to be naïve enough to look at the world in an optimistic way. That proved to be a real challenge.

In its often disturbingly vivid coverage of such themes as deadly weapons, street violence, and hate groups, *Colors* offered a disquieting contrast to the publisher's own fashion products. Even the way it was printed, on calendered pulp paper, which soaked up ink and muted the color reproductions, went counter to the brightly lit Benetton shops with happy clothes in vibrant colors. *Colors* was not Benetton's darker alter ego, but it did serve to "contextualize," as Kalman defined it, Toscani's advertising imagery. Indeed the basis for much of the criticism leveled at Benetton's advertising campaign had been the absence of context. Without a caption or explanatory text the images appeared gratuitous—shocking yes, but uninformative. The campaign signaled that Benetton had some kind of a social conscience, but the ads themselves failed to explain what it was. With *Colors* the advertisements appear as teasers for a magazine that took stands on issues of war and peace, love and hate, power and sex.

Colors explored themes routinely ignored by the mainstream press, such as "How Much?" a story about how much money entrepreneurs pay for human body parts throughout the world, and "What's Sexy," a compendium of what turns people on around the world. *Colors'* fourth, and most charged, issue was devoted to racism and expressed the need for tolerance and co-existence in the world. By avoiding sappy clichés and timeworn stereotypes, Kalman's brief editorial set the stage for a conflicting catalog of bitterness and hope: "We don't usually dwell on the bad news. And racial violence is definitely bad news. But this issue of *Colors* is about how race affects our lives and how racism can take many forms, not all as obvious as those we've presented here. These pictures are our way of showing the problem quickly and bluntly. It will take us longer to show you the solutions."

Like a serum that employs disease to immunize the body, *Colors* turned racist to fight racism. A feature titled "Who Are You?" spoke through a racist's voice to spew hundreds of slurs, epithets, and obscenities used by different ethnic and racial groups to describe their neighbors and enemies. In "So, What's the Difference?" the racist ploy of comparing and distinguishing physical characteristics was co-opted by using photographs of various kinds of ears, noses, and hair to show that physical differences are, in fact, endemic to humanity. In a stark photograph of two bleeding fingers, one black and the other white, the message that there is no fundamental difference is made vivid. In the same feature people from around the world were asked to describe difference within their various native and adopted cultures: "For the time being, I'm the only Ibo boy in Hungary. The people I work for love me for being an Ibo," replied a young boy; "I do not belong to a race. I am Egyptian. In my country it makes no difference what color you are or where you come from. The main difference here is rich and poor," said another. A disturbing feature, "How to Change Your Race," examined various cosmetic means of altering hair, lips, noses, eyes, and, of course, skin color to achieve some kind of platonic ideal. "What if . . ." was a collection of full-page manipulated photographs showing famous people racially transformed: Queen Elizabeth and Arnold Schwarzenegger as black; Pope John Paul as Asian; Spike Lee as white; and Michael Jackson's already altered features are further given a Nordic caste. "Race is not the real issue here," Kalman noted. "Power and sex are the dominant forces in the world."

But not everyone was pleased. A man in a Rolls Royce was arrested in London after smearing black paint over Benetton's store windows. He told the police that it was in retaliation for Benetton's irreverence towards the Queen. In Japan, twenty-five thousand copies of *Colors* were burned because authorities were afraid that the feature on epithets would seriously offend Japanese people, and they feared reprisals against Benetton's Japanese employees.

The racism issue of *Colors* touched raw nerves. It also proved that design in the service of a strong message could influence people. The problem was, people do not always want to be influenced in such ways. Numerous Benetton store owners were reluctant to offer the magazine; some adamantly refused. *Colors* was volatile and unpredictable. It was the first official organ of a mainstream corporation not to be dictated by demographic surveys or bottom-line policy. The magazine mirrored the passions of its editors and contributors rather than the marketplace and offered readers challenging ideas rather than safe clichés.

Language

DESIGN AS A VOCABULARY

ANHALTISCHER
KUNSTVEREIN
JOHANNISSTR. 13

GEMÄLDE AQUARELLE

KANDINSKY

JUBILÄUMS-AUSSTELLUNG

60.
GEBURTSTAG

Geöffnet:	Wochentags: 2-5 nachm.
	Mittwoch u. Sonntag 11-1
Eintritt:	Mitglieder: Frei
	Nichtmitglieder: 50 Pfg.

Walter Gropius, founder of the Staatliches Bauhaus—the state-funded school of arts and crafts—in Weimar, Germany, began his revolutionary school "not to propagate any style, system, dogma, formula, or vogue, but simply to exert a revitalizing influence on design." The Bauhaus was born in 1919. Germany had just lost a devastating world war. A fragile new republic had been established with its constituent assembly in Weimar, but despite the hopes of the Weimar Republic, the nation was in economic turmoil. The Bauhaus derived its strength from the social ferment, but ultimately suffered from the relentlessly belligerent political environment. For the Bauhaus to have been closed down only months after the Nazis came to power in 1933 suggests that it was a radical political institution at odds not only with German tradition, but also with Adolf Hitler's nationalist ideology. In fact, though the Bauhaus was built as a "Cathedral of Socialism" on a foundation that included Marxist theories about art and industry, politics per se was not primary.

The Bauhaus was established to help save the German economy by preparing a new generation of artists and artisans to deal effectively with the increasing demands of industrialization and its profound impact on society and culture. Gropius and his Bauhaus faculty sought to end the designer/craftsman's "alienation" from labor, and were dedicated to the concept of the "unified work of art—the great structure, bringing together the artist, producer, and consumer in holy union."

At the outset the Bauhaus resolved to reform society through education. It would democratize art by removing the distinction between "fine" and "applied" art, and by making art responsive to people's needs. The earliest Bauhaus manifesto offered a program that was, however, difficult to maintain given the complexities of German life. Plagued by outside critics and internal dissent, this so-called spiritual stage of the Bauhaus lasted only until 1923, replaced during its second phase (1923–1925) by new teaching methods based on quasi-scientific ideas and a machine age ethic. The third phase began when, in 1925 (continuing roughly until 1928), the Weimar government withdrew financial support, forcing the school to relocate to Dessau. It was there that Gropius built his Bauhaus school building—a monument to functionalism in which outward visual form is organically related to its internal function. It was in Dessau, too, that the workshop was transformed into a kind of laboratory program, and where, during a short spurt of economic growth, the school, having tailored its teachings to the demands of industry, developed products that rightfully represented a Bauhaus style. In 1928 Gropius retired leaving the Bauhaus to Hannes Meyer (a devout socialist) who was removed in 1931. The directorship next went to Mies Van der Rohe, who moved the school one more time before its permanent closing to an old telephone factory in Berlin.

Before its demise the Bauhaus was one of the most influential design institutions in the world in the fields of architecture, furniture, fixtures, textiles, scenic design, typography, and advertising. Its students were taught to think of themselves not as divorced from society, but as integral to it. Typographers, for example, were not aesthetic specialists nor service-oriented craftspersons, but practitioners of communications open to all possibilities—from abstract to conventional materials.

The Bauhaus typography workshop contributed ideas collected under the banner of the New Typography, the movement of progressive typographers and advertising artists who rebelled against antiquated tenets of design. This was a philosophy, not a style, based on the dictum that "form follows function," in which typography became a virtual machine for communication. The modern movement of the 1920s, though a rebellious one, reconciled contemporary and classical values by rejecting timeworn verities in favor of timeless utility. Functionalism was the hallmark of Bauhaus typography.

For decades, a tension has existed in typography between rationalism and expressionism, or rather objective versus subjective aesthetics. Jan Tschichold, who helped codify the New Typography in 1925 and eventually returned to traditional methods, wrote in his decidedly conservative *The Form of the Book*: "The aim of typography must not be expression, least of all self-expression. . . . In a masterpiece of typography, the artist's signature has been eliminated. What some may praise as personal styles are in reality small and empty peculiarities, frequently damaging, that masquerade as innovations." Yet despite this admonition, Tschichold was the chief proselytizer for a movement that attacked visual redundancy that was the byproduct of traditionalism. His doctrine of asymmetry literally stood type on its ear in an effort to garner greater attention. His predilection for sans-serif over serif faces was based on what he and other modernists believed were objective truths. Yet critics accused them of perpetrating myths to support their assertions of legibility. Perhaps the Dutch typographer Gerard Unger is correct, writing in *Emigre* #23, "Tschichold's preference for sans-serifs ... was based upon emotional considerations."

The Bauhaus and the New Typography busted the conventions of placement and layout and eliminated ornament and symmetrical composition. In place of the classical page appeared "constructed" sans-serif typefaces and bold black and red rules designed to fragment the page and control the eye. During the 1920s the New Typography was viewed as an extraordinary departure from commonplace design. Ultimately, though, even it became yet another set of rules against which to rebel.

Shadow Farmers, Shadow Pigs,

Shadow Barbers, Shadow Wigs.

W hen Lewis Carroll painstakingly curled lines of hot metal type into the shape of a mouse's tail in *Alice's Adventures in Wonderland* (1865), he engaged in typeplay that would seldom be repeated in children's books for another fifty years, and would take another sixty to become the trend it is today. Since children's books offer many possibilities for creative play it is curious that for so long children's typography remained comparatively tame. Certainly in the post–World War II period artists under the spell of modern art liberated both style and content. Following the postwar baby boom mainstream book publishers, particularly in the United States, reconsidered their audiences and took risks with subjects, styles, and, to a lesser extent, layouts. Ignoring librarians' warnings against overstepping the strict conventions that they had persistently maintained through choosing what books to buy for their libraries, publishers allowed artists and writers to push the limits of children's book art by challenging taboos—like allowing a snake to appear as a book's main character for the first time in Tomi Ungerer's 1959 *Crictor*.

As for design, in the nineteenth century a page of text was routinely set as a tightly leaded block, sometimes relieved by an initial cap or spot illumination. Picture and alphabet books, though graphically more exciting, were nonetheless typographically subdued to avoid distracting the child. For a brief period during the 1920s children's books were transformed by the modern revolution. Lazar El Lissitzky's suprematist classic, *Of Two Squares* (designed in Vitebsk in 1920 but first published in Berlin in 1922), which was based on his famous political poster, *Beat the*

Whites with the Red Wedge, was the first break from traditional children's layout and content. According to N. Khadzhiev in a 1962 essay "El Lissitzky Book Designer" (reprinted in *El Lissitzky,* Thames and Hudson, 1968), it was the first time that the artist applied the revolutionary typographic language that he would later use in adult-oriented ads and brochures. *Of Two Squares* used only symbolic abstract forms, or what Lissitzky called "elementary means," rather than representational narrative devices. Lissitzky wrote that he intended to engage all children in a thrilling game: "Don't read the story, take paper sticks, your building bricks, and put it together, paint it, build it." The book flows like a comic strip or film. "All the frames are linked by the uninterrupted movement of simple related figures in a sequence which ends in the final chord of the red square," explained N. Khadzhiev. "The words move within the fields of force of the figures as they act: these are squares, universal and specifically plastic forces are brought forth typographically."

Of Two Squares inspired Kurt Schwitters, Käte Steinitz, and Theo Van Doesburg's *The Scarecrow* (Aposs-Verlag, 1925), in which the letters *B, O,* and *X* are characters of the comic story about a pitiful scarecrow who is unable to scare anything and runs afoul of a farmer. These witty typecase anthropomorphisms, a shift from naturalism to symbolism in children's iconography, tested the limits of visual and textual comprehension. Like *Of Two Squares, The Scarecrow* was originally derived from adult typographic experiments, in this case Schwitters's own Merz nonsense poems. *The Scarecrow* was certainly in Lissitzky's mind when in 1929 he designed his second children's book, *Addition, Subtraction, Multiplication, Division,* in which capital letters were transformed into bodies and limbs of a factory worker, farmer, and Red Army soldier, each a symbolic component of Soviet society used as mnemonic tools to teach arithmetic. "This is how to use letters to put together every kind of arithmetical method—try it yourself!" Lissitzky commanded his readers. This book, however, was never published and only the dummy remains. Following Lissitzky's inspirational path, Piet Zwart created *Het Boek Van PTT* in 1938 to inform children about the Dutch postal, telephone, and telegraphic company (PTT). Full-color photomontages, three-dimensional objects, and necklaces of typographic material were combined in an anarchic but decidedly transparent step-by-step instructional guide that was as playful as it was sophisticated.

This typographic revolution did not, however, make an impact on the conventions of children's book publishing because the books were not printed in large enough quantities and generally landed on the shelves of collectors rather than children. James Fraser, editor of *Phaedrus: An Annual of Children's Literature Research,* said there was also a lack of interest in these avant-garde experiments among average readers: "I used to find ex-library copies of the avant-garde experiments in surprisingly very good condition, while copies of the standard text and picture books were tattered and worn." Indeed for substantive change to have occurred a radical shift in adult design conventions would have been necessary, which even during the 1920s when experimental design was at is zenith did not affect the children's book genre. Educators maintained rigid standards over how children were to be taught, and children's librarians generally decided which books were suitable to that task. Adults determined the conventions that governed the content and design of picture books for prereaders, picture/story books for young readers, and illustrated novels for older readers. Illustration was either realistic or fanciful, typography was straightforward and legible—any deviation from these norms was termed inappropriate. Neil Postman writes in *The Disappearance of Childhood* (Delacorte Press, New York, 1982) that "a particular form of information, controlled by adults, was made available in stages to children in what was judged to be psychologically assimilable ways." Until the advent of television (and now, increasingly, digital media) the printed book was the vessel in which this information was stored and distributed; its presentation has, therefore, always been controlled by adult assumptions about what best suited children. Left unchallenged, many assumptions were further adopted as marketing truths.

By the late 1930s children's book design was in a few instances influenced by the New Typography in the form of sans-serif typefaces in asymmetrical compositions. In *The Noisy Book* (Harper Brothers, 1939) by Margaret Wise Brown, machine-inspired Futura set with skewed line breaks approximated the sounds of household appliances and larger machines. Yet during the 1940s and 1950s forums of the American Institute of Graphic Arts codified standards of legibility for children's books to which most publishers adhered. Readability was vigilantly preserved, and change in children's book typography during the early postwar era was marked by little more than the occasional switch from typefaces like Janson or Garamond to Futura or Akidenz or Grotesque rather than adoption of constructivist, dadaist, and futurist experimental typography. Picture books were usually composed of classical book types that were rarely integrated into the art. Even an avant-garde masterpiece like Bruno Munari's *Alfabeteire* (Giulio Einaudi, editor, 1960), with illustrations that are dada-like collages of "found" letters, the sans-serif body text is discretely set apart from the images.

Yet certain anomalies did influence the field: *Funny Folks from Gardentown* (Whitman, 1938) by Tony Fraioli sidestepped typographic convention with quirky hand-drawn letterforms that complemented his witty anthropomorphic drawings of fruits and vegetables set against black backgrounds (which, incidentally, librarians considered lugubrious). Hand-drawn letterforms subsequently became more common (although black backgrounds have not). Cursive lettering for *The Story of Babar, The Little Elephant* (1933) was once criticized for being inaccessible to young readers who were unable to decipher script. Yet referring to this and even earlier cursive books dating back to the late nineteenth century, James Fraser suggested that "brighter children tried to puzzle it out or asked adults to help with difficult words until they got it." Over time, handwriting became a common means to teach script. Typewriter type, another un-childlike letterform, was associated with the adult world until *Typewriter Town* (E. F. Dutton, 1960) by William Jay Smith, a playful experiment using the typewriter characters to create images. Influenced by Lewis Carroll's mouse's tail, it was also consistent with contemporary typewritten concrete poetry for adults. In *Little 1* (Harcourt Brace, 1962) by Paul and Ann Rand, typewriter type was boldly used to complement the improvisational collages and rhythmic text. As an integral part of the book's visual personality it also made typewriter type more acceptable.

From the 1950s to the 1980s children's book design was largely overshadowed by developments in children's book art. Even books by progressive artists Maurice Sendak, Tomi Ungerer, and Leo Lionni did not unhinge typographic convention. "Typography should be seen and not heard, because reading is functional and should not be tampered with," said Lionni, whose more than forty books are set only in Century Schoolbook. He insisted that the defining element of a picture book is the *picture*, not the type. "The picture is the story, the type conveys the narrative." Yet this began to change in the late 1980s when type design became more integral to the entire children's book as the author/illustrator became more of an active participant in the design process and the computer forced the widespread re-evaluation of typographic principles in all print media. In the late 1970s, experimental typography gave adult-oriented print communications more playful veneers; constructivist, futurist, and dadaist typographics offered alternatives to classical and late modern methods.

S lodí jež dováží čaj kávu
(With the Ship that Carries Tea and Coffee)

KAREL TEIGE

The modern design movement was born in Western Europe and Russia, but didn't stay there for long. During the period of creative ferment between the world wars, Poland, Hungary, and Czechoslovakia also became capitals of the new design and New Typography. Even with the rise of totalitarianism, which brought the engines of progressive expression in Germany and the Soviet Union to a grinding halt—squelching Russian constructivism and productivism in the early 1930s and closing the Bauhaus in Germany in 1933—avant-gardists continued to work freely in Warsaw, Budapest, and Prague. Hitler and Stalin had not begun their respective occupations of these autonomous states until the late 1930s, allowing a brief respite for avant-garde art and design to develop before the war and postwar repression.

After World War I, Prague, Czechoslovakia's capital, was the crossroads for exponents of the new cultural "isms." The progressive movement of longest duration was a group called Devetsil, a confederation of left-wing writers, artists, sculptors, photographers, filmmakers, and typographers. They were known unofficially as the Czech Bauhaus, even though they were more diverse philosophically and methodologically than their German counterparts.

No one can trace where the name *Devetsil* actually came from. (In Czech the word is a pun on two roots: a botanical term meaning "spiky butterbur" and a mathematical term meaning "nine forces.") Nor is it known how many people were active members. Like other twentieth-century design "isms," Devetsil wed art to technology in an effort to unite form and function. In this respect, it was informed by the sociopolitical ideology manifest in the USSR that spread throughout Europe during the 1920s. Devetsil's leader, Karel Teige (1900–1951) was a prolific writer, poet, critic, painter, designer, and typographer whose visual models included constructivism and surrealism. An ardent socialist, he developed a concept called *ars una*, a modernist reprise of the nineteenth-century movement to integrate art into every aspect of life. In the 1920s he devoted himself to typography and "pictorial poetry," producing, editing, and designing books first in a constructivist and later in a surrealist spirit.

Teige promoted strict typographic standards consistent with those of the European avant-garde. Elementary, unadorned geometric forms devoid of any bourgeois decorative vestiges made communications more functional. In his early work, from around 1922, Teige used one basic device, a black circle, which was both eye-catching and a "word symbol" representing the avant-garde's larger rejection of archaic and contemporary superficial design trends. "The relationship between Teige's theoretical work and his typographic rules can be demonstrated by the circle," wrote Karel Srp ("Karel Teige and the New Typography," *Rassenga,* 1965). It represented a variety of things, a sun, a ball, a human head. "According to Teige the neutral geometric forms did not lose their identification with man. . . . Teige's functionalism was strongly anthropocentric." Therefore, the circle was not merely an abstract image on a page. Teige believed that abstract paintings were decorative, and therefore circles should never be used in painting because it was form without sense. The circle used in a book or journal cover, however, was endemic to the structure and meaning of text. Teige concurred with El Lissitzky's notion that the modern book should be looked at before it is read, but reading was the ultimate functional goal.

Of his many book and book jacket designs the title pages and "illustrations" for *S lodí jež dováží čaj a kávu* (*With the Ship that Carries Tea and Coffee,* 1927) by Konstantin Biebl is a unique application of constructivist form for its combination of elementary graphic devices and pastel palette, an example of how kindred designers in different parts of the world reinterpreted the language of modern design based on their own requisites.

Devetsil members longed to travel to exotic lands, and as spokesman for the movement, Teige announced, "The most wonderful thing would be to live in a fast train coach." Since Bohemia does not boarder on an ocean the members were ostensibly landlocked. Only Biebl dared make a long journey over land and sea to Ceylon, Sumatra, and Java. His book, a wanderer's travelogue in poetic verse, was not, however, illustrated with conventionally nostalgic or romantic pictures of distant places, but rather abstractly, in dynamic compositions using typecase materials, similar to El Lissitzky's typecase illustrations in *For the Voice,* Mayakovsky's book of socialist poems.

In Teige's 1927 essay, "Modern Type" (which echoes similar manifestoes by Lazar El Lissitzky and Láslo Moholy-Nagy), he argued for a radical shift in general standards, rejecting tedious layout techniques for dynamic typographic forms. He brought Bauhaus sobriety to Czechoslovakia, and though he would later be inspired by the raucous typographic and collage antics of German dada, his constructivist vocabulary inspired many young designers to leave tradition behind.

Depero: Futurista

FORTUNATO DEPERO

Redefining the spiritual and material world fell to visionaries, "men of talent and memorable fools," who led the shock troops of modernism. Inspired to action, the Italian, Fortunato Depero (1892–1960), cosigned the "Futurist Reconstruction of the Universe," a manifesto aimed at world renewal by "cheering it up" through the overhaul of everyday objects—interior decoration, clothing, publicity, mass communications, postal art. Depero was a significant part of the late first and second stages of Italian futurism, an early and exceedingly influential European avant-garde movement that altered the process of artistic production and the role of the artist in society. Futurism's founder, poet F. T. Marinetti, proclaimed in the 1909 "Futurist Manifesto" (published in the Parisian newspaper, *Le Figaro*): "United, we must attack! We must create with absolute faith in the imperishable richness of the earth! There can be no nostalgia! No pessimism! There's no turning back! Boldly, let us advance! Forward! Faster! Farther! Higher! Let us lyrically renew our joy in being alive!"

Marinetti espoused a permanent artistic and political revolution. He rejected traditionalism in favor of "the new religion of speed," mythologizing the machine—the automobile and later the airplane—as a totem of the modern spirit. Technology, though somewhat primitive in Italy, was the savior of mankind, and futurism was the avant-garde of the masses.

At age twenty-four, Fortunato (meaning good luck) Depero was already artistically formed, with a distinct stylistic personality. While he shared Marinetti's belief in "art action," Depero was engaged in considerably more playful pursuits. And, although he followed the movement's political dictates, his personal politics were based on aesthetics. "In Depero one rediscovers applied art, the happening, kinetic art, dadaist provocation, abstract painting: to sum up, a heritage of so many new directions of art," wrote Italian art historian Giorgio Ruggeri. Much of Depero's design prefigures today's postmodern and new wave eclecticism in its form and color.

Depero was an indefatigable proponent of futurism. He wrote for newspapers, promoted the futurist book, founded and directed the machine art magazine *Dinamo*, organized personal exhibitions, and worked in the theater as a set and costume designer. He was commissioned by Diaghilev to make a set and costumes for *Le Chant du Rossignol.* He invented an "onoma-language," a free word, free sounding, expressive verbal rigamarole. He represented the futurists at the 1925 Paris exposition of modern decorative and industrial art, exhibiting his life-sized mechanical men. He produced futurist radio programs. He decorated cabarets, bars, restaurants, and dance halls. With his wife Rossetta, he opened the *Casa d'Arte Futurist* in Rovereto, Italy, where he made wooden constructions, furniture, and costumes for a mass clientele. He designed futurist clothing, vests, and jackets. And in 1923 he moved to New York for three years where on West Twenty-third Street he opened Depero's Futurist House, selling everything from paintings to advertising graphics, and propagating the futurist "style" to a culture that thought of all European modernism as "futurist."

Depero triumphed with book design and production. During the 1920s the "book-object" was seriously practiced as a futurist art form—the marriage of futurist layout and typographical experimentation. For the 1927 *Biennale Internazionale delle Arti Decorative* in Monza, Italy, Depero designed a book pavilion built entirely out of giant block letters. It was a grand architectural achievement, but not as historically important as his bolted art catalog, which, along with Tulio D'Albisola's famous tin book *Futurist Words Set Free: Tactile Thermal Olfactory*, is emblematic of futurist applied arts. *Depero: Futurista*, as it was called, is a lavish compendium of his own design work (including many advertisements he had designed for Campari) covering the years 1913 through 1927. Depero was predisposed to an "Aztec deco" sensibility that was influenced by set-back skyscrapers. Depero's use of bright colors and collaged colored papers was a startling contrast to the rather conservative realism that then held sway. Reproduced in letterpress, it was bound, in machine age fashion, by two stainless steel bolts.

By 1927 Depero was recognized as an innovator. His synthesis of dynamic and expressionistic graphic forms was undeniably original. He reconciled craft, fine, and applied arts; and, believing that product advertising was the means to stimulate a dialogue with the public, he took on commissions in Italy, including a highly visible series for Campari. In the 1932 manifesto, "The Art of Advertising," Depero announced, "The art of the future will be powerfully advertising art." And he continued that "All last centuries [sic] art was advertising oriented." The suggestion being that the paintings of the past, exalting war, religion, and even love, were instruments of sales. Depero believed that the artist's individuality expressed as a selling tool was the best means to stimulate artistic dialogue with the public. Therefore, he would only work for clients (such as Campari) who gave him license. With such assignments he deliberately used the product as the source of his own iconography, inspiring, he believed, "a new pictorial taste for the image."

Peignot

A. M. CASSANDRE

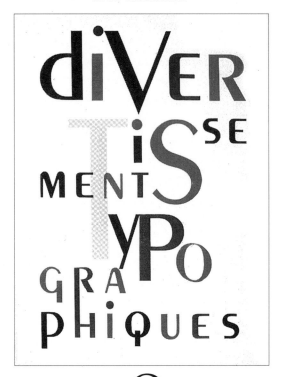

Once upon a time Paul Rand used three stylish lowercase letters on a poster promoting winter sports. This solitary word, *ski,* was the first time that the typeface Peignot was used in the United States. It was 1938 and it was the last time Rand would ever use it, but Peignot became one of the most popular letterforms of the 1930s and 1940s. It was an emblem of the age, a reflection of the Parisian *moderne* style.

Peignot, designed by poster artist A. M. Cassandre (1901–1968), still has currency as a display letter and is sometimes used to evoke the art deco period of the late 1920s to mid 1930s. Peignot was a quirky sans-serif face notable for its thick and thin body and the use of upper-case letters in its lowercase form. The typeface is famous for both its style and versatility, and its designer is well known for his significant contributions to the history of the poster, but little is known about the man for whom the face was named, Charles Peignot, or his influential Parisian type foundry, Deberny & Peignot. This is a case where the typeface is more than a mere letterform, it is a monument.

The history of graphic design usually focuses on the artists who produced the most visible and viable work, not the so-called vendors. While Cassandre's designs are celebrated, the catalyst or patron who encouraged, published, and paid for the work goes largely unheralded. This is the fate of Charles Peignot, who at one time employed Cassandre and other leading European designers including Herbert Matter, Alexey Brodovitch, and Charles Loupot. Peignot was to modern graphic design what Ambroise Vollard was to modern printmaking. He was not simply the manager of a successful type business, he was the embodiment of French typography for more than five decades. An arbiter of taste, a courageous experimenter, an adventuresome publisher, Peignot brought what one of his collaborators, the type designer Maximillen Vox, calls a "Gallic-Roman" design attitude (rooted in constant change) to the Anglo-Saxon world. Hence, Peignot's legacy is a virtual timeline of typography, technology, and modern graphic design.

In the 1920s the future of an international typography rested in German experiments. Paul Renner had designed his seminal Futura, the geometric sans-serif that became the emblem of modernity. Understanding this, Cassandre and Peignot began investigations that led step by step to the Peignot typeface (named by Cassandre). The face was the offspring of two spiritual parents: the Bauhaus and the Renaissance. After many false births, Cassandre and Peignot concluded that it would be pretentious to think of creating a completely new face and decided to work along traditional lines, while at the same time avoiding copies of what had been done. "Copying the past does not create a tradition," wrote Peignot. Cassandre had the idea of going back to the origins of letterforms. "Was there not something to be learnt from the semi-unicals of the Middle Ages?" queried Cassandre. "The idea of mixing the letterforms of capitals and lowercase seemed to us to contain the seed of new developments within traditional lines." The result was a mixture of letters, which Peignot knew would take the public some time to adjust to.

In 1937 Peignot was launched in a spectacular way as the "official" typeface of the World Exhibition in Paris. It had been chosen by Paul Valéry for inscriptions on the two towers of the Palais de Chaillot. A fabricator produced cardboard stencils for making complete alphabets, and these were used for many mural inscriptions on the exhibition stands. The response to the type was overwhelming. And like a proud father, Peignot kept tabs on its use to such an extent that weeks after Paul Rand's *Ski* poster was issued, Rand received a telegram of thanks, signed Charles Peignot.

Cooper Black

OSWALD COOPER

Every designer has used the typeface Cooper Black at least once in his or her professional life. It is as indelibly part of design as ritual is of religion. Once one of the world's most ubiquitous metal typefaces—and the heaviest, owing to its great mass—Cooper Black is a truly twentieth-century type, as emblematic as Futura or Univers. While it was not the first type to have rounded serifs, it is the most authoritative of the so-called fat faces. Used for advertising and editorial display, Cooper Black is as eye-catching as a charging bull and as loud as a carnival barker. If there had never been a Cooper Black, the world might never have known Ultra Bodoni, one of the many behemoths designed to compete in the ever-widening fat face market during the mid 1920s.

The man who designed Cooper Black is Oswald Cooper (1879–1940), Oz or Ozzie to his friends. Cooper was a native of Coffeeville, Kansas. In his teens he settled in Chicago to pursue illustration. He eventually became one of the leading practitioners of what became known as the Chicago style. In the early 1920s and 1930s American design was a mélange of regional dialects, each emanating from a big city under the influence of a single person's mannerism or the confluence of a few. Lettering, typography, and illustration were the defining media, and advertising was the primary outlet. The Boston style was attributable to W. A. Dwiggins and the New York style to Frederic W. Goudy (both of whom spent time in Chicago), but the Chicago (sometimes called the Midwestern) style was founded by Cooper. He combined calligraphic skill with typographic expertise to create advertisements that were modern in character and classic in form. While respecting tradition, he understood the needs of an expanding mass commercial market.

Cooper stumbled into his lifelong vocation by accident. He left the comforts of his Kansas home at eighteen, bound for Chicago to study at the Frank Holme School of Illustration. There he was inspired by his lettering teacher, Frederic W. Goudy, to pursue a broader practice. Goudy, the most prolific of all American type designers and director of Holme's typographic department, befriended Oz and helped him earn his tuition by assigning him jobs setting type for correspondence course booklets. This was a happy career move since Cooper had realized that he wasn't very good at drawing pictures but had a real knack for the lettering arts. Soon he was appointed as a lettering teacher.

While teaching at Holme, Cooper met a young man, Fred Bertsch, who ran an art-service agency next door to the school. Bertsch loved Cooper's work and in 1904 they entered into the perfect partnership; Bertsch, a consummate salesman, and Cooper, the gifted artist, formed Bertsch & Cooper with the goal of establishing a full-service typeshop, including typesetting, layout, copywriting, and design. But opening a typeshop was expensive even then; and while they had plenty of ambition, money was in short supply. As a small studio Bertsch & Cooper based its initial reputation on hand lettering for small local jobs and later large national campaigns. Eventually, their financial success allowed them to open the full-service shop they had dreamed of, which gave Cooper the opportunity to test his other talents. "Cooper, of course, had brilliant capacities as a craftsman in the field of printing and of advertising layout," wrote typographer Paul Standard in *The Book of Oz Cooper* (The Society of Typographic Arts, Chicago, 1949). "But in his endowment was also a gift for language, and through its discipline a power of clear and forthright expression . . . his text sought to persuade, not stampede."

The quality of Cooper's lettering was equal to the strength of his writing. Cooper's letterforms were not simply novelties, but "lessons in structural form, in free and friendly balance," wrote Standard. Cooper created as many new designs as he could, yet he had an instinctual distrust of things superficially modish and conceptually strained. "Types too dexterous, like tunes too luscious," he once waxed, "are predestinated [sic] to short careers. If William Caslon had improved his types as much as they have since been improved by others they would not have endured, for sleek perfection palls on the imperfect persons who buy and use type."

Actually, Cooper stumbled into type design almost as accidentally as he did lettering. His first type was drawn and cut, unbeknownst to Cooper and without his permission, in 1913 by one of Morris Fuller Benton's staff artists at American Type Foundry (ATF). Cooper had routinely created customized lettering in advertisements for one of Bertsch & Cooper's largest clients, the Packard Motor Car Company. The ads were so widely seen that the lettering caught Benton's eye. Type pirating was a fact of life and ads were neither signed nor attributed to any artist. Benton immediately ordered the type redrawn and founded in metal, and called it Packard. But Benton was also a man of integrity; when he learned that the original was designed by Cooper he paid a fee and attributed the design to him.

Shortly afterward, Barnhart Brothers & Spindler Type Foundry (BB&S), America's second largest, approached Cooper to design a complete family based on his lettering. Cooper did not immediately accept the offer, reasoning that he was first a lettering artist, not a type designer, and he was very busy with his own business. Bertsch, however, was not only Cooper's partner but his biggest promoter and worked feverishly to get Cooper into the limelight. Bertsch called Cooper the "Michelangelo of lettering," and urged him to accept BB&S's offer. In 1918 Cooper's first typeface was released, named Cooper, and later renamed Cooper Old Style.

In the early 1900s typefaces were vigorously marketed to printers and type shops, often through ambitious type specimen sheets designed with the same artistic flourish as period sheet music. BB&S was particularly aggressive and succeeded in popularizing Cooper's first normal-weight roman (Cooper). They further made it the basis for a continuing family. The second in the series was the famous Cooper Black, the most novel of early-twentieth-century super-bolds. BB&S declared that Cooper Black was "the selling type supreme, the multibillionaire sales type, it made big advertisements out of little ones." Cooper responded that his invention was "for far-sighted printers with near-sighted customers." Owing to its novelty, it caused commotion in certain conservative circles. "The slug-machine makers thundered against the black 'menace.' But the trend was on—the advertising world accepted the black in a thoroughgoing way and the orders rolled up in a volume never before known for any type face," wrote a type seller of the day.

Other related type designs followed in quick succession in what became known as "the black blitz." Cooper Italic was described by Cooper as "much closer to its parent pen form than the roman." Cooper Hilite was made by the simple expedient of painting a white highlight on a black proof of Cooper Black, with patterns cut and matrices engraved accordingly. "It's good for sparkling headlines; it cannot be crowded like the black, but must have plenty of 'air,'" wrote Cooper. Cooper Black Italic was completed in 1926 to cash in on the swell in sales of Cooper Black. Cooper Black Condensed was designed shortly afterward to have twenty percent less heft and be generally more useful. A complete metal font of Cooper Black weighed almost eighty-three pounds (thank heavens for transfer type) and strained the back of many a typesetter, so the condensed version was thought to save on costly chiropractor bills.

Cooper's designs initiated trends, but he refused to take part in "the itch of the times." Nor was he a fan of what in 1928 he called "the balmy wing of modernism." However, his last face, designed in 1929 for BB&S, originally called Cooper Fullface and later changed in ATF catalogs to Cooper Modern, was, in fact, consistent with the dominant styles. Of this face Cooper wrote, "This style, lately revived by the practitioners of the 'modernistic' typography, has created a demand for display letters that comport well with it—letters that reflect the sparkling contrasts of Bodoni, and that carry weight to meet the needs of advertisers, Cooper Fullface is such a letter."

In the 1930s Cooper curtailed his type design, and before his death in 1940 he turned his attention to protecting what he had created. Fighting for copyright protections for himself and all designers, he tried to convince the government that patents should be awarded for typefaces. He chided his colleagues about copying, too. Copying is shameful, he argued: "To work in the style of current trends or past periods is all right, but do it in your own way. Study the work of the leaders, but never have another's work before you when you are trying to create. There was never a great imitator—not even in vaudeville. The way to become a master is by cultivating your own talent."

Westvaco Inspirations

BRADBURY THOMPSON

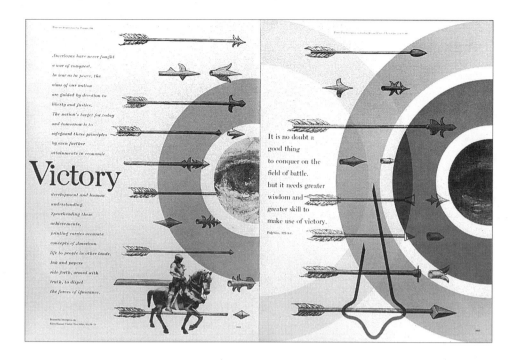

A graphic designer's influence is not measured by how many acolytes mimic his style or by how many awards he has won, but rather by what he alone has contributed to the visual language. Since such judgments are subjective, the criteria used to determine influence might be an answer to the question: If the particular designer had never existed, would the field be worse off? To be more specific, if a young man from Topeka, Kansas, by the name of Bradbury Thompson (1911–1995), had not left his job designing high school yearbooks, and had not come to New York City in the late 1930s, would a significant chapter of American graphic design history have been written?

If not for Thompson, Westvaco *Inspirations*, which in the 1930s was a paper company's spiritless promotional brochure, might never have become the bible of graphic design and textbook for a generation. If Thompson was never a magazine art director (*Mademoiselle*, *Art News*, and others), book, postage stamp, or advertising designer; if all he ever accomplished during his fifty-year career was to design and edit sixty issues of a periodical that he transformed into a journal of modern layout and typography—including special issues devoted to such themes as "Type as a Toy," "Primitive Art as Modern Design," and the phonetic "Monalphabet" (which eliminated the need for separate upper- and lowercase letters)—his place as a pioneer of American graphic design would still be locked in for the ages.

In 1938 Thompson left the American heartland without a clue that he would eventually become the art director and designer for some very influential magazines, or a teacher at Yale

University, or one of the chief designers for the United States Postal Service. He just came East to work for one of those fabled art directors in the big city that he had read about in design magazines he found in the Topeka library. From the outset he had a curiously modernist bent (curious because conservative Middle America was not a conducive environment for modern thinking).

Westvaco *Inspirations* was a compendium of what Thompson believed to be the best of contemporary practice. *Inspirations* reported on the prevailing ethos, aesthetic, and philosophy of graphic design. But it was more. Thompson promoted his vision, which wed the European modern spirit to a respect for classical heritage. "My early interest in type came from the humanist typographers," explained Thompson, "the classic types of Europe from the fifteenth, sixteenth, and seventeenth centuries. Later, *Vanity Fair* [art directed by M. F. Agha] influenced me in the use of sans-serif type—especially Futura." His appreciation for unadorned layout further evolved from studying the behemoth fashion magazines of the 1930s, while his graphic adventurism came from an intimate knowledge of printing and its potential. Thompson was never inhibited by low-budget constraints nor primitive technologies. His belief in the rightness of form was less about ideological purity than an interest in the most effective means to communicate information.

Thompson liberally borrowed from all arts—painting and sculpture, photography and drawing, realistic and abstract—to prove the limitless possibilities of the design process. One of his most well-known designs, an *Inspirations* spread titled "Kerr-choo-oo," presents type that is not read as a word but as sound. Although inspired by Apollinaire's *Calligrammes* and F. T. Marinetti's *Parole in Liberta,* it was decidedly American in its wit.

Inspirations brought classical, modern, and eclectic sensibilities together in the form of a manifesto, not the rabble-rousing kind that emanated from futurism or dada, but a soft-spoken kind—which characterizes Thompson to a T—that sought to teach rather than preach. Thompson was not radical, but modern in the catholic sense: anything was possible within his aesthetic parameters; anything was doable as long as quality was the goal. Thompson's experiments were, moreover, rooted in terra firma—the real world. *Inspirations* was a progressive's introduction to new ideas about graphic forms and their applications in the marketplace, not the clouds. Everything presented in the publication (including his convention-busting Monalphabet) was appropriate within the convention of visual communications.

The qualities that made *Inspirations* unique were rooted in its conventional production. The constraints of letterpress printing and hot metal composition stymied creative activity, but Thompson maximized the limitations, pushed the boundaries, and tested the resilience of design. One of the single most important lessons he taught through the example of *Inspirations* was that type could be made expressive, emotive, personal, and still be part of a tasteful composition. "There is no creative aspect of graphic design more enjoyable or rewarding than the indulgence in play," he once wrote.

Thompson was also smitten by French and German poster art of the 1930s, which integrated type and image as one entity. He saw these word and picture compositions as the signpost to future design possibilities. "In working on Westvaco *Inspirations* I just naturally applied all these forms," he explained. Yet he did not merely mimic existing forms.

Thompson never possessed a style per se, rather an attitude. His magazine layouts were void of artifice, but decidedly modern. His book design was based on classical models. How did he reconcile the two sensibilities? "Appropriateness," he explained. "You can't get away from tradition, if you want to bridge past, present, and future."

Lorca: Three Tragedies

ALVIN LUSTIG

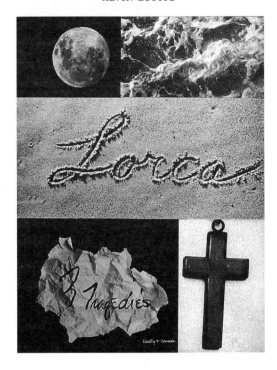

The 1953 paperback cover for *Lorca: Three Tragedies* designed by Alvin Lustig (1915–1955) is a masterpiece of symbolic acuity, compositional strength, and typographic ingenuity. It is also the basis for a great many contemporary book jackets and paperback covers. The American book jacket designers' preference, in the late 1980s and 1990s, for fragmented images, minimal typography, and rebus-like compositions can be traced directly to the stark black-and-white cover for *Three Tragedies*. This and other distinctive jackets and covers designed by Lustig for New Directions transformed the photograph into a tool for abstraction through the use of reticulated negatives, photograms, and setups.

Lustig's approach developed from an interest in photomontage originally practiced by the European moderns, and particularly the American expatriate E. McKnight Kauffer. When Lustig introduced this technique to American book publishing in the late 1940s, book covers and jackets were predominantly illustrative and rather decorative, with an abundance of hand-lettered novelty faces. The Lorca cover was a grid of five symbolic photographs tied together in poetic disharmony. Before this type of cover was introduced, European art-based approaches were not even considered by American publishers. Perhaps they were thought foolhardy in a marketplace where hard-sell marketing conventions were rigorously adhered to. Or, just as likely, the leading book jacket designers of the day were ignorant of such methods.

Lustig rejected the typical literary solution that summarized a book through one generalized image. "His method was to read a text and get the feel of the author's creative drive, then to restate it in his own graphic terms," wrote James Laughlin, the publisher of New Directions, in "The Book Jackets of Alvin Lustig" (*Print*, Vol. 10, No. 5, October 1956). Laughlin hired Lustig in the early 1940s giving him the latitude to experiment with graphic forms. New Directions' eccentric list of reprinted contemporary classics, which featured authors such as Henry Miller, Gertrude Stein, D. H. Lawrence, and James Joyce, was a proving ground for Lustig's visual explorations and distinctive graphic poetry. While attaining higher sales was always an issue, Lustig believed that he should not "design down" to the reader. Although mindful of the fundamental marketing precept that a book jacket must attract and hold the average book buyer's roving eye, Lustig crossed over into taboo marketing territory with his introduction of abstract images and small, discreetly typeset titles, influenced by the work of Jan Tschichold and other European moderns.

Lustig's first jacket for Laughlin, a 1941 edition of Henry Miller's *Wisdom of the Heart*, eclipsed the previous New Directions books, which Laughlin described as jacketed in a "conservative, 'booky,' way." At the time Lustig was experimenting with nonrepresentational constructions made from slugs of hot metal typographic material, suggesting the influence of architect Frank Lloyd Wright, with whom he studied for three months at Taliesin East. While decidedly unconventional, some years later Laughlin noted that this particular jacket "was rather stiff and severe. . . . It scarcely hinted at the extraordinary flowering which was to follow."

Laughlin was referring to the series of New Directions New Classics that Lustig designed from 1945 to 1952. With few exceptions the New Classics seem as inventive today as they were when they first appeared almost fifty years ago. Lustig had switched over from typecase compositions to drawing distinctive symbolic "marks" that owed more to the work of artists like Paul Klee, Joan Míro, and his friend Mark Rothko, than to any accepted commercial style. Although Lustig rejected painting as "too subjectivized" and never presumed to paint or sculpt himself, he borrowed liberally from modern painting and integrated the abstract sensibility into his total design.

Each of his New Classic jackets is a mix of expressionistic and analytical forms— sophisticated doodles, really—that interpret rather than narrate the novels, plays, and poetry. For Franz Kafka's *Amerika* Lustig used a coarsely rendered five-pointed star divided in half by red stripes and out of which emerges childlike squiggles of smoke—a reference to Kafka's intemperate critique of a mythic America. For E. M. Forster's *The Longest Journey* he used stark black bars that suggest a labyrinthian maze. It does not illustrate the author's romantic scene; instead the symbolism alludes to the emotive tension of the story. "In these as in all Lustig's jackets the approach is indirect," wrote C. F. O. Clarke in *Graphis* (No. 23, 1948), "but through its sincerity and compression it has more imaginative power than direct illustration could achieve."

The New Classics succeeded where other popular literary series, including the Modern Library and Everyman's Library, had failed. Each New Classics jacket had its own character, yet Lustig maintained unity through formal consistency. However, at no time did his style overpower the book. Lustig's jacket designs for New Directions demanded contemplation, they were not quick-fix visual stimulants.

Lustig was a form-giver not a novelty maker. The style he chose for the New Classics was a logical solution to the specific design problem. The New Classics did not become his signature style any more than his earlier typecase compositions did, for within the framework of modernism Lustig varied his approach, using the marketplace as his laboratory. "I have heard people speak of the 'Lustig Style,'" wrote Laughlin in *Print*, "but not one of them has been able to tell me, in fifty words or five hundred what it was. Because each time, with each new book, there was a new creation. The only repetitions were those imposed by the physical media."

Lustig's design appeared revolutionary (and so unacceptable) to the guardians of tradition entrenched at the AIGA and other book-dominated graphic organizations, but he was not the radical that critics feared. He stressed the formal aspects of a problem, and in matters of formal practice he was devout to a fault. In "Contemporary Book Design" (*Design Quarterly*, No. 31. 1954) he wrote, "The factors that produce quality are the same in the traditional and in the contemporary book. Wherein, then lies difference? Perhaps the single most distinguishing factor in the approach of the contemporary designer is his willingness to let the problem act upon him freely and without preconceived notions of the forms it should take."

Lorca: Three Tragedies exemplified Lustig's versatility and was, moreover, one of many covers for New Directions that tested the effectiveness of inexpensive black-and-white printing as it pushed the boundaries of accepted modern design. For with this and other photo-illustrations (done in collaboration with photographers because he did not take the photographs himself), Lustig customized the modern visual language to fit his preferences. Of course, he was not alone. Paul Rand produced art-based book jackets, but Lustig's distinction, wrote Laughlin in *Print*, "lay in the intensity and the purity with which he dedicated his genius to his idea vision." While the others may have been graphic problem-solvers, Lustig was a visual poet whose work was rooted as much in emotion as in form.

About U.S.

LESTER BEALL, BROWNJOHN CHERMAYEFF GEISMAR, HERB LUBALIN, GENE FEDERICO

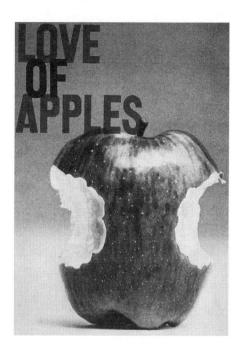

In 1955 Aaron Burns (1922–1991) was The Composing Room's type director and quality-control expert, responsible for facilitating the difficult hot metal settings demanded by agency art directors. Burns, who later cofounded the International Typeface Company, was also "a seeker-outer of people who were cutting edge," recalled Ivan Chermayeff. This was more than the typical designer and supplier relationship; Burns developed formative outlets and forums for graphic designers to express themselves through typography. Under his direction the term *cutting edge* had at times a very literal meaning. This was the period when the constraints of hot metal composition made it difficult to achieve such now common effects as tight spacing, touching, or overlapping without the designer cutting with a razor blade, repositioning the proofs, and then making an engraving of the mechanical. Burns explored any reasonable ways to push the limits of typography. One of his most satisfying attempts was a series of four sixteen-page booklets produced in 1960 titled *About U.S.*, which gave four American designers an opportunity to wed type and images without any conceptual constraints and push the edges of production in any way possible.

The four booklets (written by Percy Seitlin) were: Lester Beall's *The Age of the Auto,* where type was laboriously composed in long, thin, and contoured lines to suggest the path (or tire tracks) of an automobile ride; Herb Lubalin's *Come Home to Jazz,* a pictorial jam of jazz instruments photographed in high contrast with drop-out type in different sizes and weights running in and out of the images, suggesting the discordance of the music itself; Brownjohn

Chermayeff Geismar's *That New York,* which flirted with typographic abstraction against a New York cityscape; and Gene Federico's discourse on the *Love of Apples,* an exercise to see how close he could touch slugs of type without using a razor blade. "I wanted to try something where I used metal type in extreme ways without having to cut it—without cutting up proofs or playing with stats," explained Federico. "For some time I had known that if you stacked title gothics they would have a different look than traditional types. So the whole book was based on that simple idea."

The designers' motivations for solving the problem of filling sixteen pages were different, but each followed his own muse, not a client's. Beall, who was coming to the end of his career as a designer of corporate identity, was interested in returning to his early inspirations, which borrowed from dada and surrealism. His "essay" was concerned with the tension between typographic precision in a free-form environment. Lubalin, who was beginning to have influence on contemporary typography with visual puns and type-pictures, was attempting to bust through the confines of hot metal (which he would later do with phototype). Brownjohn Chermayeff Geismar, which had been doing conceptual design in a modern idiom since the late 1950s and was about to split up, leaving Robert Brownjohn on his own, was seeking the nexus of art and design. "Ours was impossible typesetting and useless prose," added Chermayeff. "But it was also an attempt to use typography as paint, and to explore relationships that were based on texture not language. We were doing no less than what David Carson is doing today. However, for us to be completely irresponsible required a sympathy with language." In addition to overlapping and layering through intricate film processes that were made into engravings, this typeplay mixed numbers with letterforms to make words. For Federico, an advertising art director with a special interest in type, *Love of Apples* was an excuse for a poetic polemic about nature's beauty being radically altered, as is exemplified by the line: "When we, in business, industrial America, began to get smart about apples, we packaged them and packaged them and packaged them until the apple itself became the package," which he illustrated with a photograph of an apple with a string tied around it.

About U.S. is one of modern American design's most important artifacts, both as a chronicle of the end of hot metal and as a clarion of impending photo composition. It is also one of the first public displays of conceptual and expressionistic typeplay that would alter advertising and editorial practice in the 1960s and usher in the method (or style) of design known as the Big Idea—noted for witty copywriting wed to smart conceptual typography, illustration, and photography. *About U.S.* is a snapshot of the moment when type first talked.

Ha, Ha, Ha: He Laughs Best Who Laughs Last

LOU DORFSMAN

The Columbia Broadcasting System (CBS) was the foremost American television network from the 1950s to the 1980s. No other network had such intelligent news and entertainment programming, nor had earned such public confidence. During its golden years, the "CBS eye" was a proud emblem that stood for a reputation of service and quality built by William Paley, founder and former CEO, and later, Frank Stanton, former chief of the broadcast division. Yet even inherently great programming required an equally great corporate image, an identity born of memorable graphics and compelling advertising. It can be argued that if not for the originality of its promotion CBS would have had to slug it out much harder against ABC and NBC, whose advertising rarely reached the same heights.

CBS management understood the value of a strong graphic identity, which is why in 1937 Paley hired William Golden, who created the venerable CBS trademark, and why after Golden's death in 1959 Paley and Stanton named Lou Dorfsman (b. 1918), then the promotion art director of the radio division, to take his place. Dorfsman earned the job through inspired trade advertising designed to sell advertisers on the viability of radio at a time when television was decidedly the more compelling market.

Dorfsman was the engine that drove the company's most successful advertising campaigns, and ultimately its entire graphic design program. He wrote much of his own copy and practiced the art of visual persuasion with rare wit. What his ads lacked in typical hyperbole was made up for in uncommon intelligence. He never lowered himself or his company to hard-sell tactics. He was a master of the Big Idea, a conceptual strategy characterized by understatement, self-mockery, and irony, and noted for clean design and strident copywriting wed to intelligent illustration and photography. In the more than forty years that Dorfsman managed CBS's visual identity there is not a single example where he used a typeface as novelty or decoration simply to grab attention, or abused a photograph, painting, or drawing merely for shock value. The audience was never treated as visually illiterate, and by making the public feel good about CBS's intrusion into their lives, Dorfsman instilled a pride of viewing.

Among the ads that still resonate—indeed could be reprised today without changes—"Ha, Ha, Ha: He laughs best who laughs last" is economical yet eye-catching. The word *ha* grows larger according to the Neilson's ratings response to the comedy shows of the three television networks, turning into the largest *Ha*, which represents CBS's high standing. Without the benefit of a hard-sell slogan or sensational image, but by harnessing the power of irony, Dorfsman let type alone to do the persuading. For an ad entitled "Worth Repeating, CBS News" Dorfsman used bold, disproportionately large quotation marks sitting majestically upon a pedestal of copy. These curiously abstract marks have greater shouting range than any single line of type or picture. "Dominate," a series of four advertisements used to convince potential advertisers that CBS enjoyed dominance in the ratings, was an example of "talking type." Once again, without the benefit of an image, Dorfsman used four words—"Captivate!" "Elucidate!" "Fascinate!" "Exhilarate!"—each set in a different typeface with an exclamation point dotted with the CBS eye. The copy suggested the range of CBS's programs in a market it totally controlled. Yet another exemplar was a soft-sell idea entitled "A Glossary of Television Terms," an illustrated lexicon of words such as *fish bowl, one shot,* and *audio,* that were introduced to the public through television. Cleverly illustrated, this compendium of trivia captured the interest of even the casual reader. After holding the reader's attention it smartly climaxed with the word "Leadership: The quality invariably associated with the CBS Television Network."

These ads did more than remind, inform, and persuade potential clients of the network's virtues, they increased the recognition of CBS by giving it a uniform identity, which in turn underscored the value of its corporate culture. Rarely were any of Dorfsman's designs, even the more decorative logos and trademarks, lacking an idea. In fact, if an idea was not readily apparent, he went to great lengths to concoct one. Without Dorfsman CBS would have had its eye, but with him the eye became the most positive logo in America.

Going Out

GENE FEDERICO

She's got to **go out** to get Woman's Day

the A&P magazine

...and Woman's Day isn't all she buys.

Because Woman's Day's circulation is all single copy sales,
you can be sure of 3,811,000 readers out shopping where your products are sold.

Good graphic design was long an exception to the rule in American advertising. Beginning at the turn of the century, copywriters were allowed to rein over designers and nuances of type and image were secondary to the hard sell of a product or message. Unlike European advertising of the same period, which was aggressively visual and pictorially innovative, in America it was virtually inconceivable that an art director would be much more than a glorified layout man subservient to the needs of the text. This changed in the 1930s when the advertising pioneer Earnest Elmo Calkins discovered that the effective marriage of word and picture could produce startling results. Prefiguring the "creative team" and creative revolution by more than three decades, he brought copywriters and designers together, forging a creative union. By 1939, when Gene Federico (b. 1918), a twenty-one-year old Pratt Institute graduate with a special interest in typography, entered the advertising field, a few exceptional designers had already begun to change the look (and often the content) of mainstream advertising, paving the way for a distinctly American modern style.

"Lester Beall opened my eyes to the idea that type could be used to emphasize the message," Federico said about one of American advertising's leading modern typographers. "One of his ads had the great line, 'To Hell With Eventually. Let's Concentrate On Now.' The *e* in *eventually* was very large and *now* was the same size. The simple manipulation of these letterforms allowed the reader to immediately comprehend the message." Federico's method was also based on the integration of text and image. He always worked intimately with a copywriter and played with the nuances of language. He looked for those simple elements in copy that expressed or emoted, and suggested that when a designer doesn't read the copy to catch the sound of the words, he or she runs the risk of misconstruing the typography. "If the rhythm of the words is disregarded, the copy is likely to be broken incorrectly," he continued.

Federico was more concerned with attitude than with style. Despite Lou Dorfsman's assertion that he was the prince of Light Line Gothic (admittedly one his favorite typefaces), few of his ads conformed to a single formula or evoked stylistic déjà vu. Nevertheless, one trait was dominant; his love of type. Letters served as sculptural forms placed on or against an image. Type both communicated messages and evoked a time and place.

Federico's series of advertisements for *Woman's Day*, which appeared in the *New Yorker* magazine in 1954 and were targeted at media buyers, typified his rhythmic sensitivity. One of the most well known had the catch-line "Going Out," and showed a photo of woman riding a bicycle with wheels made from the two Futura *O*s in the headline—a visual pun in the modern tradition. The goal of the ad was to persuade potential advertisers that three million-plus devoted readers went out of their way to buy this check-out counter magazine. The ads apparently did well for the client, but more importantly proved the power of persuasive visual simplicity in a field that often erred on the side of overstatement.

Man with the Golden Arm

SAUL BASS

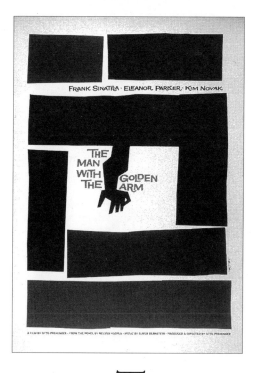

There are two Hollywoods. One, the land of fantasy and glitz. The other, the land of formula and convention. It was into the latter that Bronx-born Saul Bass (1920–1996) arrived in 1945 intent on producing unconventional advertising for the movie industry. But the odds were against him. In those days Hollywood promotion was mired in formula. Convention dictated the look and feel of posters, foyer cards, and ads. Romantic realism was a conceptual and aesthetic panacea, and the common poster showed something for everybody whether it was in the movie or not—bits of romance, action, drama, and, of course, unblemished portraits of the stars.

Bass, who had read and was influenced by Gyorgy Kepes's *Language of Vision* (1944), became a reductionist designing in a modern idiom. When he worked in the New York office of Warner Brothers, he toyed with the picture and text components of movie ads, mostly playing with scale, which was the only latitude he was allowed. Of course, it was a dead end. "I could only carry it so far, because the other ingredients had to be there," he recalled in *Graphic Design America* (Harry N. Abrams, 1989). So he packed up for Hollywood and went to work for Buchanan & Co., the agency that handled Paramount Pictures. Finally, in 1949 he designed his first breakthrough ad for *The Champion,* Kirk Douglas's seminal motion picture.

The ad was totally black with a tiny halftone and a little lettered scrawl below it. It took up about an inch and a half in the center of the page. In contrast to cluttered conventional ads, it was a real eye-opener. It was also the auspicious beginning of what evolved into Bass's expressionistic approach to Hollywood publicity, the precursor of the innovative advertising and film title sequences that he created first for Otto Preminger and, later, for Alfred Hitchcock.

In 1954 Bass designed the titles for Preminger's *Carmen Jones,* which were decidedly unique compared to the mundane lettering superimposed over backgrounds common in Hollywood movies at that time. In 1955 he made a bolder leap with the print advertising for *The Man with the Golden Arm,* which eschewed a picture of its star, Frank Sinatra, in favor of a pattern of black bars that framed a primitive woodcut-like rendering of a crooked arm. Theater owners were not pleased with the absence of the one-two punch of star portrait and heroic vignette. But one incident tells the story of Bass's subsequent success: "[Preminger] was sitting with his back to me—he didn't know I was there—talking on the phone, obviously to an exhibitor somewhere in Texas," Bass recalled in *Graphic Design America.* "The exhibitor was complaining about the ads and saying that he wanted to have a picture of Sinatra. . . . And I heard Otto say to him, 'Those ads are to be used precisely as they are. If you change them one iota, I will pull the picture from your theater.' And hung up on him." Rather than hype the film, the graphic reduced the plot, the story of a tormented drug addict, to an essence—a logo really—that evoked the film's tension.

Jumping at the opportunity to animate this simple graphic form as the title sequence for the film, Bass created a series of moving white bars on a black screen, which was transformed into an abstract ballet of erratic shapes. After a few moments the bars metamorphosed into the arm. "There was a tendency, when I did the title for *The Man with the Golden Arm* to think it worked because it was 'graphic,'" Bass explained in *Print* (1960) "but that was incidental. If it worked, it was because the mood and feeling it conveyed made it work, not because it was a graphic device." Nevertheless, by creating a graphic symbol that was effective for use in both the print campaign and the opening title sequence, Bass had introduced a new design form.

Actually, he returned to the essence of motion pictures before sound, Technicolor, Cinemascope, and other pyrotechnic advances upped the ante of filmmaking. Movies began as a purely visual medium. "We've come full circle," Bass once explained, "[we] went to a theatrical stage approach with inordinate reliance on dialogue, and now we're back again to a greater reliance on the visual, but in a way that is more real and more current with our lives today." Not surprisingly, Bass was often called upon to direct certain sequences within films where the visual scheme was more important to moving the story along than the dialog.

The Man with the Golden Arm was more than a fine piece of abstract animation. It was Bass's first movie within a movie, and it had less to do with specific aesthetics of design than a sense of the story (a key trait in Bass's later work). Yet it was not an independent effort; he believed that all aspects of a movie should fit together like pieces of a puzzle. "In every title I've done, I've been very conscious of the fact that the title has a responsibility to the film, that it is there to enhance the film, to set it up, to give it a beginning—and not to overpower and pre-empt it," he asserted in *Print.* For Bass the title was only the beginning of something, never the thing itself.

He continued making title sequences for four decades, many as memorable as the films themselves. And his work evolved from "mood-setting" animation into what he called "metaphorical live action" in *Walk on the Wild Side* (1962), where a black cat and a white cat meet, have a fight, and then part, as a metaphor for New Orleans street life. Later he pioneered the film prologue with John Frankenheimer's *Grand Prix* (1966), for which Bass traveled around the world directing camera crews in the shooting of racing sequences.

Forty years after challenging the studio's conventions and taboos, creative movie title sequences are facts of motion picture history. Indeed every designer who has ever designed film titles owes a debt to Bass. As a coda to the breadth of his influence, in 1995 director Spike Lee paid dubious homage when he copied Bass's logo for *Anatomy of Murder* as the print graphic for his own film, *Clockers*. Although Bass did not appreciate the larceny, it vividly illustrated the extent of Bass's contribution to the movie industry.

Electric Circus

IVAN CHERMAYEFF

DARLING DAUGHTERS
SWEET MOTHERS DANCE
BLACKLIGHT DYNAMITE
ACROBATS ASTROLOGERS
JUGGLERS FREAKS CLOWNS
ESCAPE ARTISTS VIOLINISTS
GROK GRAPES GRASS
UPS DOWNS SIDEWAYS
COFFEE THINK TANK
AIR-CONDITIONED
IN MORE WAYS THAN ONE
THE ULTIMATE LEGAL
ENTERTAINMENT EXPERIENCE

THE ELECTRIC CIRCUS
OPENS JUNE 28, 1967
23 ST. MARKS PLACE, N.Y.C.
EAST VILLAGE
THINK ABOUT IT.

In the mid to late 1960s the East Village in Manhattan, especially St. Mark's Place between Third Avenue and Avenue A, was the epicenter of the East Coast hippie movement. Bars, coffee houses, dance and concert halls, and headshops with names like Psychedelicatessen and Peace Eye mixed politics, drugs, and rock and roll with art and culture. Alternative theaters, like Channel One, radiated a kaleidoscope of sounds. On Second Avenue and Sixth Street the Fillmore East, the East Coast branch of Bill Graham's rock palace, headlined a youthful Grateful Dead, Jefferson Airplane, and Janis Joplin. Psychedelia stimulated by drugs like LSD and peyote was transplanted from Haight-Ashbury and acquired a New York accent.

On the West Coast Victor Moscoso, Wes Wilson, Rick Griffin, and other rock poster artists translated music into images. Encrypted by hand, nearly illegible type became a signpost, a code that conveyed the message to the young and confounded the Establishment. Hallucinogens slowed the passage of time and rendered it plastic. They transmogrified sensory modes. Feel orange! Taste purple! The psychedelic posters spoke the same undulating dialect in holistic compositions whose chromatic vibrations nonetheless took advantage of Albers's color theory.

The Electric Circus was a popular rock club in an old Ukrainian social club with a huge dance floor. Chermayeff (b. 1932) and Geismar (b. 1931) first designed the interior of the club then the poster announcing its grand opening on June 28, 1967, with words strung together in a stream-of-consciousness, ". . . darling daughters sweet mothers dance black light dynamite acrobats astrologers jugglers freaks clowns escape artists. . . ." Chermayeff was intrigued by the rambling, poetic language written by the owners of the club. Did the words describe the entertainment inside or invite the neighbors in by name?

Although not as visually elaborate as Moscoso's posters, the *Electric Circus*'s kinetic typography nevertheless reverberated with visual cues that fused form and content and added impact to the word-pictures jarred loose by the colorful language. Chermayeff's jiggly, hyperventilating alphabet wed word to image, too. At the same time, other designers like Gene Federico, Lou Dorfsman, and Herb Lubalin coaxed typeset words into visual and verbal configurations and took new liberties that the introduction of widespread phototypesetting afforded in the 1960s.

Chermayeff and Geismar met as students at Yale in the mid 1950s while doing research for papers on typeface design. In the spring of 1957 they teamed up with Robert Brownjohn to form Brownjohn Chermayeff Geismar. Brownjohn had studied with Moholy-Nagy at the Chicago Institute of Design and Chermayeff worked with Alvin Lustig in New York. They called themselves a design office instead of an art studio, which signaled a new professionalism based on problem solving and utilization of broad aesthetic resources. In those early years, before Brownjohn left the firm in 1960, the partners found inspiration in sorties to Coney Island and other urban hinterlands, immersing themselves in the sumptuousness of street vernacular. In text accompanying a photographic essay formalizing what he and his friends discovered, Brownjohn wrote, "everything of interest in this wide-open area of social uplift [the city] has been done by dead men or by amateurs, or vandals or politicians or accident or neglect or dirty old men or the makers of big, busy neon signs." ("BJ", *Eye,* Vol. 4, No. 1)

The alphabet for the Electric Circus poster began as an exploration of typographic expression in hot metal composition. In a booklet titled *That New York,* designed as an experiment for The Composing Room, Brownjohn, Chermayeff, and Geismar pushed the limits of typographic invention. They explored type as texture, stretched and distorted words and letterforms, created incongruous typographic hybrids, and layered words to the point of illegibility. If all this sounds vaguely familiar, "This and other works utilizing rubber stamps, wrong fonts, and fragmented letters preceded David Carson by thirty-five years," observed Ivan Chermayeff.

For the title, *That New York,* the designers began with a sans-serif typeface whose letterforms were overlapped and manipulated on film, in both positive and negative formats. The effect was a double-exposed image. New letterforms appeared—the *A, O,* and *R* had double counterforms and additional legs, and the *N, Y, W,* and *K* had new spiky protuberances. Using all capital letters afforded maximum play in the interstices with additional strokes added for vibrational energy.

In 1959 the firm designed the jacket for the book *Toward a Sane Nuclear Policy.* The type on the cover is stacked with uppercase sans-serif letterforms, one word per line. The top word, *Toward,* is printed twice with the second imprint offset dramatically from the first. Each of the following words is gradually more off register, culminating with the word *Policy,* which stands alone. The overlapping letters hint at the later-developed alphabet. But Chermayeff dismisses the *Sane* cover as an antecedent, saying the solution was purely conceptual and achieved through overprinting and not through the manipulation of films at all.

The alphabet was designed for the *That New York* booklet in 1960. Although it appeared in an advertisement entitled "Modern Banking is Electronic Banking" in *Fortune* magazine in 1961, it wasn't until it was applied to the *Electric Circus* poster in 1967 that it found its proper place. Chermayeff said it was "the first totally appropriate client to come up to take advantage of it." The poster won awards and was published often. Of course, it helped to have a client who intended it as an image builder for the club, not a ticket sales generator, and who neither expected or needed direct results. Although not born of the radical fringe, the *Electric Circus* poster nonetheless established an image for a club in the heart of New York hippiedom and stands as a bridge between alternative and establishment cultures.

Blues Project

VICTOR MOSCOSO

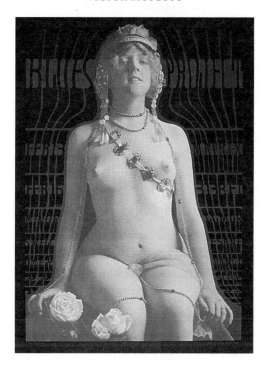

Victor Moscoso's psychedelic *Blues Project* poster is as illegible today as it was in 1967 when it, and scores of other vibrating rock posters advertising the San Francisco rock scene, first appeared. It is also as electrifying. Moscoso's posters did for graphic design what bands like the Grateful Dead, Jefferson Airplane, and Big Brother and the Holding Company did for rock music: turned up the juice and broke all the rules.

During the mid 1960s San Francisco was the vortex of the counterculture. The hippies prevailed, hallucinogenic drugs were plentiful, and rock and roll knew no bounds. Brooklyn-raised, Spanish-born Victor Moscoso (b. 1939) stumbled into this milieu and became a defining force in the distinctly American design genre known as the psychedelic poster. Characterized by illegible typefaces, vibrating colors, and antique illustrations, psychedelia was a rebellious visual language created to communicate with an exclusive community. Within a year, however, it was usurped by entrepreneurs who turned it into a trendy commercial style that appealed to a new market of youthful consumers. Before ceding the field to the so-called culture vultures, Moscoso created some of the most emblematic images of the 1960s, of which the *Blues Project* poster is one classic.

Most of the more than sixty posters Moscoso designed during a frenetic eight months in 1967 rejected publicity photos in favor of found images. For the *Blues Project* poster he used a vintage photograph of a nude Salomé. Following her contour, he hand-lettered the concert information in a typeface that Moscoso called Psychedelic Playbill (an adaptation of a Victorian woodtype).

Because he drew the letters out of negative space (whiting out all the areas between the bodies of the letterforms rather than drawing them directly), they look as if they have been carved onto the page. The figure was printed in bright orange against an acid green background; the lettering was printed in process blue. The slightly off-register trapping gave the letters a three-dimensional look in addition to the vibrating sensation produced by the juxtaposition of similar chromatic values.

The *Blues Project* poster defined a Moscoso style. Other leading contemporary poster artists, including Wes Wilson, Rick Griffin, and the team of Mouse and Kelly, had distinct visual personalities, but Moscoso's use of vibrating color was the most emblematic of the group. His brand of chromatic vibration was surprisingly derived from strict modern principles. Moscoso was schooled at Cooper Union in New York and Yale in New Haven before migrating west, and he credited his Yale professor Joseph Albers, a master of modernism, for this key discovery. Likening Albers's famous Color Aid paper exercises to the futility of learning algebra in high school, Moscoso admitted that color theory drove him crazy, but ultimately proved to be an invaluable resource. "Albers's impact really didn't show until the psychedelic poster . . . when I found myself in a situation where all I had to do was reach back to my dusty shelf, so to speak, and pull out what I had learned."

Compared to rock posters by Rick Griffin and Mouse and Kelly, each of whom practiced an obsessively precisionist, macabre comic style, Moscoso was a master of simplicity. Despite what appeared to be layers of graphic complexity, his visuals were strategically composed and purposefully designed. While being stoned may have added to the enjoyment of the *Blues Project* poster, the design was not drug-induced chaos. Moscoso was a highly disciplined rebel. He consciously rejected all the rules he learned during his time at college when he admired Paul Rand, won a cash prize for designing a roman alphabet based on the Trajan inscription, and rendered Chancery Cursive and Caslon from memory just for kicks. But the *Blues Project* poster was indicative of a complete understanding of balance, proportion, and color. The poster may not directly conform to any modernist theory, but it was influenced by contemporary design thinking.

Moscoso's first rock poster for The Family Dog dance hall, a picture of a gargoyle on the top of Notre Dame with psychedelic type overprinting the image, was an admitted flop. "I had seven years of college—I could have been a doctor," he said about the process of self-re-evaluation that resulted in a creative epiphany. He realized that none of the self-taught poster artists were encumbered by the rules of good design, so Moscoso reversed everything he had formally learned. The rule that a poster should transmit a message simply and quickly became how long can you engage the viewer in reading the poster? Five, ten, twenty minutes? Don't use vibrating colors became use them whenever you can and irritate the eyes as much as you can. Lettering should always be legible was changed to disguise the lettering as much as possible and make it as difficult as possible to read. Moscoso called this "a world turned upside down." But acting on these ideas he created a body of work that altered the language of a generation.

Best of Jazz

PAULA SCHER

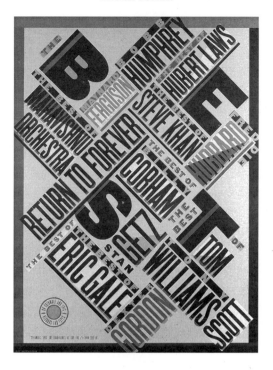

With the *Best of Jazz* poster, Paula Scher (b. 1948) introduced young American designers to forgotten design languages and inadvertently unlocked the floodgates for unknowing designers to pilfer historical artifacts as decontextualized scrap. With the Reagan presidency in 1980 national sentiment turned toward nostalgic and old-fashioned feel-good graphics that fed a longing for past innocence. This provided, consciously or not, a fertile environment for a new wave of historical derivation in design, which ultimately became known as "retro." For a generation of designers and consumers disconnected from their visual past, the *Best of Jazz* poster appeared fresh and unprecedented.

Early in her career, Scher was inspired by Push Pin Studios' reprise of passé styles such as Victoriana, art nouveau, and art deco. She turned to type from illustration shortly after coming to New York, citing a self-assessed inability to draw well. As an art director at CBS Records from 1975 to 1982, Scher commissioned conceptual illustrators and combined their surrealist styles with eclectic and often historic typography that echoed the illustration. The effect was a holistic integration of type and image in the manner of nineteenth-century posters.

In the late 1970s, the record industry hit the skids economically—sales slumped, costs soared, and inflation took its usurious bite. "I could no longer put all of our money into imagery," Scher stated in an interview in *Mixing Messages* (Princeton Architectural Press, 1996), "so the type came forward." About that same time Russian constructivism was being revisited in books and exhibitions. Scher, who had long collected and admired old graphic styles, quickly assimilated the revolutionary language.

Scher may have begun the *Best of Jazz* poster with an anthropological dig through the Russian avant-gardist's visual vocabulary, but she ended up with a distinctive tapestry woven of personal affinities, problem-solving pragmatism, and New York derring-do. The letterforms are not Cyrillic, but, oddly enough, nineteenth-century sans-serif woodtypes borrowed from old Victorian type catalogs. The Russian artists had located their constructions in the weightlessness of white space even as they concretized that same space as a formal element. Scher, conversely, confines this poster within a border then packs it with a feverish riff of letterforms that energize the surface plane and metaphorically mimic the improvisational nature of jazz itself.

Scher borrowed the constructivist's strong geometric composition, thrusting diagonals, and signature colors: red and black. High contrast is apparent between the bold, black capitals that spell out *BEST* and the smaller, busier typography. Overlapping colors, surprints, and knockouts make the most of the limited color palette. These elements may explain why the poster was popularly perceived as constructivist, but there was also an unmistakable resemblance to Victoriana in the tightly packed, nearly cluttered arrangement of type, the woodtype typography itself, and the slant toward ornamentation. Although it was a hybrid of two historical forms, the result was fresh-faced, decidedly contemporary, and, yet, eerily familiar, much like a child whose genetic code descends from but ultimately transcends that of its parents.

Effectively reinterpreting historical style is harder than it looks. To create unique graphic imagery inspired from the past involves juggling a number of currents: the inspiration and historical context of the original work; the resonance of the source material in its original time frame and the interpretations it might be given when restaged in a contemporary setting; and the designer's own personal style and taste. But where are the boundaries when designers treat past aesthetic vocabularies as a storehouse of motifs to be used willy-nilly for their gratuitous impact on contemporary audiences? Far from any universal agreement, historical appropriation ranges from the clearly ethical—inspiration, influence, homage, reinterpretation, quotation, and parody—to the blatantly unethical—mimicry, copying, imitation, and plagiarism.

Some of Scher's historically inspired inventions have veered perilously close to copying an original, as with the 1986 Swatch advertising parody of Herbert Matter's 1938 poster for the Swiss Tourist Bureau. With tongue in cheek, Scher assembled most of the same visual elements as Matter did, with the notable addition of a hand and wrist wearing two Swatch watches, which are, not incidentally, made in Switzerland. The capricious nature of the product dramatized in the monumental style of Matter's poster created a humorous juxtaposition and sense of absurdity that appealed to Scher's wit. It was a chance to play with the 1950s this-will-change-your-life type of advertising. In an interview with Dick Coyne of *Communication Arts* (May/June 1986), Scher explained, "Whether or not people get the joke or understand the basis of it—I hope they do— that's the fun for us [Scher and then-partner Terry Koppel], and one reason why we both love to design." They acknowledged Matter in a credit line at the bottom of the ad.

Historical reprise has been a mixed blessing. At once it serves to educate designers about history, making them more open to learn about past eras and epochs, but also sanctions easy formal solutions devoid of originality. While some critics argue that overt borrowing from the past tends to trivialize both past and present by promoting rote design, others argue that the introduction of these reprises serves to enliven the field by offering more creative options. Where history is intelligently absorbed the results are invisible. Where history is used effectively as a model, a sense of appropriateness is usually apparent. But where history is just a cut-and-paste procedure, the result is almost always a cliché.

Basel Kunstkredit 1976/77

WOLFGANG WEINGART

By itself, typography is as boring as hell,"
stated Wolfgang Weingart, the man who stood Swiss typographic design on its head. "What
makes it exciting is how you interpret it." The tenets of Swiss design, later the International
Typographic Style, emerged from the traditions of the Bauhaus, the New Typography of the
1920s and 1930s, and de Stijl. Sans-serif typography and objective photography—photographs
that do not seduce or make exaggerated claims—were positioned on an underlying mathematical
grid of verticals and horizontals in a harmonic relationship derived from objective and functional
criteria.

Switzerland's neutrality in World War II provided a sanctuary for pioneering designers Max
Bill and Theo Balmer to continue their explorations begun at the Bauhaus. A booming postwar
economy heightened industry's demand for publicity and the rationalist design ethic prospered,
spreading to Germany, Basel, and Zurich, and eventually to the design community at large. Emil
Ruder and Armin Hofmann began teaching at the Allegemeine Gewerbeschule (Basel School of
Design) the same year, 1947, establishing their own version of typographic principles based on a
correct balance between form and function, the sanctity of readability, and the belief in an
absolute and universal graphic expression.

After a three-year apprenticeship as a hand typesetter with a small printer in Stuttgart,
Wolfgang Weingart met Armin Hofmann by chance in 1963 when he inquired about his and
Ruder's classes at the School of Design in Basel. Although he studied briefly with both teachers a

year later, Weingart considers himself an educational orphan, a failed student of Ruder's and underexposed to the teachings of Hofmann, who left for India shortly after Weingart arrived. "I had a special understanding with Ruder and he let me use the workshops whenever I wanted," Weingart said in an interview in *Eye* (April 1991).

In this pristine academic environment, the perpetually restless Weingart began to question: Why does type need to be flush left and ragged right? Why do paragraphs need to be indented? He didn't want to reject all that came before, just expand it. In 1968 the Advanced Course for Graphic Design was started, and Weingart was offered a position on the typography faculty. His contributions to graphic design's lexicon are considerable: wide letterspacing, layering of photographic and typographic imagery, solid bands and blocks of reversed type, grids implied then violated, underlining, unconventional mixing of type sizes and weights, diagonal type, and using geometric shapes and typographic units as illustrative devices—all elements that would later be adopted as contemporary mannerisms. Is Weingart pleased? Hardly. He would condemn this list as "design cream" that has been skimmed off and used as disembodied fragments by designers who don't think for themselves. "I never intended to create a 'style,'" Weingart said. He did intend to discover a new visual attitude and method of experimentation based on a solid teaching foundation.

Weingart's posters for the Basel Kunstkredit (art fair) document his investigations. The *1976/ 77* poster is a hallmark of typographic and spatial play, and visual proof of his philosophy that typography exists in a triangular relationship between the design idea, typographic elements, and printing technique. Photographic fragments of a building and interior architecture allude to illusionistic space, a snippet of reality. The camera lens image is photographic, too, but frontal and flattened in space. For contrast Weingart used the tools of print technology, enlarged halftone dots and moiré patterns, as aesthetic elements to interrupt the reading of the "reality" of the photographic images and reinforce the true nature of the poster—ink on paper.

Diagonals draw the viewer into the space, both through the perspective of the architectural references and the directional nature of the geometric shapes. Graphic devices, grids, and solid blocks of typography are embedded in the graphic imagery, sometimes overlapping other images, other times tucked behind. The effect is one of layering, or put another way, of spatial dialogue between illusionistic three-dimensionality and the two-dimensional activity of the surface. The result is disorienting, complicated, and dynamic, but it is not chaotic. A solid vertical and horizontal axis underpins the geometric thrusts and girds against the photographic allusions to spatial depth, reminding the viewer of the surface plane. Weingart tinkered with visual pathways, tested readability by partially obscuring letterforms, and left the viewer with a nonlinear, holistic conglomeration.

Weingart is not a theorist, but a practitioner for whom technology is the ultimate challenge. He embraced it as both a partner and a friend, garnering techniques from his own investigations and experiments. He pioneered sandwiching and juxtaposing film positives in the darkroom to form a seamless union between imagery, typography, and technology, a technique that prefigured the computer. He acknowledged the computer has "speeded things up," but with an ironically peevish attitude for an alleged technophile. He still maintains that basically "there's nothing it can do that can't be done by hand, or film montage. It hasn't produced a new visual language."

As a teacher, Weingart's influence radiates beyond his own oeuvre. In 1972 he organized a lecture tour through Switzerland, Germany, and the United States, illustrating his threefold manifesto to expand typographic alternatives through syntactic, semantic, and pragmatic considerations. Prophetically, he concluded his remarks by confessing his program completely neglected the study of texts, which would find full flower in the next decade's passion for semiotics, the study of signs and sign function. Early students like April Greiman, Willi Kunz, and Dan Friedman, after studying with Weingart in Basel, returned to the United States to teach and practice. This extended spirit of aggressive exploration eventually coalesced as the new wave in America.

Weingart's style was appropriated during the late 1980s and early 1990s. At first he said imitation was a stimulant, an incentive to keep one step ahead. Now he says, "My work is a quarry. People see a stone they like, appropriate it and work it until there's nothing left." He still teaches but no longer designs. He is far from distraught, though. "No, I had to stop, in order to let the things that I produced sink in, and wait until the next, real explosion comes, so that designers in the new decade can copy me again."

Cranbrook

KATHERINE McCOY

Accused of being a cloistered atmosphere polluted by its own freedoms, the graphic design program at the Cranbrook Academy of Art has certainly been in the forefront of design criticism for the past twenty-four years. One might expect to find guerrilla theoreticians lobbing graphic cherry bombs at mainstream modernism, but, in fact, Cranbrook's influence did not come from launching manifestoes; it developed by creating a stimulating environment where graphic experimentation altered the conventional practice of graphic design. According to Katherine McCoy (b. 1945), chairwoman of the graphic design program from 1971 to 1995, the work done during that time can be loosely organized into three "clusters of concerns": the expansion of modernism's formal language (1971–1979), a short middle phase characterized by "high formalism" (1980–1981), and a third, poststructuralist stage (1982–1995). Criticism notwithstanding, Cranbrook's explorations served as fodder for rigorous discourse that helped define and expand the profession during the 1980s.

Although Cranbrook embraced the Bauhaus notion of unity between art and industry, as early as 1940, when Charles Eames became chairman of the department of industrial design and Eero Saarinen and Harry Bertoia were on the faculty, Cranbrook had replaced the rigidity of Bauhaus ideology with a more complex, eclectic approach in which personal directions were encouraged. It was in this context that Katherine and Michael McCoy became co-chairs of the design department in 1971. In what started out as a part-time position, Katherine was responsible for two-dimensional design and Mike the three-dimensional design of furniture, interiors, and products.

How did the institution that Paul Goldberger described in the *New York Times Magazine* (April 1984) as "part artist's colony, part school, part museum, and part design laboratory" become an experimental crucible for American typography during the 1970s and 1980s without a plan, much less a manifesto? In this unstructured environment the focus and impetus for learning came directly from the students, who were highly motivated self-starters. "We always encouraged students to read," explained McCoy (*Eye*, No. 16, Vol. 4). McCoy kept an ever-expanding department bibliography, but texts were not assigned; students were encouraged to research, ruminate, and formulate with an eye to developing their own conceptual strategies. Cross-fertilization was a way of life between departments (art, photography, and architecture) and people. Students worked cheek by jowl in studios with faculty and each other as dorm rooms and cafeterias became laboratories for high-spirited discussions.

McCoy was reluctant to describe the evolution at Cranbrook as a progression. It was more like spontaneous combustion, but there was an overarching philosophy that confronted graphic design's traditional dilemma—form versus content—head on. "Form is not the enemy of content, and form can become content as well as a container of content," she explained. For McCoy, her 1989 *Cranbrook Design* poster symbolizes this reconciliation and pluralism. Visually, word pairs stretch the length of the poster anchored to the center, their dialectic reinforced by color and layout. Layered beneath the word pairs are collaged image-fragments of student work, echoing the bilateral symmetry with two-dimensional design projects on the left and three-dimensional projects on the right. The deepest information layer is the See-Read-Text-Image diagram that unites the poster formally, and semantically suggests multiple interactions between the elements.

To structure the phases during her tenure at Cranbrook, McCoy used a simplified communication model based on a 1949 linear-progression schematic developed by Shannon & Weaver. Although Shannon's model was later replaced by more sophisticated ones, "the sender › message › receiver" chain identified the core elements of communication as a basic linear interaction. McCoy, whose background is in industrial design, came to Cranbrook as a problem-solver and modernist. In the early years, 1971–1980, the program focused on the message part of Shannon's equation, expanding the modernist notion of the transparent designer communicating a clear and precise message to an audience. The entire lineage of Swiss work was examined, from Karl Gerstner and early Müller-Brockmann, Hans Neuberg and Emil Ruder to the later "high Swiss" of Ruedi Rüegg, Odermatt & Tissi, and Wolfgang Weingart's "mannered Swiss." Despite this thoroughness, the Swiss vein was just one of many being explored at the time.

As a result of working with Ed Fella, a self-taught commercial artist with a highly personalized graphic style, McCoy's modernist tendencies expanded to include an understanding and sympathy for the "low end" of commercial art and the vernacular. McCoy brought Fella into the program at Cranbrook to participate formally in critiques and informally in spontaneous interactions with students. This sparked investigation into other commercial vernaculars and books like Robert Venturi and Denise Scott Brown's *Learning from Las Vegas.*

In 1978, *Visible Language,* a scholarly journal devoted to exploring the role and properties of written language, dedicated a volume to contemporary French literary aesthetics and engaged Cranbrook in a collaborative effort to design the volume, titled "French Currents of the Letter." Daniel Libeskind, head of Cranbrook's architecture department, worked with McCoy and select students, giving them a crash course in French linguistic theory.

Deconstructionism, a term that would later become Cranbrook's albatross, is a part of poststructuralism, which, in turn, is a response to structuralism, an earlier movement in French literary theory. Led by Ferdinand de Saussure, structuralism posited that signs, rather than being isolated elements with self-contained meanings, are culturally interdependent parts of an overall network whose meaning is derived from the relationships between the parts. Deconstructionism was introduced to the United States through the writings of Jacques Derrida, which were translated into English in the late 1970s. Derrida suggested that a cultural construction, such as an idea, a value, or a sentence can be disassembled, or taken apart, and decoded—its parts examined for "meaning." The parts can be reassembled into another whole that may, then, take on a different meaning. The rearrangement of the parts into various wholes opens a way of exploring the complex nature of signs and moves communications into the complicated landscape of multimeaning, layered contexts, thus marking a shift from binary, yes–no signification to a more subjective, multidimensional interpretation of meaning.

For the *Visible Language* project, McCoy and students Richard Kerr, Alice Hecht, Jane Kosstrin, and Herbert Thompson created a typographic analog to the text. The essays began with traditional layouts. Progressively the space between the words and lines was expanded and footnote material was repositioned to interact unconventionally with the text. The final essays appeared to be pages of floating words visually punctuated by black horizontal bands of marginalia that so dislodged conventional reading order that the viewer was forced into alternative reading patterns. Vertical and diagonal pathways opened up, causing words and phrases to reassemble themselves through new juxtapositions that jarred conventional meanings. It offended almost everyone, drawing rage and ridicule from designers still committed to the modernist canon of simplicity, legibility, and problem solving.

The investigation of formalist expression culminated in 1980–1981 with the high formalist phase. Here the emphasis shifted, in Shannon's model, from the message to the sender. The classic student exercise in typography, to take a semantically neutral message like a weather report or recipe and explore its presentation through typographic and compositional variations, had evolved into what became known as the "label" exercise. After some classic warm-ups, the projects started with a Yellow Pages ad or a product label that was subjected to visual analysis, typographic variations, and most controversially, subjective interpretations of the original object or ad. The designer was no longer just a translator, but a commentator, partner, and participant in the delivery of the message.

The third, poststructuralist phase (1983–1995) grew out of a restlessness and dissatisfaction with mannered formalist manipulations. Although the *Visible Language* project in the late 1970s touched on deconstructionism, it wasn't until the mid 1980s, with the classes of 1985/87 and 1986/88, that an active interest in linguistic theories really flourished. Driven by student inquisitiveness, McCoy called this period the "theory-of-the-week-club—structuralism, poststructuralism, deconstruction, phenomenology, critical theory, reception theory, hermeneutics, letterism, Venturi vernacularism, postmodern art theory." McCoy resisted, asked questions, and challenged both students and theories. As Jeffery Keedy, a student at the time, recalled (*Eye*, No. 16, Vol. 4) she kept saying, "But what does it look like? How you do make it work as a design tool?" She admitted to being skeptical at times, but always remained committed to the mutual search, if not the mutual conclusions.

In the poststructuralist period at Cranbrook, the emphasis in Shannon's model of communication changed again, now from sender to receiver. The traditional notion that text was to be read (a linear, encoded, left-brained activity) and images were to be seen (a holistic, experiential, right-brain activity) was questioned. Text became cross-functional and took on an expanded capability to communicate beyond its functionality, moving into the realm of the illustrative (type as image), atmospheric, or expressive. Similarly, images could be "read," sequenced, and combined to form more complex information patterns.

Concepts like multiplicity, layers of embedded information, viewer-controlled text and imagery, and nonlinear progression, which were characteristics of Cranbrook's experimental design in the late 1980s, have become bywords of multimedia, the new graphic design frontier. McCoy saw graphic design as a pluralistic activity, one in which the components of Shannon's model still apply, but no longer in a linear fashion. The imperative was for integration and cross-functioning of all the elements. "I think this approach fits modern society because the contemporary world is subtle and complex. Simple black-and-white dualisms no longer work."

Is graphic design graduate school a hermetically sealed research and development laboratory or a pseudoprofessional environment with training wheels? Those who would attack Cranbrook for being the former, need to consider the impact on the design profession of alumni like Lorraine Wild, Nancy Skolos, Tom Wedell, Lucille Tenazas, and Jeffery Keedy. Cranbrook didn't intend to launch a revolution in theory-based graphic design. In fact, Katherine McCoy didn't even want to teach. So why did she stay for twenty-four years? "Because it is such a flexible situation. . . . If you want change you can change. The only real requirement from the administration is that you attract good students and produce strong graduates who find their way in the profession."

The Discreet Charm of the Bourgeoisie

YURI BOKSER

On August 19, 1991, the day that hard-line Russian communists ousted Mikail Gorbachev in the famous short-lived coup, Yuri Bokser (b. 1954), a thirty-seven-year-old Russian poster artist, boarded an Aeroflot jet at New York's Kennedy International to return to his besieged Moscow knowing that he might be arrested. Bokser—one of Moscow's leading film-poster designers, who also designed unpublished political posters critical of Lenin, Stalin, and Gorbachev—had just finished a short stay in New York where he received assignments from the *New York Times* and *Rolling Stone.* Warned against returning home, he had little choice: his wife and children had been left behind because temporary entry visas to the United States were difficult to get in those days, and his life's work was there, too.

Bokser, born in Tashkent in 1953 into a Jewish family with roots deep in the Russian soil, had drawn cartoons for exported Soviet magazines that had looser restrictions than internally distributed media, but he wanted to do something more meaningful, like posters. "This was impossible because I could not make the kinds of posters that the official publishing houses would print," he once recounted. "I made two or three attempts at that and failed miserably." It was not his plan to become a nonconformist, but through the underground artists at the Moscow Art Institute he had seen Polish magazines like *Projekt,* the Swiss *Graphis,* and some American design journals. "I was inspired by the freedom in that work, and also in American art in general," he said.

Bokser made his first unofficial poster around 1981, a few years before *perestroika* (the new openness) took hold. It was for rock-musician friends and was printed in a small quantity. "But after that I didn't make another poster for a long time," he recalled. Bokser's first success came when Reklamfilm, the USSR's oldest film promotion company, changed leadership when its chief art director was caught taking kickbacks from artists. His replacement decided to use new artists. Bokser was the first of the newcomers, then, one by one, came his friends. Nevertheless, having an art director who was sympathetic to expressive and symbolic art—surreal, allegorical imagery with hidden references and meanings—did not immediately change the way things were done. "It was very difficult in the beginning because Reklamfilm had to get permission to print each poster from the department of film distribution, which demanded that everything be conventional." Ironically, the films did not have to sell or make money, so in any other context more freedom would have been possible.

Bokser's breakthrough came when an editor at Reklama Cine did what Bokser referred to as "a very strange thing" by printing a small quantity of one of his formerly prohibited posters. The image for Luis Buñuel's *The Discreet Charm of the Bourgeoisie,* showing a slice of salami in the shape of a heart, was exhibited both in- and outside of the USSR—the first time since the constructivist art of the 1920s that such a symbolic treatment had replaced the official Russian pedantic representation. The public response was so positive that it encouraged a shift in the policy of the film distribution department. As if by waving a magic wand, a new style of conceptual film posters, which owed more to the Polish tradition of illustrative poster art than to Russia's constructivist legacy, were produced at prodigious rates. Each of the regular Reklamfilm artists produced between twenty and thirty posters annually. For a few years, the posters were printed in quantities that exceeded one hundred thousand and could be seen everywhere, providing a festive atmosphere to the otherwise drab Soviet cityscapes.

Bokser was not, however, content just to do film posters. He turned to social art that rejected the style known as socialist realism, which he argued was really "socialist romanticism." His satiric jabs at the Soviet establishment, especially the failings of perestroika, became well known. "I was skeptical about perestroika almost from the beginning," he explained at the time. "It quickly became merely a new slogan. Of course, it's better than Stalinism." Indeed under Gorbachev the promised freedoms were rationed; the majority of Bokser's social commentaries were prohibited from being printed by the official publishing house and in many instances could not even be shown in exhibitions. Leaders of the Artists Union, to which Bokser belonged, would not allow certain critical representations of Lenin and, especially, Gorbachev to hang since they feared losing their positions. "In our country it is normal," he said. "I do not feel offended by these people. I can understand the pressures brought to bear." Yet Bokser continued to do unpublished critical works for a small coterie of friends.

Bokser insisted that he was always free to do his work as long as he did not expect the controversial works to be published. But he also admitted that exercising total freedom in the USSR was never easy. So he remained true to the ideals of reform, despite the fact that the inevitable shift to a market economy proved deleterious to his art. Shortly after returning to

Moscow in 1991, he wrote that "there has been less work during the past two years, and I am afraid that the great cinema period of Soviet posters will be over. With capitalism everything depends on money, including film. And now the film distributors want *Rambo* movies and *Rambo*-styled posters, which is really socialist romanticism all over again. My fellow artists and I deceived the system for five years. Now, some younger artists will come along and do the *Rambo* posters, but not us."

Template Gothic

BARRY DECK

If period typefaces such as Broadway from the 1920s, Helvetica from the 1960s, or Avant Garde from the 1970s had been designed at any other time in history, would they have been as emblematic of their times? Or were they such total products of their eras that the question is moot? When William Caslon designed his only sans-serif typeface back in the early 1800s, it was considered an aesthetic monstrosity. Had it been created in the 1920s, however, when geometric sans-serif faces stood for progressive ideals, it would have been accepted without question. Typefaces, like automobile and clothing design, contribute to the Zeitgeist. But what makes the character of a particular type so endemic? "The process by which particular typefaces come to embody the look, mood, and aspirations of a period is mysterious and fascinating," wrote Rick Poynor in *Eye* (No. 6, Vol. 2, 1992).

Timing may not be *everything*, but it does have a lot to do with why typefaces appeal to the public's taste at any given moment. It certainly explains why CalArts graduate Barry Deck's (b. 1962) Template Gothic (1990), a vernacular-inspired yet futuristic-looking typeface, became the most emblematic font in an epoch replete with emblems. At the time of Template Gothic's inception graphic design was experiencing technological shifts that altered methods and mind sets. Modernism was being challenged by a growing number of heretics opposed to its dogma; universality had become the hobgoblin of cultural diversity; and Swiss-influenced typography had become cold and trite. Template Gothic was one designer's attempt to explore alternative influences that were more or less deemed taboo. "The design of these fonts came out of my desire to move beyond the traditional concerns of type designers," Deck explained in *Eye* (No. 6, Vol. 2, 1992), "such as elegance and legibility, and to produce typographical forms which bring to language additional levels of meaning."

Some designers hold the traditional approach as sacrosanct as any religious doctrine. "Type is rigid and implacable," wrote Frederic W. Goudy in *Typologia* (1921). But others see the past as a foundation upon which to build new traditions. "We've had five hundred years of movable type now we have mutable type," conceded Matthew Carter in *Fine Print on Type* (1990). This mutable type requires mutable typographic rules. As Katherine McCoy wrote in *Design Quarterly* (No. 148, 1993), "Gone are the commercial artist's servant role and the Swiss designer's transparent neutrality. . . . Forms are appropriated with a critical awareness of their original meaning and contexts. This new work challenges its audience to slow down and read carefully in a world of fast forward and instant replay. . . ."

After twenty years of grid-locked design, reappraisal was inevitable. Rudy VanderLans and Zuzana Licko of Emigre had already opened up the laboratory doors, while academic hothouses, such as Cranbrook and CalArts, were encouraging students to push the boundaries. Conventional typeface design reprised or adapted historical models while strictly adhering to the tenets of balance and proportion. Conversely, the "new" typography started from zero. Without the benefit of precedent to guide them, type designers sought more eccentric influences both from exotic and mundane sources. Template Gothic was literally taken off the wall. "There was a sign in the laundromat where I do my laundry," Deck said. "The sign was done with lettering templates and it was exquisite. It had obviously been done by someone who was totally naïve." Although the stencil was itself professionally designed, manufactured, and commonly sold in stationery stores, the untutored rendering of the ad hoc laundry sign exemplified a colloquial graphic idiom that many designers viewed as a foreign language.

Designers have for a long time dug up and collected visual detritus from the street as a kind of deep background. Even the moderns appreciated old hand-painted signs as quaint artifacts from an era before sophisticated design methods brought light and order to the world. Given the postmodern ethos for revaluation, many of these same artifacts were elevated to monuments of visual culture. In much the same way that the Trajan Column in Rome provided the ancient inscriptions for the subsequent design of roman letters, the template inscriptions that influenced Deck were the basis for a distinct alphabet. Deck did not simply mimic the original, he built an aesthetic principle that challenged the prevailing concerns about legibility and accessibility.

Perhaps the best reason for Template Gothic's success was that it evoked the present *and* the future. A composite of low- and high-tech, it combined the vernacular traits of the mass-produced stencil and the futuristic character of early computer lettering. At the time it was released it captured the conscious and unconscious needs of designers to break from the recent past. In addition, Template Gothic is a curiously workable—user friendly—mélange of irregular, tapering strokes, thick and thin bodies, and inconsistent weights, or what Deck called the "distortive ravages of photomechanical reproduction." Conceptually playful and experimentally serious—purposefully imperfect—Template Gothic is a postmodern discourse on the standards and values of typographic form. It is also a distinguished display and text face with tremendous versatility.

Manson/Mason

JONATHAN BARNBROOK

O n the surface, the spiky roman typeface
Manson, reminiscent of medieval inscriptions and replete with crucifix-ated *T*s and *O*s, exudes a
kind of mysterious Gregorian atmosphere. But Jonathan Barnbrook's typeface is more than a
family of quirky letterforms, it is a case study of how and why typefaces are named, and the
relationship that a user has to both the name and face. Christened after mass-murderer Charles
Manson, according to Barnbrook in *Emigre* (No. 23, 1992), this is merely a "different way of
looking at the naming of a typeface." Shortly after it was introduced, Manson was criticized not
for its form, but its name. One of the letters to *Emigre* read: "In a time of random violence,
individual, organized, and institutionalized, why are you naming a typeface after Charles
Manson? As part of our media culture, in fact a well-respected one, what kind of humor are you
projecting? What kind of responsibility are you neglecting? This is no subtle joke. We are
shocked at your inhumanity and callousness."

Although Barnbrook's description of Manson in *Emigre* did not sufficiently address the
reason for celebrating this particular criminal, he did offer this: "While reading the word *Manson*,
associations with other words such as *mason* and *mansion* might be evoked, names that do not
relate somewhat to the elegant look of the typeface. The surname Charles also sounds quite
sophisticated. But then you realize that its the name of a mass murderer and you re-assess your
attitude to the typeface." Barnbrook's doublespeak may not do justice to his seductive
medievalized Roman derived from his 1991 design of Exocet, based on a primitive Greek stone

carving. Nevertheless, taken at his word, this is not merely a novel or gratuitously named typeface, but rather a test of what motivates someone to choose a particular type.

The name Manson forces the user to address a fundamental relationship. What, for instance, does the face signify? Aesthetics aside, why would someone buy a font with such a namesake? Apparently the name is more experimental than the typeface design itself, for it tests the limits of signification and association. While most typeface names are comparatively benign, something called Manson cannot avoid conjuring up images of violence and criminality, in the same way that *Nixon* conjures deception and deceit. Given this name, the quirky letters are no longer just the distant relations of ancient Greek inscriptions, but are kissing cousins of the swastika tattoo carved into Manson's forehead or the words *Helter Skelter* that were drawn in blood on the walls of Sharon Tate's home.

Bowing to criticism, however, and thereby eschewing the issues that Barnbrook initially sought to raise, the 1995 Emigre Fonts catalog included a specimen of Manson renamed Mason; perhaps suggesting the Order of Masons, which itself has a cultist underpinning, or the ethno-centric comedian Jackie Mason, who has a large cult following, or more likely it refers to a stone mason, from whence the inscriptions derived. But despite revisionist nomenclature, the name Manson not only sticks, but also gives the face an aura, if not a meaning, that it would not have had if it were originally called Mason. As proof, two recent book jackets for *The Death of Hitler* and *The Violence of Our Lives: Interviews with American Murderers* used Manson/Mason for what critics of this nomenclature would assert were the wrong reasons: to signify and/or dignify violence. Although only designers who know the name, not the average reader, will actually get the reference, the impetus to use this face was its name, which when linked to these specific titles reinforces the idea that this typeface represents violence.

Typefaces are given names either to define otherwise abstract letterforms according to purpose (e.g., News Gothic), or to celebrate the face's maker or inspiration (e.g., Benguiat), or to sell a particular fashion (e.g., Cubist Bold). In the 1930s, A. M. Cassandre named his transitional sans-serif Peignot after Charles Peignot, the design impresario who helped launch his career; Frederic Goudy called one of his numerous type designs Deepdeen after his rural New York State retreat. And Milton Glaser called his popular display face, originally used on his *Dylan* poster, Baby Teeth because of the physical relationship to a baby's pearly whites (yet it could easily have been called Stairstep for the same reason). The majority of classical text faces are named after their designers: Garamond, Bodoni, Firmin Didot, Baskerville, Caslon, Gill, Cooper, and Bernhard are the major street signs of typography. Naming a face after its creator is one way to ensure immortality, or at least notoriety.

Identity

DESIGN AS SIGNATURE

Flight

E. McKNIGHT KAUFFER

Edward ("Ted") McKnight Kauffer (1890–1954) was one of Europe's most prolific and influential advertising artists of the 1920s and 1930s, certainly as innovative as his more celebrated French counterpart, A. M. Cassandre. In England, where he lived and worked, Kauffer brought advertising art into the twentieth century, yet in America only a few knew of the Montana-born expatriate's achievements.

Kauffer was sent abroad at the behest of Professor Joseph McKnight (the young man's mentor from whom he took his middle name). If he had not gone he might never have become a poster artist and graphic designer, and if he had not been introduced to Ludwig Hohlwein's poster masterpieces in Munich and attended the Academie Moderne in Paris, his life would have taken a much different turn. Before crossing the Atlantic he stopped in Chicago where he was profoundly influenced by the Armory Show, the landmark exhibit that gave Americans their first exposure to the burgeoning European avant-garde—it had opened first in New York and then Chicago to critical, if not dismissive, reviews. Kauffer didn't know what to make of the unprecedented Picassos, Cézannes, Duchamps, and Matisses on view: "I didn't understand it. But I certainly couldn't dismiss it," he wrote some years later. Eventually, these paintings would inspire his own benchmark work entitled *Flight* (1916), which in 1919 was adapted as a poster for the London *Daily Herald* with the title *Soaring to Success! The Early Bird,* the first cubist advertising poster published in England.

The art capitals of Europe beckoned, but the clouds of war loomed, and in 1914 Kauffer

161

became a refugee with just enough money in his pocket to return to America. Instead of sailing straight home, however, he discovered England, and with it a tranquillity he had not experienced in America. "I felt at home for the first time," he wrote. Kauffer volunteered to serve in the British army but was ineligible because he was an American citizen. Instead he did a variety of menial jobs while waiting for painting commissions to come along.

At this time Kauffer met John Hassall, a leading English poster artist, which led to a meeting with Frank Pick, the publicity manager for the London Underground Electric Railways. Pick was responsible for the most progressive advertising campaign and corporate identity program in England. He had the vision to both unify the Underground's graphic system and diversify its publicity, thus making it more efficient and appealing. He commissioned Edward Johnston to design an exclusive sans-serif typeface and logo for the Underground (both are still in use) as well as England's finest artists to design posters for its stations. Kauffer's first Underground posters, produced in late 1915, were landscapes rendered in gouache or poster paints advertising picturesque locales. These and his 140 subsequent Underground posters, spanning twenty-five years, evidence Kauffer's evolution towards modernism.

During his first year in England, Kauffer became a member of the London Group, a society of adventuresome painters who embraced cubism. He refused to abandon painting for his new advertising career, but rather questioned the growing schism between fine and applied art. "He could see no reason for conflict between good art work and good salesmanship," wrote Frank Zachary in *Portfolio* #1. In fact, he was dismayed by the inferior quality of English advertising compared to work being done on the continent. During the 1890s there had been a period in which the "art poster" flourished in England, exemplified by Pride and Nicholson (known as the Beggarstaff Brothers), yet this flicker of progressivism was soon snuffed out by nostalgic fashions. Although Kauffer's earliest posters were picturesque, they were hardly sentimental; he intuitively found the right balance between narrative and symbolic depiction in prefigurations of his later abstract images.

It is likely that Kauffer saw the first exhibit of the vorticists in 1916, and that this avant-garde movement of British futurists, who worshipped the machine, had an impact on his own work. *Flight,* in its minimalism and dynamism, echoed the vorticist's obsession with speed as a metaphor for the machine age. This is "Kauffer's major work," wrote Kauffer biographer Hayward Haworth-Booth, "[and] also the finest invention of his entire career." The image departed just enough from direct quotation of cubist form as to become the basis for a personal visual language. "He had a child-like wonder and admiration for nature," continued Haworth-Booth referring to how Kauffer based this image not on imagination, but his first-hand observation of birds in flight. However, *Flight* might not have become an icon of modern graphic design if Kauffer had not submitted it in 1919 to *Colour* magazine, which regularly featured a "Poster Page" where unpublished maquettes were reproduced free-of-charge as an inducement for businessmen and advertising agents to employ talented poster artists. The poster was seen as one means of helping England get back on a sound commercial footing after the war. *Flight* was bought by Francis Meynell, a respected English book publisher and printer who organized a poster campaign for the Labour newspaper, the *Daily Herald*. Meynell interpreted that the soaring birds represented hope, and Kauffer's novel design somehow suggested renewal after the bloody world war. The poster was hung everywhere, and soared its maker into the public eye. Kauffer soon received commissions to design campaigns for major English wine, clothing, publishing, automobile, and petroleum companies, most notably Shell Oil and Shell Mex.

Kauffer argued that nonrepresentational and geometrical pattern designs "can effect a sledge hammer blow if handled by a sensitive designer possessing a knowledge of the action of color on the average man or woman." He believed that the artist's job was to foster an appreciation of diverse visual stimuli that transcended the conventional marketing tricks. Nevertheless, even Kauffer had to lead clients by the hand: "In most cases it has not been possible to give me full freedom," he wrote, "and my clients have gone step by step rather than by leaps, but by this slow process we have argued and discussed each advance until our opposite points of view have reached a synthesis, and it is because of this mutual understanding that I confidently expect England to progress to international distinction, not because of myself but through the new talent that is making way in many directions. . . ." His own productivity is evidence that certain businessmen appreciated the communicative power of unconventional form, but even in such a receptive milieu (particularly when compared to American advertising) there were hostile critics who referred to Kauffer's abstract designs as "McKnightmares."

Despite these occasional barbs, critics realized that Kauffer made significant inroads in the applied arts, first in the application of cubist form, and then after 1923 when he realized that vorticism no longer offered viable commercial possibilities and he entered his so-called jazz style, in which he created colorful, *art moderne* interpretations of traditional form. In 1927 he took a three-day-a-week job at Crawfords, the largest advertising agency in England, which lasted two years and marked the end of his jazz style and the move towards modernist photomontage, influenced by German and Russian advertising of the time. Kauffer expanded on this revolutionary vocabulary, and in his own work he replaced diagonal with rectilinear layouts, crushed his type into parallelograms, used positive/negative lettering frequently, and most importantly took up the airbrush to achieve the streamlined effect that characterized his work of the 1930s. Kauffer was further involved with the popular new medium of photomurals, and developed the "space frame" to give an illusion of multiple vantage points on a single picture plane.

Kauffer was called the "Picasso of advertising design." Critic Anthony Blunt wrote: "Mr. McKnight Kauffer is an artist who makes one resent the division of the arts into major and minor." And in the introduction to the 1937 Museum of Modern Art exhibition catalog of Kauffer's posters, Aldous Huxley praised Kauffer's primary contribution to modern design: "Most advertising artists spend their time elaborating symbols that stand for something different from the commodity they are advertising. Soap and refrigerators, scent and automobiles, stockings, holiday resorts, sanitary plumbing . . . are advertised by means of representations of young females disporting themselves in opulent surroundings. Sex and money—these would seem to be the two main interests of civilized human beings. . . . McKnight Kauffer prefers the more difficult task of advertising products in terms of forms that are symbolic only of these particular products. Thus, forms symbolical of mechanical power are used to advertise powerful machines; forms symbolical of space, loneliness, and distance to advertise a holiday resort where prospects are wide and houses are few. . . . In this matter McKnight Kauffer reveals his affinity with all artists who have ever aimed at expressiveness through simplification, distortion, and transposition. . . ."

No longer are postage stamps staid icons of officialdom, they are outlets for exceptional design, striking imagery, hilarious wit, even biting satire. Yet no other form of graphic design is as sacrosanct or more indicative of a nation's character. With the exception of a national flag no other official design is more politicized. Postage stamps are more than mere currency, they are a nation's signboard. They commemorate the most important issues and events, and they are potent instruments for propaganda when they carry messages designed to influence, inspire, and move.

What appears on stamps is usually determined by committees. In the United States a citizens advisory panel comprising experts in various areas of popular culture, sports, and art advise the Postmaster General what stamps to issue. Special interest groups are known to lobby as vociferously for stamp recognition as for congressional legislation. Stamps are the most widely recognized collectible, and in certain nations the field of stamp collecting is a major industry. The postal agencies of larger nations have become veritable stamp dealers either to supplement their national budgets or to subsidize their postal services. In countries where the postal service is privatized, such as The Netherlands, brisk sales can mean the difference between profit and loss.

Designing postage stamps is not easy. With the eyes of a nation focused on the result, these images are intensely scrutinized. When the Croatian artist Boris Bucan designed his nation's first air mail stamp he came under fire. Since this breakaway Yugoslav republic had very few commercial airplanes, he designed a stamp that showed a paper airplane against a blue sky.

Although the stamp was published, his sarcasm went unappreciated by countrymen who petitioned for its recall. Conversely, there were few if any notes of displeasure when the Dutch designer Rick Vermullen, of Hard Werken Design in Rotterdam, designed a preprinted paid postcard for the Royal PTT Nederlands on which he included a picture of himself in a comic pose. Vermullen was commissioned to design a stamp that somehow represented the users of such cards. After conducting research, he determined that ninety-five percent of preprinted postcards were used by sweepstakes players and contestants to enter quizzes and games. He therefore decided to show a quiz master (Mr. Vermullen himself) standing over a TV screen that projects the seventy-cent value of the stamp in large numerals. The seven is decked out like a crossword puzzle, while the zero is a dart board, representing a game of chance. The quiz master holds up two prizes: In one hand money and the other hand flowers. The image is printed outside of the formal stamp area, giving it the appearance of a coupon.

The Royal PTT Nederlands is one of the most progressive postal agencies. Back in the early 1930s its visionary director, Jean François Van Royen, commissioned avant-garde designers Piet Zwart and Paul Schuitema to create advertisements and stamps that transcended convention by employing their distinctive use of typofoto (collage and New Typography). Under Paul Hefting, art director of the art and design department, the PTT continues to push the limits of the postage stamp tradition in terms of marketing, management, and design. Since the PTT was privatized less than a decade ago, emphasis has been placed on increasing the amount of stamp sales by creating designs that people are compelled to buy for utilitarian and aesthetic reasons.

In addition to the conventional postage stamps, PTT encourages designers to take unique approaches to commemorative, cautionary, and information stamps. They lead the way in commissioning internationally known graphic artists to extend the boundaries. French designer and former principal of Grapus design collective Pierre Bernard designed a series of Red Cross stamps; British designer Neville Brody designed stamps for a national flower exhibition; Belgian cartoonist Ever Mullen designed a series of child welfare stamps; and American Robert Nakata of Studio Dumbar in Den Haag designed stamps commemorating 150 years of travel on the Dutch railways. Nakata's design is indicative of the creative license afforded by the PTT. To suggest the idea of travel, Nakata used the famous *Kiss* by Rodin to signify both arrival or farewell. To ground this metaphor behind the sculpture the roof of a railway station platform is visible.

To stimulate sales to collectors and users stamps must elicit intellectual or emotional responses. That distinctive stamps are designed annually indicates that the world's postal services understand that the public has tastes that can be served by stamps. That many of these are designed by inventive graphic designers proves that this art for the masses is by no means crass.

McGraw-Hill Paperback Covers

RUDOLPH DE HARAK

If modernism imposes coldness and sterility, as critics have argued, then Rudolph de Harak (b. 1924) must have done something wrong. A devout modernist, his work for public and private institutions has been uncompromisingly human. For proof take 127 John Street, a typically modern skyscraper in New York City's financial district. Before de Harak designed its entrance-level façade it exuded all the warmth of glass and steel on a winter's day. But with the installation of his three-story-high digital clock (composed of seventy-two square modules with numerals that light according to hour, minute, and second), the mysterious neon-illuminated tunnel leading to the lobby entrance, and the bright canvas-covered permanent scaffolds that serve as sun decks, 127 John Street was transformed from a modern edifice into a playground.

De Harak's innovative addition to the John Street building enlivened a faceless street; likewise his inspired exhibition designs for museums and expositions have transformed didactic displays into engaging environments. Dedicated to the efficient communication of information, he used detail the way a composer scores musical notes, creating melodies of sensation to underscore meaning. His exhibits were indeed symphonies that both enlightened and entertained. His exploded diesel engine, the centerpiece of the Cummins Engine Company Museum in Columbus, Indiana, in which virtually every nut and bolt of this complex machine was deconstructed in midair, was evidence of the designer's keen ability for extracting accessible information from even the most minute detail. And yet while his exhibition design explored the rational world, his graphic design uncovered the subconscious.

Although de Harak deliberately employed neutral typography to anchor his design, the hundreds of book jackets, record covers, and posters he created between the opening of his design office in 1952 and its closing in 1990, are evidence that throughout his career he expressed *emotion* through type and image. While not the raw expressionism of the most fashionable designers of the 1990s, de Harak employed abstract form ever so subtly to unlock alternative levels of perception. He related this practice to abstract expressionism, which in the early 1950s he wholeheartedly embraced, and while this may be difficult to see amid his orthodox, systematic design, the nearly four hundred McGraw-Hill paperbacks he designed in the early 1960s bring this relationship into clear focus. De Harak's rigid grid was, in fact, a tabula rasa on which both rational and eccentric imagery evoked ideas. The subjects of these books—philosophy, anthropology, psychology, and sociology, among them—offered de Harak a proving ground to test the limits of conceptual art and photography. At the same time he experimented with a variety of approaches inspired by dada, abstract expressionism, and, ultimately, op-art.

His on-the-job research helped push the design practice towards an art-based theory. With one eye on the international typographic style, the other was focused on pushing the bounds of letterform composition. Following in the tradition of poetic typography of the 1920s, de Harak imposed his own levels of legibility through experimentation with various forms of letter and word spacing.

He built his typographic scheme on Berthold's Akzidenz Grotesk from Berlin. This bold European typeface effectively anchored de Harak's design and gave him a neutral element against which to improvise with a growing image repertoire. His early experiments, including fifty covers done for Westminster records, were the basis for the decidedly modern book jackets that he designed for Meridian Press, New Directions, Holt Rhinehart and Winston, and Doubleday. And all the approaches he developed during the late 1950s led to his opus, the McGraw-Hill paperback covers that became laboratories for his experiments with color, type, optical illusion, photography, and other techniques. More important, these covers would define his design for years to follow.

McGraw-Hill paperbacks were emblematic of 1960s design. At this time the international typographic style and American eclecticism were the two primary design methodologies at play in the United States. The former represented Bauhaus rationalism, the latter 1960s exuberance. De Harak was profoundly influenced by the exquisite simplicity of the great Swiss modernist Max Bill, but as an American he wanted to find a vehicle for reconciling these two conflicting sensibilities. Just as he resisted the hard-sell approach in advertising, he also rejected the eclectic trend to make typography too blatantly symbolic. "I never saw the need to put snowcaps on a letterform to suggest the cold," he offered as an example of the extreme case. Instead he worked with a limited number of typefaces, at first Franklin Gothic and News Gothic, preferring it over Futura, then Akzidenz Grotesk, and ultimately Helvetica. De Harak believed that Helvetica gave him all the color, weight, and nuance he required to express a variety of themes and ideas.

The McGraw-Hill covers were pure visual communication. Since de Harak did not allow for anything extraneous, each element was fundamental. Yet as economical as the covers were, each was also a marriage of expressionistic or illusionistic imagery and systematic typography, the same repertoire of elements that de Harak would use in other graphic work where he was known for reducing the complex without lessening meaning.

Dylan

MILTON GLASER

Bob Dylan arrived in New York in January 1961 at the age of twenty-one. In five years he produced seven albums and came to symbolize a generation caught between the unprecedented consumer prosperity that followed World War II and the Cold War's chilling rhetoric of mutually assured destruction. The 1960s generation adopted Dylan, projecting onto him its collective hope and cynicism. On July 29, 1966, it was reported that while riding his motorcycle on the back roads in Woodstock, New York, the back wheel locked, and Bob Dylan was thrown over the handlebars and seriously injured. Rumors abounded. Some thought he was dead, and some thought it was a ruse to cover up a recovery from an overdose. Whatever the truth, the words and the music stopped.

After six months without any new Dylan material, Columbia Records was in a nervous panic. To fill the gap, Columbia unilaterally decided to issue a greatest hits album pieced together from previous album cuts. Creative director Bob Cato and art director John Berg had a dramatic, backlit photo by Roland Scherman of a closely cropped profile of Dylan playing the harmonica, his wild hair bathed in a corona of light. Dylan had previously rejected it as cover art. But because he was in breach of contract, Dylan could no longer control what his recording studio did.

It was further decided to include a free poster in each new greatest hits album. Columbia decided to use the Scherman photographic profile on the album cover, but needed someone to design the poster. The Scherman profile triggered Berg's memory of Milton Glaser's (b. 1929) playful and inventive silhouettes that captured the essence of gesture and content through minimal means.

The hallmark of Glaser's work was an aggressive mining of visual artifacts and archetypes from diverse and unexpected sources. In addition to silhouettes, Glaser was working with black-ink contour lines, creating flat shapes and enriching them with adhesive color films, echoing the simple iconography and directness of comic books. He was interested in Islamic miniatures and was intrigued by the psychedelia emerging from the West Coast. Long before postmodernism, Glaser understood that design is essentially a vernacular language, and he delighted in discovering obscure typographic forms. On a trip to Mexico City he was so captivated by the letterforms on a small advertisement for a tailor that he photographed the sign and returned home to invent the remainder of the alphabet, which became the typeface Baby Teeth.

When the request came from Berg to design the poster of Dylan along with a package of pictorial reference, including copies of the Scherman photograph, it didn't strike Glaser as anything extraordinary—and time was short. So he did what he was already doing, rather effortlessly and entirely intuitively.

First, the memory of a powerful icon surfaced, a self-portrait by Marcel Duchamp—a profile torn from a single piece of colored paper and placed on a black background. Dylan's hair became an inductive mélange of Persian-like forms. Dylan's name, executed in Glaser's own Baby Teeth typeface, rested in the bottom right corner of the poster, a warm brown against a black background, unusual in its subtlety. The geometric letterforms contrasted sharply with the mellifluous hair and sinuous profile. Glaser admitted to being consciously intrigued by the notion of opposites: the hard, reductive edge of Dylan's profile contrasts with the expressive nature of the hair; bright, whimsical color reverberates off the dense, solid black.

In the original sketch (his only sketch), Glaser positioned a harmonica in front of Dylan's mouth, as in Scherman's photograph. When Berg saw the sketch, Glaser recalled, he said "Simplify, simplify." What he meant was, "Get rid of the harmonica." Eliminating the harmonica created a white negative space nearly equal to the black silhouetted profile. This increased the visual vibration of the whole piece and focused more attention on the "coastline" of Dylan's profile. Glaser went directly to finish. Six million *Dylan* posters were printed and included in the album, making it the single most reproduced image Glaser ever created, aside from his I ♥ NY™ campaign.

NeXT

PAUL RAND

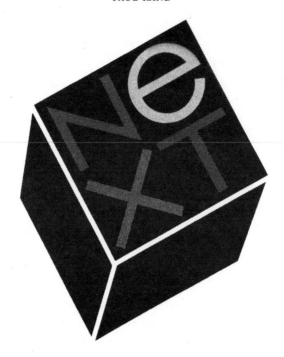

It is difficult enough to invent a meaningful corporate logo, sign, or mark to express conventional business issues without having to depict the future as well. However, that is what was demanded of Paul Rand (1914–1996) when in 1988 he was commissioned to design a logo for NeXT, an educational computer company headed by Steven Jobs, the founder of Apple Computer Company. Although NeXT's new product was cast in secrecy, the corporate name alluded to its futuristic positioning—not simply a *new* computer, but the *next* wave of information processing for the educational market. With only a few clues, Rand was given a month to devise a logo that would embody as much symbolic power as the memory of a silicon chip.

Rand had made identity systems out of whole cloth many times before. He created time honored marks for IBM, UPS, and ABC. In each he found the most identifiable graphic forms: stripes for IBM, a gift box atop a shield for UPS, the repetition of circles for the lowercase letters *abc*. Designing such charged—and lasting—logos is not magic, but it does take an acute understanding of the nature of perception and the ability of translate that into a visual form. "Logos are *aides de mémoire* that give you something to hook on to when you see it, and especially when you don't see it," explained Rand. And the problem with the word NeXT was that it was not depictable. "What are you going to show? A barber shop with somebody pointing, 'You're next'? It's simply not describable in typographic terms."

Graphic devices that represent the future, such as the arrow, were made meaningless by overuse, but the NeXT computer was contained in a black cube, which gave Rand the idea he needed. He decided to frame the word in a cube to evoke the product itself. However, at the time the logo was introduced to the public, the computer's shape and form were completely secret. "It was understandable only as a cube, nothing else," he explained. "But without that reference point, I would have had to devise something out of the blue." In fact, for Rand it was not so much a question of having a reference point as using that reference point. "The client mentioned the cube to me when I was given the problem, and I'm sure the other designers who worked on the logo must also have heard about it," Rand presumed.

The NeXT logo was successful in part because the cube was symbolically related to the product itself, but Rand insisted that the shape was only important in sparking the idea. "Some reference was made to it being like a child's block," he continued. "I really think that is one of its virtues and part of its charm. However, the logo is not designed to be charming, it is designed to identify."

Before the logo could do the job, however, Rand had to sell the mark to Jobs. For this he had a pronged strategy. The first was to present only one logo. This underscored his own confidence in the solution and deflected indecision on the part of the client. The second was to "speak" only through a presentation booklet that concisely explained the rationale and showed the applications of the logo. Jobs had seen all the timeworn futuristic clichés—arrows, clouds, lightning bolts—in the book. However, he was unprepared for Rand's twenty-page book, entitled "The Sign of the Next Generation of Computers *for Education . . .*"

From the beginning of this limited (fifty copies), Platonic document, Rand announced his premise: "What should a logo for NeXT look like?" he asked in text set in Caslon, which led into a concise narrative that condensed decades of communications history into ten minutes of reading time.

First he introduced the concept of type itself: "Choosing a typeface as the basis for the design of a logo is a convenient starting point. Here are two examples: Caslon and Bifur. Caslon is an alphabet designed as far back as 1725 by William Caslon. It appears to be a good choice because it is both elegant and bookish, qualities well suited for educational purposes. . . ." He described the nature of his faces, their quirks and virtues, and concluded by admitting, "Attributing certain magical qualities to particular typefaces is, however, largely a subjective matter."

Next he defused the client's need to sample a variety of typefaces: "One reason for looking at a number of possible typefaces is to satisfy one's curiosity. Another, and perhaps more meaningful one, is to study the relationship of different letter combinations, to look for visual analogies, and to try to elicit ideas that the design of a letter or group of letters might inspire." He offered some examples that were intended to pique the reader's interest, and offered this warning: "Personal preferences, prejudices, and stereotypes often dictate what a logo looks like, but it is *needs*, not wants, *ideas*, not type styles which determine what its form should be. . . ."

Then Rand took a representative typeface and set it in caps to explain why this particular iteration was unsuccessful: "Set in all capitals, the word NEXT is sometimes confused with EXIT, possibly because the EXT grouping is so dominant. A combination of capitals and lowercase letters alleviates this problem." And after winning the argument, he provided a textbook example of a more successful application: "Here are some possibilities which explore the use of lowercase letters. The *e* is differentiated so as to provide a focal point and visual contrast among the capital letters which, otherwise, consist only of straight lines. Happily the e also could stand for: education, excellence, expertise, exceptional, excitement, $e = mc^2$, etc."

This brief lesson in typographic style segued into an explanation of how a mark should function: "Ideally, a logo should explain or suggest the business it symbolizes, but this is rarely possible or even necessary. There is nothing about the IBM symbol, for example, that suggests computers, except what the viewer reads into it. Stripes are now associated with computers because the initials of a great computer company happen to be striped. . . ." And then he introduced the idea underlying his version of NeXT: "A logo takes on meaning, only if over a period of time it is linked to some product or service of a particular organization. What is essential is finding a meaningful device, some idea—preferably product-related—that reinforces the company name. The cube, in which the computer will be housed, can be such a device because it has visual impact, and is easy to remember. Unlike the word Next, it is depictable, possesses the *promise of meaning*, and the *pleasure of recognition*."

Understanding that questions would arise concerning the application of the cube, Rand talked about versatility: "This idea in no way restricts its application to any one product or concept. The three-dimensional effect functions as an underscore to attract the viewer's attention." Once established that the cube was the appropriate form, Rand addressed the basic structure of the logo: "Splitting the logo into two lines accomplishes several things: it startles the viewer and gives the word a new look, thus making it easier to separate from common usage. And even more importantly, it increases the letter size two-fold, within the framework of the cube. For small space use, a one line logo would have been too small to fit within this same framework." Rand showed that readability was not affected because the word was too simple to be misread. "Moreover, people have become accustomed to this format with such familiar four-letter word combinations as LOVE."

He concluded his primer with a down-to-earth analysis: "The adaptation of this device to miniaturization—tie tacks, charm bracelets, paper weights, stickers, and other promotional items is endless. It lends itself as well to large-scale interpretation—signs, exhibits in the shape of cubes, in which the actual exhibit is housed, as well as exhibit stands. For printed matter, its infinite adaptability and attention-compelling power is self-evident."

Upon presentation, Rand did not utter a word, he just sat silently watching as Jobs read. "The book itself was a big surprise." Jobs recalled, "I was convinced that each typographic example on the first few pages was the final logo. I was not quite sure what Paul was doing until I reached the end. And at that moment I knew we had the solution. . . . Rand gave us a jewel, which in retrospect seems so obvious." Moreover, as it turned out, Rand's user-friendly teaching aid underscored Jobs' own commitment to the process of education.

Restaurant Florent

M&CO.

NOVEMBER
SOUP   BOUDIN & WARM TARTS

GUSTY WINDS
HIGH SUPPER 40S TO MID 50S
LOWS UPPER 30S TO MID 40S

FLORENT
OPEN 24 HOURS 989 5779
WATCH FOR HEAVY RAINS

WEAR YOUR GALOSHES

MNCO

In 1986 a chef named Florent Morlet opened an inexpensive French restaurant in New York City's unsavory meatpacking district. Without any investors and little capital, he rented a funky old luncheonette that had recently gone out of business. His intent was to remain unpretentious (and still appeal to an exclusive clientele), yet Restaurant Florent did require the basic promotional materials, such as menus, business cards, and a sign. For these graphics he hired M&Co., a New York firm known for experimental commercial art. Tibor Kalman (b. 1949), M&Co.'s creative director, suggested that Florent keep all the fixtures, furniture, utensils, and the sign that the previous greasy spoon had left behind. "Let the restaurant design itself," said Kalman.

The menu designed itself too. Kalman decided that to be consistent with the restaurant's overall ambiance the menu should look like a printer had thrown it together. He would have gone to a place where they print typical Greek coffee shop menus, "but we felt that the result wouldn't be quite as effective as what a job printer might do, because those other printers are imitating designed things," he explained. Instead the menu looks as though it had been pieced together in a few hours using random type from a letterpress type case. Nevertheless, it took two months to design. "If we weren't trained designers it would have taken less time," said Kalman. "The difference between something really wonderful and really horrible is very close."

M&Co. designed Florent's first announcement using a mundane exterior photograph of the restaurant (the kind used for common diner postcards). For the second they made an original design and printed it on a coarse chipboard paper stock. Kalman decided to illustrate the idea of a restaurant through little pictographs lifted straight from the Manhattan Yellow Pages. The result was a kind of rebus with a chair representing the restaurant, a truck representing the address, a gun representing New York City, and an old Bell Telephone Company logo representing, well you know. "Our vocabulary was based on dumb, really obvious, generic images used for most commercial advertising," explained Kalman. But the goal was not nostalgia. In fact, Kalman insisted that the difference between nostalgia (or kitsch) and appropriation is ultimately how the finished product is filtered through the designer. Nuance is the key.

Early versions of advertisements for Florent employed quirky iconography, too. One showed a raw steak, another a simple salt shaker (both had the restaurant's name but no address or phone number). As Restaurant Florent's popularity increased additional moneys were available for larger ads. M&Co. created a different ad every week, all orchestrated to create a distinct mythology. Inexpensive stock photos and studio shots of found objects conveyed a variety of ideas, the most emblematic of which was a common three-dimensional menu board left over from the greasy spoon days, complete with misspellings of the day's specials. Others showed arrows pointing to the shirt of a customer, humorously indicating what specials had been spilled that day, a parody of an ecological chart. The most fashionably design-conscious ad used words in the manner of dadaist typography of the 1920s to illustrate Florent's food and drink menu.

Many restaurants and businesses have consistent identity campaigns, but Restaurant Florent stands out for two reasons: it was a pioneering effort in vernacularization (the return to commonplace elements of commercial art), and it was a successful performance of various talents brought together as a repertory producing the equivalent of scripted and improvisational graphic design.

Disney World Signage

SUSSMAN/PREJA

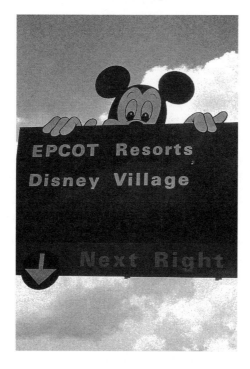

Walt Disney World in Orlando, Florida, is not a Mickey Mouse operation. It is as large as San Francisco and as diverse as New York's five boroughs. By comparison it reduces the original Disneyland in Anaheim, California, founded in 1955, to the status of mere amusement park. Disney World is the escapist capital of the world with attractions like the Magic Kingdom, a fantasy theme park modeled after Disneyland; Walt Disney Village and Pleasure Island, a mammoth resort and shopping mall; Epcot Center, a world's fair–scaled projection of the future; and UA/MGM Studio, a Hollywood movie set come to life. These realms are separated by large greenbelts and connected by a north-south axial highway and arterial road system, which like any interstate requires precise way-finding management. But precision is only one concern of Michael D. Eisner, Walt Disney Inc.'s chairman and chief executive officer.

Eisner's widely publicized strategy of growth brought with it a Medicean patronage of art and architecture. His commissions to postmodern architects Michael Graves, Frank Gehry, and Arata Isozaki reflected a commitment to the unique and unusual. Paul Goldberger, architecture critic of the *New York Times*, called Disney Inc. "a corporate patron like no other." Hence, the commission given to Sussman/Preja and Company—the creators of the carnival-modern graphics of the 1985 Los Angeles Summer Olympics—to design Disney World's road signs, buses, and gateways underscored Disney's commitment to distinctive design, down to the smallest detail.

In 1986 Eisner thrust Walt Disney Inc. into a developmental frenzy that included expansion of its film, publishing, and resort operations in the United States and Europe. Unlike most American cities of comparable size, where poor planning has ruined skylines and made ingress and egress confusing at best, Disney believed in coordinated development. A responsibility for the total comfort of visitors, both in the attractions and on the roads, meant that as Disney World grew, a new environment that facilitated mobility and identified Disney World as an integral and accessible entity was needed.

"In the beginning our signage was like everywhere else in the country," said Eisner about their original "liver-colored" road signs that also serve as the National Park Service standard. But beyond his apparent preference for nonconformity, Eisner admitted, "I drove myself around Disney World but routinely got lost. If I couldn't find my way who could?" The desire for a contemporary look, plus the development of new hotels and attractions were good enough reasons for Eisner's decision to change the entire system. But he also offered a more fundamental rationale: "When Walt Disney World was originally built, the Magic Kingdom was up at the extreme north of our property. I'm told that the [development group] felt that if they signed at the beginning of the property, kids would get so excited about going to the Magic Kingdom they'd be frustrated to find a fifteen minute drive ahead of them." With the new growth it no longer took fifteen minutes to get to a Disney attraction, making a uniform signage system not only more appealing but, in fact, quite necessary.

Based on their success with the graphics program for the 1985 Summer Olympics, Deborah Sussman (b. 1931) and Paul Preja (b. 1930) of Sussman/Preja and Company were invited to propose ideas. When they were awarded the commission, Wing Chao, senior vice president of planning, architecture, and engineering of Disney Development (the division administering to all areas other than the design of the thematic attractions) had one simple request: "I wanted their wildest ideas and craziest notions. They shouldn't hold anything back." Sussman was glad to oblige. "We showed them a hundred ideas for the one that got built, but that was part of the fun," she said.

Understanding how the signs could be more efficiently used was key to an effective design solution. Sussman took charge of the design team, Preja led the analytical phase, Scott Cuyler did much of the initial creative work, Robert Cordell was the in-house project manager for all Disney work, and Debra Valencia worked on the typography during the refinement stage. April Greiman, a frequent collaborator with Sussman/Preja, consulted on various aspects of the signage. The design problem was also opened to other designers in their office.

At the outset the designers needed to be familiar with the rather complex layout of Disney World. "We didn't know what Epcot was," admitted Sussman. "Or that the Magic Kingdom was essentially the same as Disneyland. Or what Pleasure Island was and how it related to the Magic Kingdom" Indeed most outsiders are also unaware that these diverse attractions fall under one umbrella. After their initial research was completed, Sussman issued a statement that became the blueprint for her vision. In it she said, "there is the world and then there is Disney World," suggesting the scope and limits of the problem.

The first planning decision was to simplify the signage requirements yet attend to every complex detail. "We decided to establish a series of discrete districts, similar to boroughs," Sussman said about the initial stage, "which affected how many of the previous signs we could effectively eliminate. Instead of having to erect a separate sign for every component of Disney World, we could group them into discrete categories that were headed by these districts. That, of course, affected things like size, typography, and nomenclature. Before this, every sign began with 'Walt Disney World,' followed by the name of the attraction and other pertinent information. It was like reading a long menu— by the time you get to the end you forget what the other entrées were. Similarly, by the time you've finished reading the road sign [if you can read it at all] what you probably remember is the heading. That indicates a tremendous amount of redundancy."

The new plan reduced the number of messages under the district name, which then was eliminated on the signs nearer to the attraction. A hierarchy of signs was established and designed accordingly; it included large highway signs, secondary message markers (like what frequency to turn the car radio to for Disney World's exclusive channel), off-highway directionals, and so on. The next step involved the three basic aesthetic components: color, typography, and form. "We agreed with the Disney people who felt that they had enough images in Disney World already," Sussman continued. "But we did, however, want to evoke the spirit of Disney. Our challenge was how to do it without imitating or, as Frank Gehry said 'co-opting, or being co-opted by' these famous Disney icons. Our answer was to look at the simplest vocabulary possible."

Sussman selected Univers type because of its numerous size and weight variations. As for color, "Mickey is black and white, plus red and yellow. Yet from these colors you can't make a whole signing system—at least we didn't think that we could," she said. Ultimately green was introduced, as well as purple for its playful spirit. As for form, Sussman played around with various cut-paper configurations, and Scott Cuyler devised the angular post used for some of the highway signs, which took on a kind of postmodern, or Disney Deco, flavor. But in the end it was Mickey's profound influence that made the difference. Without literally looking like Mickey Mouse, the addition of a black circle (in which directionals were placed) onto the otherwise rectangular signboards became an indispensable graphic signature. "It worked immediately," Sussman said about the simple yet brilliant composition. "And when we made the signs that had two circles, it was unmistakably Mickey."

The concept went to Eisner for final consideration, who, according to Sussman, said upon first glance "'If I had to make a decision today, I'd say yes.' But since this was a major commitment, he wanted to test it out while looking at some other ideas." Eisner loved the colors, and even suggested they be copyrighted so that no one else could use them. But he also wanted to know what else could make the signs "more Disney." An obvious suggestion was to put Mickey's hand in the black circle in place of the arrow. "We tried it out as a full scale, on-site sign," Sussman explained, "but we felt strongly that it didn't work. The hand just does not want to become an arrow." Since Eisner liked the idea, Sussman was a little worried that he would insist on going with it. "But," she said, "when we showed it to him he admitted that we were right." Another option was to use a silhouette of a Disney character or part of one sticking out of a diagonal sign for off-highway use. However, the feeling at Disney was that visitors would either steal them or stop to have their pictures taken next to them, which would ultimately impede the flow of traffic. In the end they decided on one special series of highway messages featuring Mickey on three sequential overhead signs spread over a few miles. The first showed two yellow gloved hands reaching over the sign, Kilroy style; in the second, two round black ears peeked up; and finally, in the third, Mickey's smiling face peered over.

Like an old Burma Shave sign, these teasers span Disney World's main highway. Elsewhere 775 other signs of all descriptions, even the commonplace markers indicating stop, yield, and speed, are set atop colorful stanchions and pylons that are not only efficient, but also playfully decorative. How have the signs fared with the public? "They have gotten good response," Eisner said proudly. "I don't know whether it's because people now know where they're going or that they really like the look." In creating an environment that reflects its time, communicates a purpose, and defines a corporation that since its inception has devoted itself to celebrating the imagination, Sussman/Preja joined other architects and designers who transformed Disney World into a festival of late twentieth-century design.

The Public Theater Posters

PAUL DAVIS

The revolution was already in full swing when in the late 1950s Paul Davis (b. 1938) entered the fray. Some renegade illustrators and art directors had already begun to revolt against the saccharine realism and sentimental concepts in most American magazines and advertising. Although Davis was not among this first wave, he was swept up by it. By the early 1960s he had developed a distinct visual style—a unique confluence of primitive and folk arts—that brought a fresh, American look to illustration. In a relatively short time he was among the most prolific of the new illustrators, and his style had a staggering impact on the field.

Davis developed an interest in American primitive painting and folk art as well as in the hand-lettered wooden signs that defined eighteenth- and nineteenth-century American commerce. "An artist of the caliber of [the nineteenth-century Pennsylvania primitive] Horace Pippin, whom I still think is one of the most undervalued American painters, was making honest observations of American life," he said about the search for a native culture. "The 1950s were a particularly nationalistic time, especially in the arts. People were talking about what is American. Europe was still the acknowledged leader in the arts, and many people did not believe that Americans even had a culture." In 1959 Jasper Johns showed his flag paintings for the first time. They were unmistakably American. Davis remembered going to the Whitney Museum biennial exhibitions where Larry Rivers and Robert Rauschenberg were shocking people with their new American visions.

One of Davis's many stylistic evolutions occurred between the late 1960s and early 1970s with a cover for the left-wing arts and politics journal *Evergreen*. He rendered a religious depiction of Cuban revolutionary Ernesto Che Guevara, whose exploits in South America had become mythologized by the American New Left. In this image Davis eschewed the Early American conceit for a synthesis of Italian religious art and socialist realism. "I was trying to make the image of a martyr," said Davis about this artifact of the era. "I didn't realize the potency of the symbol at the time. But when the cover and later the poster appeared, *Evergreen's* offices were firebombed [by Cuban émigrés]."

With this image he began a formal shift from the stiffness and motionlessness of his primitives to a more photographic sensibility. "I tried to erase the traces of American primitive art because it was becoming a trap," he admitted. "I wanted to rid my work of all the elements that referred to other styles. And within a year or two after this, I had eliminated a lot of self-consciousness from my work." Soon Davis began to "depend more on the beauty of objects," and depicted scenes rather than ideas.

Davis's most significant contribution to American graphic design is his theater posters. His rendition of *Hamlet* and subsequent posters for Joseph Papp's New York Shakespeare Festival done during the mid 1970s challenged the conventions of contemporary theater advertising. First, they were not encumbered by the usual bank of "ego" copy. "Those early posters didn't say anything: No Joe Papp; No Shakespeare Festival; No actors. I didn't even sign them at first (and only self-consciously used my initials when I first began to do so). The only lettering was the title of the play and the name of the theater, though we realized later that it wouldn't hurt to mention that this was, in fact, a Shakespeare Festival production and began to include a logo." Second, without mimicking style, Davis's posters referred to the late nineteenth-century European tradition of poster art, which was ignored by contemporary posterists.

His Public Theater posters were stark, employing a central image with simple type either stenciled or silkscreened directly on the artwork (as he did on *Hamlet* in collaboration with art director Reinhold Schwenk) or seamlessly integrated into the composition (as with the *Three Penny Opera*). "The history of the Shakespeare Festival posters says a lot about the way the posters are used," he said. "I have often made comments in the posters about the way posters look on walls and in the environment in which they are hung. Many of my posters for the festival have had that self-conscious quality about being a poster." One example, *For Colored Girls Who Have Considered Suicide When the Rainbow Is Enuf*, showed the main figure with the title lettering scrawled on a tiled subway wall where, in fact, the poster was intended to be hung. The third, and final challenge to conventional theater posters was his basic methodology. Davis read the play, went to the rehearsals or readings, and talked to the actors and directors. "They seemed to think," he said, "that I was doing this revolutionary thing by actually reading the scripts."

The Public Theater

PAULA SCHER

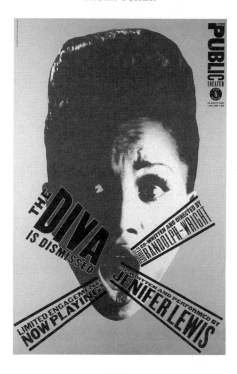

Paula Scher (b. 1948) is not a native New Yorker, but she has acquired the self-assured, sarcastic, and abrupt elocutions of one. Scher believes that the best way to communicate to New Yorkers is to shout. "What better way to get a message across than for someone to yell something like 'I'm pregnant!' down a corridor; it's better than the Internet," she said. And this is exactly how she designs for The Public Theater. She shouts with type—boldly and unmistakably.

Scher's posters for The Public's 1995 season, only a component of a larger shouting campaign, have been included in virtually all the design annuals and shows, but one has to be a New Yorker (or at least from the environs) to truly appreciate the impact of The Public's language on the public. This is not the typically benign illustration sandwiched between layers of billing and flowery hyperbole. Rather, Scher's cacophony of disparate woodtypes, silhouetted photos, and bright, flat colors is more akin to the two-color rag bond or oak tag bills produced by job printers or run off at Kinkos to advertise circuses, county fairs, prize fights, and dance bands—the kind that are stapled and wheat pasted every time the New York sanitation authority's back is turned. Scher's scheme, inspired by today's street graphics and yesterday's Victorian playbills, was purposefully designed to appeal to a broad audience, from the inner city to the outer boroughs, especially those who have not been attracted to the theater before and for whom the typical "Broadway style" of advertising says exclusion.

Scher's street-based campaign supported the vision of The Public's creative director, George

C. Wolfe, the director of such plays as *The Colored Museum, Angels in America*, and *Jelly's Last Jam*. After taking over in 1993, three years following the death of impresario Joseph Papp, The Public's director for more than twenty years, Wolfe has completely reshaped the institution—its season, staff, lobby, advertising, and mission—to be more inclusive of those persons and communities for whom theatergoing has not been an option. "I want to have the kind of plays in The Public where the whole building becomes a giant snapshot of where America is," he said in his rapid, syncopated cadence. Although Papp, who coined the name The Public Theater, welcomed the public during his significant tenure, and introduced a diversity of plays and playwrights, such as David Rabe, Caryl Churchill, Miquel Pinero, Ntozake Shange, David Mamet, and George C. Wolfe, himself, the theater's traditional audience was still essentially what one critic described as "uptown white." Wolfe, on the other hand, wanted total inclusivity. "I want to take populist culture and elevate it, and bring elitist culture to a populist level," he stated with missionary zeal. So to change both the perception and the reality, as an adjunct to producing plays that addressed the experiences and lore of African-Americans, Hispanics, Asians, and gays, Wolfe dramatically changed The Public Theater's distinctive visual persona, which for twenty years had been based on Paul Davis's iconic painterly posters. "I was looking for someone who could give The Public an in-your-face unity," he continued. "I wanted something combustible and dynamic."

Scher's debut was somewhat of an improvisation. The day she learned that she and her Pentagram/New York team had been selected, she was also informed that Wolfe immediately needed to begin advertising The New York Shakespeare Festival, The Public's long-running, free summer performances of Shakespeare in Central Park. With little time, Scher had to create a coherent scheme that not only advertised the plays, but also signaled both the beginning of Wolfe's era and the Shakespeare Festival's relationship to the whole Public institution, comprising Central Park's Delacorte Theater, five separate theaters in The Public's headquarters in the old Jacob Astor Library, its Broadway productions, and additional public events, which, Wolfe explained, "were originally tied together by Papp's personality," but now required an organized system. Rather than ponder the virtues of one design scheme over another, Scher was forced to create what would become The Public's visual identity based on one of its many component parts. Nevertheless, she turned a necessity into a blessing. The idea to focus solely on typography as the organizing principle was a response to Wolfe's mandate to "cleanse the visual palate" and thereby eschew illustration entirely. Wolfe liked Scher's earlier Victorian- and constructivist-inspired compositions done in more or less appropriate contexts, but nothing could have been a better fit than this assignment; for here she could revive her favorite Victorian woodtypes—the ones that can be seen from a block or more away—on real playbills, posters, and billboards, not as mere pastiche, but as functional design elements.

The Shakespeare Festival graphics were based on a simple format. Key words like *free* and *live* were greatly enlarged, satisfying Wolfe's desire to address the public in a direct, no-nonsense manner, like sale signs in supermarket windows. Likewise, enlarged fragments of the titles of plays set in bold gothics, like the words *wives* for *The Merry Wives of Windsor* and *gents* for *The*

Gentleman of Verona, drew attention to a linguistic mystery and provided a distinct contemporary identity that Evan Shapiro, director of marketing for The Public, said was like giving a news report rather than an ad spiel. "The approach is not complacent," he added, "it says we're here, come see us, or we're coming to get you." The typographic posters were placed on telephone stalls around New York, hung in commuter railroad stations in the environs, and on a few select billboards. They were intended to draw passersby into a visual game of deciphering the meaning of the words. If they missed on the first try, the ads were positioned close enough that on second glance the message was revealed. Flyers and handbills with this ersatz call-to-arms typography were also sniped around town in a blitz of paper promotion that is typically New York.

Language by its very nature is a communal thing, and Wolfe and Scher, who have their own personal shorthand, believed that the syncopated sounds formed by the truncated titles and phrases communicated through bold type, dark rules, and bright colors would develop into a conversation between the people of New York and The Public Theater.

The cornerstone of The Public persona was its logo, a combination of Scher's visual/linguistic elements that shouted the word *public,* which was spelled out in a sampling of black woodtype letters in weights ranging from heavy to light set against a white field; the words *The* and *Theater* are there, but subordinate to the dominant word/idea. In addition to the main logo, Scher designed round logos, or what Wolfe called "tokens" (The Public is built over the Astor Place subway station) for individual theaters. The next level in the hierarchy of communication were accordion-folded flyers that when completely unfolded (to a length of around two feet) revealed the entire season's programs in a typographic array reminiscent of Victorian theater bills, a sharp contrast to the usually quiet treatments of most mainstream theatrical subscription materials.

An exception to the pure typography rule were the posters for the individual plays, many of which included photographs—such as the emblematic silhouette of tapmaster Savion Glover on the poster for that tongue-twisting titled musical, *Bring in da Noise, Bring in da Funk,* which sandwiched him between a jumble of letterforms, somewhat akin to a wall of graffiti.

Wolfe wanted his posters to be like old LP album covers, and Scher, who designed albums for CBS Records in the 1970s, has certainly obliged by making them very graphic. But while most of her posters owe a spiritual debt to street graphics, they do not look like anything else on the street. One needs only to look at construction hoardings where sniped posters for *Blade to the Heart* and *The Diva Is Dismissed* were hung; both had the allure of untutored street graphics, but stood noticeably apart. The *Blade* poster, for example, featured an enlarged process-color photo of a boxer in a typical fighting stance with the large dots of the color plates knocked out of register in a pun on the punch drunk nature of the play's protagonist. The *Diva* poster showed the huge face of Jennifer Lewis, whose one-person show this was, with a kinetic propeller of type coming from her open mouth. The forms were somewhat vernacular, and therefore beckoned, but it was the subtle wit that gave them resonance and fostered memorability.

Information

DESIGN AS GUIDEPOST AND PATHWAY

Catalog Design Progress

LADISLAV SUTNAR

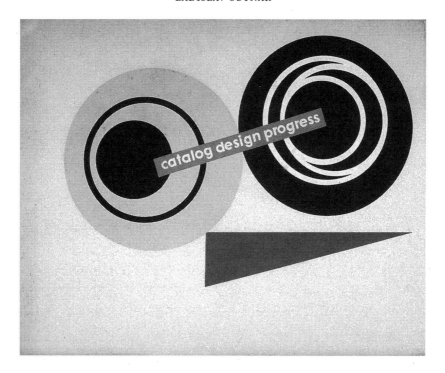

Even before the advent of the "information age" there was information. Masses of it begging to be organized into accessible and retrievable packages. In the 1930s American industry made an initial attempt to introduce strict design systems to business, but the Great Depression demanded that the focus be on retooling factories and improving products, which spawned a new breed of professional: the industrial designer. In Europe the prototypical industrial designer had already established himself, and the graphic design arm of the modern movement was already concerned with access to information as a function of making the world a better place. The mission to modernize antiquated aspects of European life led directly to efficient communications expressed through typographic purity. This revolutionary approach to design began simultaneously in Germany, Russia, and Holland, and swept through Eastern Europe as well. Ladislav Sutnar (1897–1976), a graphic, product, and exhibition designer, led the charge in Czechoslovakia years before emigrating to the United States.

Sutnar was such an enthusiastic propagandist for industrialization that he was introduced to Karl Löndberg-Holm, the publicity director of the Sweet's Catalog Service, the largest American industrial catalog publisher, who instantly arranged for Sutnar to become his art director. Löndberg-Holm quickly became the other half of Sutnar's brain. Their collaboration was to information design what Gilbert and Sullivan were to light opera or Rogers and Hammerstein were to the Broadway musical. Together they composed and wrote *Catalog Design* (1944) and

Catalog Design Progress (1950). The former introduced a variety of radical systematic departures in catalog design, the latter fine tuned those models to show how complex information could be organized and, most importantly, retrieved. More than forty years after its publication, *Catalog Design Progress* is still an archetype for functional design. Sweet's Catalog Service was a facilitator for countless, disparate trade and manufacturing publications that were collected in huge binders and distributed to businesses throughout the United States. Before Sutnar began its major redesign around 1941, the only organizing device was the overall binding, otherwise chaos reigned. Löndberg-Holm had convinced his boss, Chauncey Williams, the president of F. W. Dodge, to order an entire re-evaluation from logo (which Sutnar transformed from a nineteenth-century swashed word, *Sweets,* to a bold *S* dropped out of a black circle), to the fundamental structure of the binder (including the introduction of tabular aids), to the redesign of individual catalogs (some of which were designed by Sutnar's in-house art department).

Sutnar was one of the first designers to design double spreads rather than single pages, an aspect of his methodology that is so common today that in retrospect the fact that it was an innovation could easily be overlooked. A casual perusal of Sutnar's designs for everything from catalogs to brochures from 1941 on, with the exception of covers, reveals a preponderance of spreads on which his signature navigational devices force the users to follow logically contiguous levels of information. Through these spreads Sutnar was able to harness certain avant-garde principles and therefore injected visual excitement into even the most routine material without impinging upon accessibility. While his basic structure was decidedly rational, his juxtapositions, scale, and color were rooted in abstraction. Underlying Sutnar's modern mission was the desire to introduce aesthetics into, say, a plumber's life.

The Medium is the Massage

QUENTIN FIORE

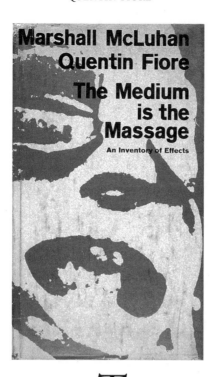

T*he Medium is the Massage* by Marshall
McLuhan and Quentin Fiore (b. 1920) is the touchstone of media lore and doctrine from the
1960s. It was required reading for everyone concerned with what McLuhan dubbed the "electric
age," or how technology in general, and new communications media specifically, would alter
people's lives. McLuhan was a philosopher and prognosticator whose books *The Mechanical
Bride, The Gutenberg Galaxy: The Making of Typographic Man,* and *Understanding Media: The
Extensions of Man,* explored the evolution of technology and its effects on the way mankind
thinks, acts, and reacts. He was revered by some, attacked by others. Critics called him a fake,
charlatan, and savant, arguing that his ideas were simplistic, obtuse, and contradictory. McLuhan
countered that contradiction was endemic to contemporary life; contradiction was the metaphor
for television, a medium that allowed a person to ponder two or more ideas at one time.

McLuhan believed that the invention of printing had shattered community by destroying the
oral tradition. He argued that writing and reading were solitary acts that conflicted with tribal
unity, memory, and imagination. Electronic media, television mostly, was destined to return us to
a global village, allowing individuals once again to take an active role in the communications
process. Media were extensions of human activity (e.g., the wheel was an extension of the foot).
Television, he insisted, would allow for greater individual participation.

Was this genius or hocus-pocus? Critic Marvin Kitman referred to this book as "The Tedium is the Message." Indeed *The Medium is the Massage*'s contents by McLuhan and graphics by Fiore came under harsh criticism. But this should not eclipse the historic nature of Fiore's work.

The Medium is the Massage (the title comes from mass-age, a double-entendre used to underscore McLuhan's notion that media are so pervasive that they work people over like a masseuse) was the first book for the television age. *New York Times* critic Eliot Freemont Smith wrote that the large format of the hardcover took on "the aspect of a TV screen." Fiore, who initiated the project with the help of Jerome Agel, a book packager, designed it as a kinetically flowing collection of word bites and iconic images set in economical (Helvetica) type. He underscored McLuhan's ideas with what might be called a series of literary billboards—double-page spreads with large call-outs and blurbs. McLuhan described them (perhaps sarcastically) as "collide-oscopic interfaced situations."

The Massage heralded a number of firsts: the first time that a paperback preceded the hardcover version into the marketplace; the first time such cinematic visual pacing was applied to American book design; the first book coordinated by a "producer," Jerome Agel, who takes credit for orchestrating its "sound and music." And although not a first, most important, was the close conceptual relationship between the designer and writer—like those of Lazar El Lissitzky and Vladimir Mayakovsky, John Heartfield and Kurt Tucholsky, Guylas Williams and Robert Benchley. Although the collaborators were not in constant contact during the creation of the book, Fiore was in tune with McLuhan's thinking so that the concrete presentation of McLuhan's often complex (and contradictory) ideas was made accessible.

Fiore was born in New York in 1920. He had been a student of George Grosz at the Art Student's League and of Hans Hoffman at the Hoffman School. He was a devotee of classical drawing, papermaking, and lettering and began his career before World War II as a letterer for graphic designer Lester Beall (for whom he designed many of the modern display letters used in ads and brochures before modern typefaces were available in the United States) and for Condé Nast, *Life*, and other magazines (where he hand-lettered headlines for editorial and advertising pages). He left lettering to become a graphic designer, and for many years designed all the printed matter for the Ford Foundation in a modern but not rigid style. Since he was interested in the clear presentation of information, he was well suited as a design consultant to various university presses, and later to Bell Laboratories (for whom he designed the numbers for one of Henry Dryfuss's rotary dials). In the late 1960s he also worked on Homefax, an early telephone facsimile machine developed (but never marketed) at RCA/NBC, where he coordinated an early electronic newspaper.

Fiore predicted the widespread use of computer-generated design, talking computers, and home fax and photocopy technologies. He also predicted the applications of the computer in primary school education long before its widespread use, and accordingly in 1968 he designed two hundred computer-like "interactive" books for school children to help increase literacy skills. McLuhan's philosophy was a logical extension of Fiore's own practice.

The second coproduction with McLuhan was, by Fiore's own admission, less successful than *The Massage*. *War and Peace in the Global Village: An Inventory of Some of the Current Spastic*

Situations that Could Be Eliminated with More Feedforward was assailed by one critic as a crankish, repetitive, and disjointed tome in which McLuhan's puns had become a nervous tic. McLuhan based his book on the bewildering idea that war is a result of the anxiety aroused when changing metaphors in perception fail to yield up familiar self-images. Fiore's design was a mosaic of disparate imagery and text, which struggled with little success to reign in McLuhan's humorless meanderings. Fiore next worked on a book with Buckminster Fuller, entitled *I Am a Verb,* which could be read from front to back and back to front. Each are emblematic of the times.

Jerry Rubin's *Do It!* was also designed in the manner of *The Medium is the Massage.* Although universally panned by the critics, it became a bible of the 1960s. Fiore worked directly with the former yippie leader, typographically emphasizing certain ideas in a manner vaguely reminiscent of the dadaists and futurists. Photographs were also used as icons and exclamation points and strewn through the text to add sight and sound to an idea or pronouncement. Fiore was as anarchic as possible while still working within the constraints of bookmaking. His design was ahead of its time, but he believed that the methods he adopted were simply the most appropriate ways to convey the information. "They were just jobs, each requiring special treatment," he said.

New York Subway Map

VIGNELLI AND ASSOCIATES

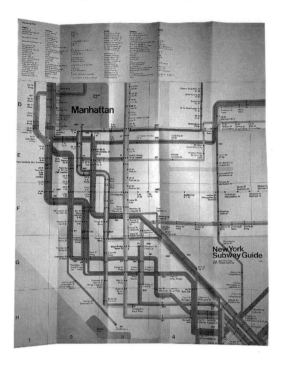

At the end of a meeting in the early 1990s where Vignelli and Associates presented a comprehensive redesign of the subway train interiors for the New York Transit System, one of the members of the selection committee asked, "Mrs. Vignelli, you once said in your book [*Design: Vignelli*] that it is not pleasant to work with the Transit Authority. Why do you want to be involved in a project like this again?" Without hesitating Lella Vignelli responded, "Because we are socially responsible." The unpleasantness referred to was the design of the New York City subway map in 1970, one of Vignelli and Associates' most well-known and difficult achievements.

In 1965 Massimo Vignelli (b. 1931) moved to the United States from Italy and cofounded Unimark with Bob Noorda, a Dutch graphic designer and former art director at Pirelli in Milan. In the early 1960s Noorda designed informational graphics for the Milan subway system, which helped Unimark get the job to create signage for the New York Subway in 1966, and which later led to designing the map.

Vignelli's training as an architect in Italy in the mid 1950s and his study with the Swiss graphic designer Max Huber made him a veteran of the grid. In those early years Vignelli also began a long-lasting friendship with Umberto Eco, author of *The Name of the Rose,* and one of the top semioticians in the world. "We were analyzing everything according to a semiotic grid. It was just natural for us, like the ABCs." Semiotics is the study of symbology, the notion that every sign (word, letter, image, number, etc.) is arbitrary and has meaning only when it represents an idea or thing. Vignelli sees the semiotic grid as a relationship between semantics (the meaning of the information), syntactics (its visual representation), and pragmatics (the effect of the sign on the receiver). It's a closed-loop system to make sure a design clearly and consistently represents the proper message and that the audience receives that message as intended.

For Vignelli the semiotic grid is the *sine qua non* of communication design and the perfect tool to untangle the jumble the subway system had become by the 1960s. The IRT, BMT, and IND had grown sporadically into 714 miles of track with some 465 stations. The signage project began with an analysis of the traffic flow to identify points of decision and levels of information. From that, Vignelli devised a modular system of signs each designed as individual units, like the letters of an alphabet, which were then hung together to form informational sentences. Mathematical precision and rationality informed every part of the system from the prefabricated signs in lengths of one, two, four, or eight feet, to the typography that was similarly modulated with the smallest type on the informational panels one-half the size of the type on the directional panels, and that one-half the size of the typography on the station identification signs.

Vignelli wanted to hang the signs from thick black support bars that he believed would unify the information. This echoed his earlier work for the Piccolo Teatro (1964) in Milan, a poster that featured his signature style of tightly spaced sans-serif typography and introduced the concept of "information bands," information separated by wide black rules, which became characteristic of his designs in the following years. The Transit Authority never installed the black support bars, but rather painted black bars across the tops of the panels.

In 1971 Massimo Vignelli left Unimark and with his wife Lella established Vignelli and Associates and Vignelli Designs in New York. Lella was named president of Vignelli Designs, the branch of the firm responsible for product and furniture design. Vignelli and Associates was commissioned to design a map for the subway system that would untangle the web of train lines on the existing one. Vignelli had initially envisioned an interrelated system of maps: an overall system map, a geographic map indicating the relationship of the subway to the geography, a detailed neighborhood map to re-orient the traveler upon arrival at a new destination, a pocket map, and what Vignelli calls a "verbal map"—intended for the main stations that featured written directions from point A to point B in language that Mama would use, "Take train #6 to 59th Street, transfer to train RR and get off at Times Square." Pointing out that fifty percent of the population is verbally oriented and fifty percent is visually oriented, Vignelli's verbal map directly addressed the needs of the public. Although one was implemented in Grand Central Station, the verbal maps were shelved, along with the neighborhood and geographic maps, victims of budgets and bureaucracy.

But the overall system map and the pocket map survived. Researching and learning from previous underground system maps, like Beck's London Underground map, Vignelli, too, organized his subway map on a grid, orienting the "spaghetti work" of the railways to the verticals, horizontals and forty-five-degree angles of the page. Each line had a different color, bright primary colors, and either a number or letter designation appearing at the beginning, at the end, and at intervals along the route. Every station was listed. Every stop had a dot. A dot on the line indicated the train stopped at that station. No dot, no stop. The web of lines dominated the background of white abstracted land masses, with the surrounding waters a mid-range gray, and parks designated with geometric forms in a darker shade of gray. The map was distorted, with the central, more congested areas larger and the outlying areas truncated. Vignelli used layering, separation, and color to differentiate the planes of information. This system of representation clarified what was important to the traveler: how to go from point A to point B. The map bypassed the literal and focused on the relationships inherent in the information and at the same time exemplified the essence of orthodox modernist principles.

Soon after the system map was put into effect, the official at the Transit Authority who originally commissioned Vignelli and Associates retired. His replacement called for a new map. He criticized the Vignelli map for lacking reference to the natural geography: the water was not blue, the parks were not green. Vigorous campaigning to retain the award-winning map eventually failed to convince this new official who, as Vignelli described, "had the knife by the handle." The map was replaced in 1979.

Iconography

DESIGN AS INDELIBLE SYMBOL

The Swastika

Few symbols have had as much impact on humankind as the swastika. No other known symbol in the primitive or civilized world is as old; scholars argue that it predates the Egyptian ankh (the symbol for "life"). No other mark has turned up in so many distant and different cultures, suggesting an enormous migration or diaspora of peoples joined by a common belief or understanding. Yet no symbol in recent memory elicits such fear and loathing while at the same time such reverence and respect. Arguably not even the Latin (or Christian) cross exerts as much raw emotional power throughout the world today.

This hooked cross, also referred to as a sun-wheel, which gets its name from the Sanskrit word *svastika*, meaning "well being," "good fortune," and "luck," and resembles the Indian mystic figure *svastikaya*, a "sign of benediction," was adopted by Adolf Hitler in the summer of 1920 as the emblem of the nascent National Socialist Workers Party (the Nazis). Refashioned by Hitler to maximize its inherent graphic power, the *Hakenkreuz* (the German word for hooked cross), emblazoned on armbands and flags, represented this nationalistic political and social movement. From that moment, this venerable symbol was forever associated with the most heinous crimes perpetrated by man.

"The fact that an ignominious fanatic placed a swastika on his battle flag is insufficient reason for ignoring this symbol's historic significance," wrote Henry Dreyfuss in *Symbol Sourcebook: An Authoritative Guide to International Graphic Symbols.* He suggested that the swastika must not be totally rejected because it was co-opted by a madman and embraced by a blind nation. Indeed, the swastika has not entirely lost all of its former mystic significance. It is still employed in rituals in some Eastern and Far Eastern cultures. But more important, as the single most charged symbol of the twentieth century its history should not be overlooked by designers who can learn valuable lessons from how and why it was used.

Before 1920 the swastika's symbolism was convoluted, but was at all times benign. Even in the United States it was indigenous to cave dwellers—one was found in the excavation of a prehistoric tomb in what is now Ohio. During the nineteenth century certain native American tribes embroidered the mark on blankets and ceremonial attire, and decorated pottery and ceramics with it. It was adopted as a ubiquitous design motif and was still in currency until a few years after the Nazis came to power in Germany in 1933. The swastika as a good luck symbol was adopted by American merchants and manufacturers on packaging, wrappers, and in advertising. It was frequently used as an architectural ornament, and was also popular as an ornament or border in prewar typeface books. The swastika was as common a graphic design motif in the 1920s and 1930s as the lozenge, leader dot, and sawtooth rule are in contemporary design.

Hitler was a wannabe architect, painter, and dabbler in commercial arts, but as leader of his movement he was the quintessential art director too. His understanding of symbolism, propaganda, and design is clear upon reading excerpts from *Mein Kampf* ("my struggle"), in which—though it was written in stupifyingly formal prose replete with euphemisms and epithets that enforce his own self-styled heroism—he convincingly argued the need for a powerful symbol/emblem/logo for his nascent party. "The lack of such symbols," he wrote, "had not only disadvantages for the moment, but it was unbearable for the future. The disadvantages were above all that the party members lacked every outward sign of their belonging together, while for the future it was unbearable to lack an emblem that had the character of a symbol of the movement and that as such could be put up in opposition to the communists." Hitler recalled the first time he witnessed a large communist party rally, where he saw a sea of red on flags, scarves, and flowers among the one hundred thousand in attendance. "I personally could feel and understand how easily a man of the people succumbs to the suggestive charm of such a grand and massive spectacle," he wrote.

It is uncertain who actually suggested that the swastika be adopted by the Nazis—Hitler likes to take the credit—but its redesign as the party emblem and flag are documented fairly well in *Mein Kampf:* "Suggestions were made from all sides which, however, were better meant than they were successful," wrote Hitler. "For the new flag had to be as much a symbol of our own fight as, on the other hand, it had to have an effect as great as that of a poster. . . . In hundreds of thousands of cases, an effective emblem can give the first impetus for the interest in a movement." Hitler's brief color analysis in *Mein Kampf* read like a term paper on semiotics: "White is not a color that carries people away. It is suitable for associations of chaste virgins, but not for the overpowering movement of a revolutionary time. . . . [Black] is also not thrilling enough. . . . White and blue was out of the question, despite the wonderful effect from the aesthetic point of view, as the color of a German individual state and of a political orientation directed at particularistic narrow-mindedness that did not enjoy the best of reputations. . . . [Black, white, and red] this color composition . . . is the most resplendent harmony that exists."

Hitler was never satisfied with the results of his open competition to design the flag, in which all party members were invited to take part: "I had to reject, without exception, the numerous designs that in those days were handed in by circles of the young movement and that mostly had placed the swastika on the old flag. I myself—as leader—did not want to come forth immediately with my own sketch, as it was quite possible that someone else would produce one that was just as good or even better." In fact, according to Nazi lore the form that the party adopted was ostensibly designed by Dr. Friedrich Krohn, a dentist from Starnberg whom Hitler never acknowledged by name in *Mein Kampf*, but about whose design he wrote, "[it] was not bad at all, and besides that approached my own design very closely, except that it had the mistake that the swastika was composed in a white circle with curved hooks. Meanwhile, I myself, after innumerable attempts, had put down a final form: a flag with a background of red, with a white circle, and in its center, a black swastika. And this then was kept."

Although Hitler gave credit to a Munich goldsmith, Herr Füss, for designing the party's badge (similar in design to the flag) he neglected to credit Wilhelm Deffke, a leading German logo and trademark designer for having refined and stylized a version of the swastika before 1920. According to a former assistant, Deffke was branded a "cultural bolshevist" by the Nazis, but in a recent biographical note on her employer she wrote: "Deffke came across a representation of the ancient Germanic sun-wheel on which he worked to redefine and stylize its shape. Later this symbol appeared in a brochure which he had published, [The Nazis] chose it as their symbol but reversed it. . . . Needless to say, this was done without any thought of copyright or compensation to the 'cultural Bolshevist.' In September 1935, this symbol was incorporated into the Third Reich's flag. It is ironic that the design chosen for the national emblem and the ruling party was rediscovered and refined by a man whom the regime later persecuted. . . ."

The swastika would not have been adopted if Hitler did not want it, nor would it have been applied so effectively. Even the most vociferous opponents of Nazism agree that Hitler's identity system is the most ingeniously consistent graphic program ever devised. That he succeeded in transmuting an ancient symbol with such a long-lasting historical significance into one that was even more indelible is attributable to his mastery of the design and propaganda processes. Yet, the Nazi emblem's good design does not redeem the corruption of a party and a nation that embraced it. "As National Socialists we see our program in our flag," wrote Hitler in *Mein Kampf*. "In the *red* we see the social idea of the movement, in the *white* the national idea, in the swastika the mission of the fight for the victory of the idea of creative work which in itself is and always will be anti-Semitic."

Hitler's death and Germany's defeat in 1945, twenty-five years after the symbol was adopted, may have stopped the Nazis' crimes against humanity, but no amount of cleansing can wash the blood off the swastika. Unless the history of the Nazi era (1933–1945) is totally rewritten—and the danger of that is ever present—the swastika will remain forever the most powerful logo of the age, the manifestation of evil and hate.

1939/1940 New York World's Fair

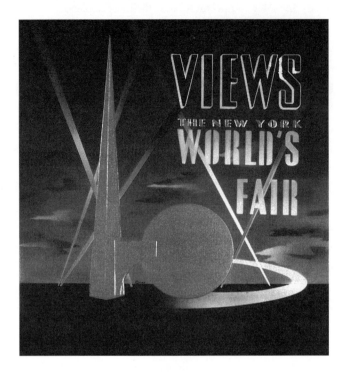

Sometimes at night I lie awake in the dark and try to recapture the vision and the sound of The World of Tomorrow," wrote Meyer Berger in 1940, shortly after the World's Fair closed. "I try to remember how the pastel lighting glowed on Mad Meadow in Flushing: soft greens, orange, yellow, and red; blue moonglow on the great Perisphere and on the ghostly soaring Trylon. I think with a sense of sweetened pain of nights when I sat by Flushing River and saw The World of Tomorrow reflected on its onyx surface, in full color, and upside down. . . . "

The 1939/1940 New York World's Fair was an extraordinary experience for the reported fifty million visitors who passed through its futuristic gates and gazed at its majestic centerpiece, the Trylon and Perisphere. It was the most ambitious international exposition since the phenomenal Crystal Palace housed the first New York World's Fair in 1853. Not just a trade show, it was endowed with mythic qualities; it was the "Fair of the Future," "The World of Tomorrow," and "The Dawn of a New Day." It was a masterpiece of showmanship, the epitome of stagecraft—a real-life Land of Oz indelibly etched in the memories of those who attended and in the imaginations of those who did not. It was more than a collection of exhibits; it was a wellspring of innovation in corporate identity and promotion.

In 1935 the fair's 121 incorporators decided to put an end to a decade of municipal malaise, marked by the stock market collapse and subsequent economic depression, with the most elaborate demonstration of scientific, technological, and human ingenuity that the world had ever seen. As the guidebook announced: "This Fair of Tomorrow is a promise for the future built with the tools of Today, upon the experience of Yesterday."

Towards this end New York's park and highway czar, Robert Moses, gave his blessing. The fair corporation took as its sight the once beautiful tidal basin of the Flushing River, which had been turned into a festering bog and ash dump by one Fishhooks McCarthy and his Brooklyn Ash Removal Company. Miraculously it was transformed into Flushing Meadow, the park of the future. Heralded as a "scientific victory," it was the most ambitious environmental reclamation project of its time.

Consistent with the theme committee's precept that "super civilization ... is based on the swift work of machines, not on the arduous toil of men," the fair was a mélange of provocative, often symbolically designed pavilions (some representing *architecture parlante,* or billboard architecture—a building whose exterior look revealed its interior purpose, such as the Aviation Building shaped like a dirigible hanger) that were organized into thematic zones covering all aspects of human activity in which man and machine were somehow wed: Transportation, Production and Distribution, Communications, Community Interests, Government, Business Systems, Food, Medicine and Public Health, Science and Education, and Amusement.

Democracity, the Fair's central theme exhibit, designed by Henry Dreyfuss, was an idealized projection of America in 2039, an interdependent network of urban, suburban, and rural areas. Viewed from two moving circular galleries, the viewer was given a bird's-eye view of Centeron, a perfectly planned, modern, riverside metropolis that could accommodate a million people but, in fact, had no inhabitants because it was used exclusively as the hub of commerce, education, and culture. The mellow yet authoritative voice of H. V. Kaltenborn in a recorded narration, underscored by music written by William Grant Still and conducted by Andre Kostelanetz, told visitors about a population that lived in commodious high-rises amidst suburban garden developments, or Pleasantvilles, and in light-industrial communities and satellite towns called Millvilles, rimmed by fertile and profitable farming zones or greenbelts—all linked, of course, by modern express highways and parkways. "This is not a vague dream of a life that might be lived in the far future," wrote Robert Kohn, chairman of the fair's Board of Design, "but one that could be lived tomorrow morning if we willed it so."

Democracity was suitably housed in the Perisphere, an enormous white futuristic temple that also served as the fair's indelible, architectural trademark. Designed by Wallace K. Harrison and J. Andre Foulihoux—who had also been involved in the design of Rockefeller Center—the Perisphere was the largest "floating" globe ever built by man: 180 feet in diameter and eighteen stories high, twice the size of Radio City Music Hall. The theme center emerged after more than one thousand sketches and models, and despite its new forms, the design was not without precedents, including Bauhaus and constructivist references.

Each hour more than eight thousand spectators entered the Perisphere through the Trylon, a triangular obelisk 610 feet high, larger than the Washington Monument, ascending on the two largest escalators ever built to a 65-foot-high bridge that led directly into this visionary extravaganza. Six minutes later they would exit down the Helicline, an 18-foot-wide ramp with a stainless steel underbelly. Ironically, this futuristic trademark was built with common steel and clothed in the imperfect materials of the day, including gypsum board that would flake and crack, and required continual maintenance. Even Harrison commented that "in many ways, it was more beautiful when it was just steel."

Selling the public on modernity, and more importantly on coming to see it incarnate in Flushing Meadow, was a task as monumental as building the fair itself. No sales pitch was as persuasive as the one extolled by the view from the Perisphere as visitors left *Democracity*. That first elevated view of the fairscape was a stunning advertisement for the rightness of the future—or so the planners hoped. Laid before Mr. and Mrs. Average American in all its colorful splendor was the World of Tomorrow today. Equivalent to more than 370 city blocks, it included more than two-hundred modern and moderne buildings curiously laid out according to a nineteenth-century *beaux-arts rond-point* system of radiating streets and fanlike segments extending like spokes from a central hub.

The fair vividly represented and profoundly utilized the new, distinctly American field of industrial design. Industrial designers were industry's predominant form-givers, whose "faith was . . . based on moral conviction," wrote historian Francis V. O'Connor, "that the public good was to be attained by the universal adoption of a certain rightness of form in all matters from the design of cities to the styling of pencil sharpeners." The lighting stanchions, monumental fixtures, and most of the kinetic exhibits were imaginatively designed by these gifted proponents of the new streamline aesthetic. Among them were Raymond Lowey, Walter Dorwin Teague (who was an original member of the design board), Henry Dreyfuss, Donald Desky, Egmond Arens, Russell Wright, Gilbert Rohde, and Norman Bel Geddes.

Lowey, who before establishing himself as an industrial designer was a commercial artist following the dominant *moderne* style, conceived of the Chrysler Corporation and Transportation exhibits; Teague, who was also a skilled but pedestrian commercial artist, designed seven exhibits including those for Kodak, U.S. Steel, Consolidated Edison, Dupont, National Cash Register, and Ford; Desky applied surrealism to the Communications exhibit and Russell Wright did likewise for Food. Of all these, however, the most memorable was the brainchild of a one-time scenic designer, Norman Bel Geddes. His theatrical extravaganza for General Motors, called *Futurama*, was housed in architect Alfred Kahn's seven-acre-square streamline monument, and was the most ambitious and visionary multimedia educational entertainment built for any fair.

The fair was also the most crassly merchandised event the world had ever known. Among the thousands of souvenirs were toys and games, ranging from kazoos to paint sets, all emblazoned or molded in the shape of the Trylon and Perisphere. Despite the predominance of cheaply manufactured trifles, the fair committee insisted in their press releases that the quality of these articles was guaranteed by the "artistic prominence and skill of their designers."

The efforts of the World Fair's planners should not be dismissed as merely a vain effort to predict the future. Despite its failures, the 1939/1940 New York World's Fair was not an empty metaphor, but rather a colorful, though temporary, beacon of hope. The Trylon and Perisphere symbolized the real world of tomorrow for a nation about to enter a storm of conflict and gave its visitors the stuff of memories that neither war nor time could erase.

Air Corps U.S. Army

JOSEPH BINDER

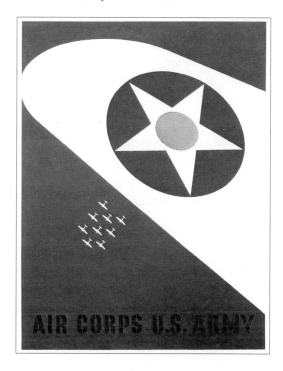

The modern poster had its start in Paris a few years before Viennese designer Joseph Binder (1898–1972) was born. Yet he became one of its later pioneers, introducing a cubist-inspired style that employed sharp edges of color to define forms. Binder emigrated to the United States in the late 1930s. His long-running campaign for A&P Coffee (1939) and emblematic posters for the New York World's Fair (1939) and particularly the U.S. Army Air Corps (1941) defined a modern American graphic style.

Binder rejected any direct influence from his contemporaries: "I always worked alone—no one ever influenced me," he claimed. But he was inspired by industrial progress. He was born in Vienna a year after the secessionists disrupted the complacency of the bourgeois art establishment. His hometown became a wellspring of modern art and design. At the beginning of the twentieth century the influence of industry was reflected by the contemporary Austrian architects Otto Wagner, Joseph Maria Olbrich, Josef Hoffmann, and Adolf Loos. Nourished in this environment, Binder was instinctively drawn to and understood the requisites of posters. "We live in modern times of life and mind. Everything moves faster today," he wrote in an unpublished memoir. "In poster design we need the same speed to put the message across effectively."

Binder opened a design studio in Vienna in the early 1920s. It was large because the original drawings for the six-foot-four-inch by twelve-foot-seven-inch posters had to be produced in actual size and covered a whole wall. From 1925 to 1929 he was a freelance designer for the Julius

Meinl Company, Vienna's leading importer of coffee, tea, and related products, for whom he created advertising, trademarks, and labels. His unifying vision, dubbed the Meinl style, was celebrated by the leading design publications, the *Studio* and *Gebrauchsgraphik*.

Binder believed that style was a transmission code. He developed an emblematic hard-edged style that he encouraged others to freely mimic. "I am here to introduce this style," he announced at a lecture in New York City in 1938. "In the short weeks I am [here] I want to furnish an explanation of exactly what 'modern commercial art' means." But at the time his mission was difficult. American advertising was governed by copywriters who preferred the word to the image and distrusted modern graphic approaches. Binder's first major assignment for the J. Walter Thompson advertising agency was a successful, albeit lackluster, series of billboards for Ballantine's beer, and many of his early American assignments were to comp experimental ideas that never saw the light of day. Undaunted by the reluctance of American business, Binder eventually secured some profitable accounts.

Among his most well-known commissions, the *Air Corps U.S. Army* poster, which won first prize in a Museum of Modern Art competition, signaled a new utilization of space. Noteworthy for its minimal imagery and simple graphic forms, today it is dated only by the silhouettes of propeller-driven aircraft. A yellow wing set against a grayish blue sky offsets the red, white, and blue Air Force logo. The entire image is stylized to ensure memorability. Binder did not self-consciously try to "be of his time," a trap that many lesser stylists fall into, but his works are nevertheless clearly tied to their epoch.

Binder built his design philosophy on the fundamental idea that "the artist should contribute to the development of the modern style instead of indulging in realistic representation of past periods and vain attempts to imitate the works of former times." He believed that the new industrial style was descended from painting, but its function was "to convey the essence of the advertising message in the shortest and most impressive way. . . . It is the artist's task to transfer the clear and constructive shape of the objects as he sees them to the two-dimensional surface. . . . Realism should be left to photography. The artist must not compete with the camera. . . . Therefore the artist must abandon realistic representation and take up styling." Modern design was, therefore, not in competition with technology, but enhanced what the machine could achieve.

Stylization was chiefly based on geometric forms—which is necessary for reducing and abstracting any object from a tree to a human head. "Every form in nature has a very strong and definite construction for it has 'grown,'" Binder wrote. "Every plant has gradually and organically developed. . . . The fine artist renders in his picture the atmosphere and pictorial value of a pine or a palm. But the designer must understand its proportions and emphasize its natural construction. On the other hand, he must reduce the complicated details of the object which make the picture distinct." Binder also believed that color was an important aspect of styling, and taught his students that the artist must "surpass the optical effects of nature with a limited number of colors."

Binder wed cubist form and Bauhaus theory, and wrote frequently about these issues. On shapes: "The sphere and cube are selected as they will simplify the possibilities in design. [As artists we] like to bring the visible world into rules, as scientists have always done. A design will be most attractive when it gives the essentials in a concentrated form." On color: "The same concerns the use of color. Planes of pure color are placed side by side, characteristic of the object. The perspective must not upset the balance. Light and shade must be kept simple." On perspective: "If we draw perspective as it appears in nature, then the effect is too weak. We must strengthen this effect. This will be obtained by simplifying, for which two possibilities can be applied; the orthogonal or the parallel perspective." On proportion: "The individual differences between similar forms are determined by proportion. Height and width create opposites." And on *surprise*: "[Everyone will say that they] saw a blue cow. Such are the enormous possibilities not yet explored. What is small render large, and vice versa. Space adds legibility."

Today Binder's works may appear dated, but his method is an appropriate learning tool. In 1964 the psychologist Rollo May, Binder's longtime friend, summed up his practice: "Most artists have an antagonistic point of view toward Western society and its civilization. Binder's work has the feeling of relationship with modern sciences. . . . Binder always had a positive point of view toward modern science and technical development in relation to his aims in artistic achievement . . . where all established conceptions are stripped from word until the essence of the word is clarified. I feel it is this essence in Binder's art which is so apparent."

Shooting Targets

One need not be a marksman to appreciate the simple beauty of shooting targets. For function and utility they are among the most perfectly designed graphic forms; nothing could be more economical than the black concentric circles surrounding a bull's-eye. If the archetypal target did not date back to antiquity it would epitomize the modern marriage of form and function—as designed by a Bauhaus master perhaps. The fact is, no form is more modern than geometric form. A circle is a circle, an oval is an oval whenever it is produced.

The target was a visually eye-catching device used in Russian constructivist ads and posters during the 1920s. In the 1930s Western advertising-arts magazines referred to "scoring a bull's-eye" with stark, modern graphics. Such mainstream products as Odol, Tide, and Lucky Strike use targets on their packages. And the vivid geometric form continues to be used in contemporary design and illustration. However, the standard shooting target was not originally, nor has it been subsequently, designed by any individual designer. Its formal attributes were born of necessity. In ancient times the *targe*, as it was called, was a light circular shield protecting the foot soldier from arrows. The shooting target, which simulated that shield, was made from a bundle of wood formed into and painted with circles and hung from a tree or easel.

Jasper Johns transformed the target into pop art in 1960, and today antique dealers sell shooting gallery targets as naïf art. Yet targets have primarily served a utilitarian function. Wade Jackson who oversees the firearms training program at the FBI Academy in Quantico, Virginia, said "the target is a tool that helps perfect the fundamentals of marksmanship." In the 1930s and 1940s the classic FBI target was a cartoon version of the stereotypical criminal; a pug-faced, Caucasian male of undetermined ethnic origin aiming his pistol at point-blank range. The central shooting area of this target, from the chin to the diaphragm, was lightly shaded to guide the shooter's aim to that part of the body where he could effect what law enforcement terms a "cessation of voluntary activity." In the 1980s the "FBI Silhouette," an outline of a male torso that stands upright either at attention or with one hand on hip, replaced the caricature and has been more or less officially adopted by most American law enforcement organizations. Scoring numerals are positioned along contoured rings, akin to a topographic map, indicating the various hit zones resulting in "rapid incapacitation."

"The numbers on the targets," explained Agent Jackson, "are worked out in ballistic workshops where scoring agenda take the arbitrary nature out of the process." But it is not necessary for a target to be a human figure. "The fundamentals of marksmanship." Jackson asserted, "will get you where you want regardless of the target itself." Actually, in the 1980s the FBI switched to the FBI-Q, or the so-called "Coke bottle," a simple rendering of a thin neck and fat body that eschewed human resemblance but provided a proper hit zone. Jackson speculated that since there is no FBI design department dedicated to target research, the redesign of the FBI-Q and Federal Firearms QIT (Quick Incapacitation Target) was probably the work of "one persuasive guy in the organization."

Targets are designed to be ripped, torn, and shot apart. In this sense even the basic circular target evokes an eerie quality that is difficult to detach from its graphic grace and elegance. Yet it is this very tension between the target's form and function that makes it so intriguing, indeed hypnotic. In the hands of a marksman it is an efficient tool, but in the eyes of the designer a target is harmony and balance.

Darkie Toothpaste

For more than six decades Darkie has been the best-selling toothpaste throughout Asia. Manufactured in Hong Kong and Taiwan by Hawley & Hazel, part-owned by the Colgate-Palmolive Company, its leadership was challenged in 1990 not by a new and improved competitor, but by the Interfaith Center on Corporate Responsibility, which argued that the trademark of a grinning black minstrel promoted racial stereotyping. Spokespersons for Colgate-Palmolive initially insisted that the product name and design were not offensive to Asian people. However, the company ultimately gave in to mounting protest from the West and ordered Hawley & Hazel to change the image. The redesign featured a young, well-dressed black man in a top hat and a new name, Darlie.

An American visiting a Far Eastern metropolis might well be shocked by the sight of billboards showing the original smiling, bug-eyed minstrel advertising Darkie toothpaste. Since the mid 1960s Americans have become sensitive to derogatory stereotypes. Yet these deep-seated images have been difficult to extinguish even here. Racial and ethnic stereotypes have no higher purpose than to simplify, dehumanize, and degrade people, yet many such stereotypes have been used for mass market product identification, advertising, and as trade character mascots. Although the Darkie controversy occurred continents away, it recalled a period in American history when stereotypical images of Jews, Irish, Italians, Chinese, and African and Native Americans were exploited by manufacturers and merchants to sell products.

From the cigar-store Indian to the Gold Dust Twins (two comical African pygmies who were trademarks for a leading detergent), stereotypes have pervaded popular art. The practice has all but ceased, but vestiges of benign racist trade characters remain, including Aunt Jemima, the former plantation mammy who over the years has been transformed into a housewife, and the Cleveland Indians logo, the comic heathen with the foolish grin.

In the early twentieth century, ethnic and racial trade characters were accepted symbols of national brand campaigns. A 1915 issue of the trade journal the *Poster* reported that among American housewives, the most popular, indeed friendly, brand identifiers were the Armour Meat Company and Cream of Wheat chefs, both black men, and Aunt Jemima, precisely because of the customer's identification with them as warm character trademarks. Today Aunt Jemima is so positively engrained in the popular subconscious that rather than retire her entirely, her handlers have taken the bandanna off and given her a mainstream persona.

Stereotyping was common from the end of the Civil War through the 1890s, when the population expanded in urban areas and more goods and services were required to feed and clothe them. Enterprise and competition grew at a fast pace; numerous advertising techniques were employed to make a large consumer base aware of mercantile options. The earliest forms were typographic space ads, bills, and broadsides composed by job printers. Then, as printing technology improved and color printing became economically feasible, more specialized commercial artists took responsibility for the design of advertising, including trade cards, posters, and collateral ephemera. Racial and ethnic caricature was one of the most commonly practiced graphic leitmotifs. Comic physiognomic distortion was used with impunity for both political and social satire, and as entertainment in forms such as Currier and Ives print series *Darktown*, *Judge's Blackville*, *Puck's* mildly Jewish humor book *Pezneez* (a transliteration of *business* in a Yiddish dialect), to name a few. Comic artists, including Thomas Worth, F. W. Opper, R. F. Outcault, F. M. Homrath, A. B. Frost, and E. W. Kemble, also developed character trademarks to sell soaps, patent medicines, writing inks, and washing machines. Racial stereotyping in the service of commerce was a benign graphic convention not intended to deride, or so the artists may have believed. It was a right-of-passage, a tax levied upon all entrants to the melting pot.

The process might be called democratic. Every major immigrant group was indiscriminately pilloried by caricaturists—a curious badge of distinction. Ultimately, however, most immigrant groups were allowed to enter the mainstream, stereotype in tow. Often the groups themselves used similar self-caricatures in their own media. But not so, African and Native Americans. Stereotypes of the Native American "heathen" or "noble savage" continued unabated, while African Americans were saddled with various slave images (Uncle Tom, Mammy, etc.). The black minstrel image, the birth of black face, was so popular that white performers would put on burnt cork to entertain in theaters that otherwise restricted black people.

The grain of truth on which stereotypes were developed made racial and ethnic caricature both dangerously insipid and useful to merchants. Blacks, for example, were used to identify certain food staples because on the plantation they were either cooks or picked similar crops in the field. Playing off skin color, they were also used to advertise soap products, like the Pears Soap ad showing a black child being scrubbed so thoroughly that he turned white. Images of the "noble savage" adorned patent medicines and tobaccos, the former because they were hyped as Indian remedies and the latter because Indians grew the weed. Although the noble savage was not as denigrating as other racial caricatures, it was, nevertheless, a false stereotype that oversimplified the plurality of Native American tribes and nations. While caricatured Jews, Italians, and Irish were not as gainfully employed as trademarks, they appeared often on "soft-sell" trade cards that showed generic vignettes on the front side with more specific advertising copy on the back, and were given away with merchandise. Usually in these often comical scenes, hooked-nosed Jews were shown with pawnshop balls, Italians were organ grinders, and Irish had simian characteristics.

Some historians argue that racial and ethnic stereotypes represent early indigenous American humor. With the different waves of immigration each new group threatened the previous one, making hostility inevitable. Humor was a means of letting off steam. By extension, product identification was an even more widespread means of assimilation. Yet over a long period of use graphic symbols come to represent certain truths. Such is the case with racial and ethnic stereotypes. Artists who simplify, distort, and exaggerate physical or behavioral characteristics have significantly influenced popular perception. Early American myths of race and ethnicity developed, in part, from the popular arts. While contemporary graphic artists and designers are more inclined to understand the ramifications of their work, the lessons of the not-so-distant past underscore the potential power of graphic design. The Darkie controversy proved that the strength of stereotypes must not be underestimated.

Does It Make Sense?

APRIL GREIMAN

D*esign Quarterly* #133 (1986) was no ordinary magazine. Although disguised as a common thirty-two-page magazine format, upon opening, the issue unfolded accordion style until, when finally extended and opened, it metamorphosed into a single-page poster, measuring approximately two by six feet. *Design Quarterly*, then edited by Mildred Friedman, was a publication of the Walker Art Center in Minneapolis directed toward the international design community. Each issue focused on a single theme, and, in 1985, *Design Quarterly* invited April Greiman (b. 1948), a pioneer of computer-generated design to design an issue of the magazine about her work.

Instead she transformed the magazine into a poster, a life-size digitized, nude self-portrait. Greiman's eyes are closed and her left breast is cloned onto the right side of her body. Another close-up of her head, this one with eyes wide open, projects from the vertex of her feet under the heading "the spiritual double." Superimposed type and image ideograms were dispersed over the surface of the poster, and photographs of dinosaurs, outer space, hieroglyphs, formulas, weather pattern symbols, and disembodied miniature hands performing mysterious acts all orbit around the meditative, naked Greiman. A tally stick, simultaneously suggesting a time line and growth chart, underscores the length of the poster and emphasizes the physicality of the oversized page. In addition, time line entries mark major scientific innovations, including "Electricity 1831," "Relativity Theory 1905," and "Man on the Moon 1969" as well as "Birth of April Greiman 1948." The scale below the hash marks reads in ticker tape fashion:

"proton.neutron.electron.moron.milli.micro.nano.pico.kilo.mega.giga.tera.order.chaos.play.dream. dance.make sounds.feel.don't worry.be happy."

The reverse side renders tales of dreamlike narrations in floating text boxes, a Zen koan, ambiguous, large-scale photographs, and an agonizing step-by-step record of the process of working with the new computer technology.

Flight of fancy or logic puzzle? Did it make sense?

Greiman's poster was a compendium of the preceding decade—a nation bloodied by the Vietnam War saw the rise of feminism, Eastern religion, consciousness-raising, spiritual awakening, and reinvigorated interest in Jungian archetypes and dream symbology. It was also a formalist autobiography. Graphically, designers grew restless with the absolute order and clarity of the reigning classic Swiss modernism. In the early 1970s Greiman studied with Wolfgang Weingart and Armin Hofmann at the Basel School of Design in Switzerland where a spirited climate of innovation and research nourished inventive typographic experiments: extreme leading, wide letterspacing, typographic weight changes mid word, alternative text divisions— pushing typographic expression toward the personal, expressive, and, occasionally, humorous. Technically, *Does It Make Sense?* was dazzling.

As director of visual communications at CalArts in 1982, Greiman had early access to state-of-the-art video and digitizing equipment formerly used by Nam June Paik. The Macintosh computer was introduced in 1984. By 1986 the collage in *Does It Make Sense?* involved no conventional paste-up; it was composed and assembled as a single document in MacDraw and printed out as it was designed on screen, tiled out on 8½" x 11" sheets of bond paper. It was a feat only dreamed of until then; the ability to bypass conventional paste-up production methods. The text function of the MacDraw program for the first time allowed direct composition of text in relation to the digitized video images.

Before *Does It Make Sense?* bit-mapped type and imagery had been an anathema to designers; the computer was arcane, expensive, and unfriendly. With its publication, the design world was challenged to take another look. Decontextualized images, thematically mixed texts, apparent non sequiturs, floating text blocks, typography set in mirror image, humor, and personal juxtapositions were all recontextualized and revoiced as Greiman's own in a pyrotechnic meld of form and content. It was rendered coherent by the digital medium.

The personal computer would eventually open opportunities for new levels of authorship for designers. Although the role and legitimacy of personal expressiveness in graphic design is still being evaluated, *Does It Make Sense?* is a touchstone: the creation of self-referential statements and compositions through the medium of professional graphic design.

Style

DESIGN AS AESTHETICS AND FORM

Goudy Stout was designed in 1930 by Frederic W. Goudy, one of America's otherwise foremost type designers. Why the equivocation? Because Goudy Stout was a frivolous typeface. "In a moment of typographic weakness I attempted to produce a 'black' letter that would interest those advertisers who like the bizarre in their print. It was not the sort of a letter I cared for . . . ," admitted Goudy.

Even luminaries blunder when they succumb to the unpredictable tastes of the marketplace, consequently a rather long list of talented designers have perpetrated typographic crimes and misdemeanors, placing many ill-advised typefaces into currency. Among them are Hermann Zapf's Sapphire, Emire Reiner's Floride, Morris F. Benton's Hobo, J. Hunter Middleton's Plastica, A. M. Cassandre's Acier Noir, and Roger Excoffon's Calypso.

Benton's Hobo, which has been on typositor for many years, has aged poorly. When issued by the American Type Foundry and Intertype in the early 1920s, Hobo had fashionable characteristics that made it a viable advertising display face. Its vertical strokes and curved bars with the variation of stress on different letters gave it a quirky character and eye appeal; the elimination of all lowercase descenders saved on space. In the right designer's hands Hobo isn't half bad as a decorative alphabet, but used incorrectly, which is usually the case, the results are abominable.

With all the elegant typefaces extant, why are so many of the ugly specialty faces used? Or more to the point, why were they designed in the first place?

Typography is a handmaiden to commerce, and as Goudy suggested, pleasing the client is at least one of the typographer's raisons d'être. Decorative, ornamented, or novelty typography dates back to the early nineteenth century and the Industrial Revolution. Commerce was expanding its boundaries. A primitive form of print advertising replaced the tradesman as the primary hawker of goods. In *Printing Types: An Introduction* (Beacon Press, 1971) Alexander Lawson wrote: "Early in the nineteenth century English type founders produced a variety of embellished types designed to emphasize their unique characteristics for the single purpose of attracting attention. Fat faces, grotesques, and Egyptians—decorative types when compared to the romans that had undergone but minor changes since fifteenth-century Italy—were not flamboyant enough for the new requirements of advertising display."

Type founders discovered that virtually any unusual design would be purchased by job printers for advertising, broadsides, and packages. Initially the ornamented types were inline or outline versions of the Didot and Egyptian styles, but designers soon switched from altering existing faces to creating more unique and outlandish inventions. Letterforms mimicked the appearance of Gothic architecture, and were intricately designed with filigree like that applied to cast-iron machinery. Type echoed the Victorian's penchant for extravagant decoration.

Some of these alphabets were reproduced from letters in ancient manuscripts, but most were conceived by artists and produced at great expense. A somewhat arcane, but nevertheless important, distinction must be made between ornamented typefaces and the so-called fancy faces. Since designers of the latter were prone to derive inspiration more from common sign painters than from monastic scripts, fancy faces did not resemble book illumination, but rather vernacular lettering.

Concerning fashions in typefaces, a 1879 issue of the *Typographic Advertiser* offered the following: "We change, tastes change, fashions change. The special furor is now for bric-a-brac— antique pots and platters, Japanese oddities, and Chinese monstrosities. But fashion's rule is despotic, as so, yielding to her commands, we have prepared and show in this number some oddities to meet the taste of the times. . . . As printers no doubt desire to be in fashion, we trust they will approve our course by sending in orders for them, that their patrons also may catch the infection. . . . "

The infection eventually disappeared. As the Victorian era came to an end the passion for extreme ornament faded. A renewed interest in typography of classic origin contributed to the demise. In *The Practice of Typography* (1900), Theodore Low De Vinne offered this eulogy: "Printers have been surfeited with ornamented letters that did not ornament and did degrade composition, and that have been found, after many years of use, frail, expensive, and not attractive to buyers." However, De Vinne further noted that "more changes have been made in the direction of eccentricity than in that of simplicity. Fantastic letters were never in greater request, but they rarely appear as types in books. To see the wildest freaks of fancy one must seek them not in the specimen books of type founders, but in the lettering made for displayed advertisements and tradesman's pamphlets." Although traditional typographers now eschewed ornament, a new breed of professional, the commercial artist, was creating hand-drawn, often one-of-a-kind, novelties for use on a plethora of printed matter.

At the turn of the century, designers working in the art nouveau style rejected the nineteenth-century excesses, but replaced it with "floriated madness," which was eventually rejected by those designers who sought yet another style. The vogue for the decorative letter was somewhat eclipsed during the 1920s by the canon of purity and functionalism espoused by the Bauhaus and described by Jan Tschichold in his book *The New Typography* (1928). However, despite the proliferation of functional sans-serif types like Futura, advertisers required eye-catching type to appeal in an increasingly competitive market.

During the 1920s and 1930s, the era of *art moderne,* a multitude of quirky types were issued by the major German, American, English, Dutch, and French type foundries and promoted through extravagant type specimen sheets. Many of these faces symbolized modernity.

Type design has traditionally been based on past models, and typographers today are archaeologists digging through antique typebooks for faces suitable for revival or adaptation. While the revivalists pay homage to the past, the computer mavens are looking towards the future. But the future of quirky typography is déjà vu. Primitive, low-resolution bitmap forms have offered numerous possibilities for quirky typography equaling the worst produced during the nineteenth and early twentieth centuries, but in the right designer's hands, there is also an unlimited variety of fascinating concoctions.

The Great Gargantua and Pantagruel

W. A. DWIGGINS

An admirer said of William Addison Dwiggins (1880–1956): "There are few American designers whose work can be revisited after decades with more pleasure and instruction." Dwiggins—or Dwig or WAD or Bill, as he was known—was a renaissance man: typographer, type designer, illustrator, author, puppeteer, marionette designer, book jacket and book designer. He was the missing link between the aesthetic movement and commercial art, an auteur in that he developed an unmistakably distinctive graphic style that informed the practice of his epoch, from the 1920s to the 1950s. To give further buoyancy to his reputation, on August 29, 1922, in an article in the *Boston Evening Transcript,* Dwiggins was the first to use the term *graphic design* to describe his broad design practice.

Dwiggins's passion for design pervaded everything he touched (and wrote). His work was an extension of his self. "One stood quietly apart waiting for him to look up," recalled Dorothy Abbe, his long-time colleague, about his intensity, passion, and humanity. "Presently he swung from his stool. With a final glance at the piece that absorbed him, he reached for tobacco and, filling his pipe, slowly turned toward you, smiling his welcome. This was ever his way—the smile, the slow unhurried steps, emphasized by the simplicity of his dress, always in white. Not only did he move slowly, but he worked slowly in the sense that the first effort was usually discarded, to be written, or drawn, or carved, again and again. And yet in this quiet, patient manner he brought into being more than most people even dream of."

Among the countless projects completed during his long career, the shelf backs (or spines), title pages, and illuminations for a five-volume boxed set of Rabelais's *The Great Gargantua and Pantagruel* (1936) reveals his virtuosity. In this book Dwiggins wed respect for tradition with passion for the new. In Dwiggins's work, the classics served as foils for a contemporary decorative vocabulary that synthesized medieval, oriental, and Mayan visual forms. Although his motifs are described as *art moderne* (art deco), they were only remotely related to this machine age international style. Actually, Dwiggins developed a distinctive manner that was later adopted by other purveyors of commercial style. Dwiggins did not conform to the times, rather the times conformed to him.

The Limited Editions Club publication of *The Great Gargantua and Pantagruel* is certainly one of the finest on Dwiggins's own shelf. Even when compared to the unique spines he designed for numerous other classics, these exuded a certain magic through their composition. Every aspect of the books' conception, production, and manufacture from the deep green color of the cloth bindings and slipcase to the conceptual acuity of the lighthearted illustrations to the composition of neo-baroque ornament to the curvaceous hand lettering on the title and chapter breaks made this a readable confection. Over time it has become a kind of fetishistic design artifact.

George Macy, the irascible publisher of the Limited Editions Club, commissioned a three-volume set; Dwiggins urged him to divide the text into five separate volumes (*The Great Gargantua and Pantagruel* was written as five books under one cover). This number gave Dwiggins the opportunity to create a virtual stage on which the characters in the books could play. Dwiggins tied the five volumes together through the spine illustrations. Separately each spine had its own integrity, but together they became a frieze of the book's leading characters. Dwiggins further created individual title pages, which he precisely hand lettered in pen and ink in actual-size layouts, often in more than one version, as if titles for a play or film. Title page design was a time-honored part of bookmaking, and Dwiggins respectfully played with the medium by busting through the rigid constraints. Inside the books he designed vignettes that illuminated the text, but not in the conventional mimicry of a passage or line. Personally inscribed on the flyleaf of Dorothy Abbe's copy Dwiggins wrote: "Although the . . . vignettes might be considered gothic I tried to avoid a gothic overtone in this book." He succeeded in designing a book that, though set in another time, was not merely relevant, but vital.

In Hingham, Massachusetts, far from the capitals of commercial art and design, Dwiggins remained an iconoclast for his entire life. But few mavericks were ultimately as influential. He inspired imitators, yet none were able to recreate his panache. Dwiggins was the quintessential designer and experimenter of his time. "Modernism is not a system of design—it is a state of mind . . . a natural and wholesome reaction against an overdose of traditionalism," he wrote. "The graphic results of this state of mind are extraordinary, often highly stimulating, sometimes deplorable." Dwiggins pushed the boundaries when necessary, while standing for tradition. He once wrote that he lived for a single purpose: "the game is worth the risk."

Vanity Fair and Fortune Covers

PAOLO GARRETTO

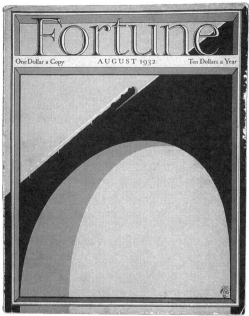

Paolo Garretto (1903–1983) was a prolific cartoonist, caricaturist, and poster artist who worked for magazines from the mid 1920s to the late 1940s. During his peak in the mid 1930s, every week at least one major periodical or poster hoarding featured an image that he produced. For *Vanity Fair*, just one of his primary outlets, he designed more than fifty covers and was known as one of *Vanity Fair*'s graphics triumvirate, which also included Miguel Covarrubias and William Cotton.

Although he was friends with *Vanity Fair*'s legendary art director M. F. Agha (1896–1978), Garretto was originally commissioned in 1930 by one of the magazine's editors, Claire Booth Brokaw (later Claire Booth Luce). His caricatures for *Vanity Fair* were uniquely styled and defined the times when they were made. Overtly influenced by cubism and futurism, his style grew more out of a naive instinct than premeditated borrowing. Which came first, a dominant style or a personal one? Garretto was a leader not a follower. His covers for *Fortune*, the legendary finance magazine that pioneered poster-like covers, veered from caricature/design to pure design in an illustrative mode. These were grand visual statements.

Garretto's graphic approach was based on simplification of primary graphic forms into iconic depictions and loose but poignant likenesses. Vibrant, airbrushed color was his trademark, and he also experimented with different media to create exciting new forms, including experiments with collage and modeling clay that proved fruitful. Without his superb draftsmanship, what is now pigeonholed as deco styling would surely have been a superficial conceit, but his conceptual work was so acute, and his decorative work was so well crafted that he eschewed these pigeon-holes. Writing in a 1946 issue of *Graphis*, Orio Vergani described Garretto's ingenuity this way: "Once the constructive theme of his images is discovered Garretto proceeds to the invention of the media necessary for executing them. I believe he has painted, or rather, constructed his images with everything: scraps of cloth, threads of rayon, with the bristles of his shaving brush, with straw, strips of metal and mill board, with iron filings and sulfur, tufts of fur and wings of butterflies. His colors are born of a strange alchemy of opposed materials in the light of an artificial sun, he seeks for the squaring of shade as others have sought for the squaring of the circle."

Garretto was born in Naples, Italy, in 1903 but had a peripatetic childhood because of his father, a scholar and teacher who traveled extensively. When he was twelve years old his family moved to Philadelphia where, before he mastered English, he would communicate with his teachers through drawings. At the outbreak of World War I he returned to Italy and moved to Florence because his father was a reserve officer in the army. After the war, and amid the throes of great social upheaval, the family moved to Rome—a hotbed of cultural activity and political revolution. In Rome, Garretto would go nightly to the Caffe Aragno where the intelligentsia assembled; there he would sketch portraits on the marble table tops. One portrait of F. T. Marinetti, the founder of futurism, and another of the thespian Pirandello served to get him a job doing cartoons for a local newspaper.

The postwar years were marred by struggles between communists and fascists. Garretto hated the bolsheviks, he says somewhat romantically, for the murder of the Czar and particularly his little son Prince Alexei. But, closer to home, the bolsheviks had attacked his father at a veterans rally, beaten him, and stole his medals. Although his father "turned the other cheek and forgave his enemies," Garretto was not so forgiving. At the age of eighteen he joined the Vanguardists, the fascist youth organization. In those days fascism was an anti-establishment movement and an alternative to communism. Although he has since renounced those years as childish folly, at the time he was committed to the cause. He even designed the fascist uniform (because he said that he disliked the disheveled look of the fascist partisans). And when Mussolini saw him and a few of his friends in a formation dressed in their spiffing splendor, Il Duce appointed Garretto one of his personal bodyguards. And a great honor it was too until he learned that the position was for life. The elder Garretto, who was adamantly opposed to Paolo's involvement with the fascists, eventually helped obtain a permanent discharge, allowing him to go back to school, earn his architectural degree, and ultimately travel to England, where he became a sought-after caricaturist.

At age twenty-two Garretto received steady work from Dorland, Europe's largest advertising agency. His work was published regularly in the eight major British pictorial magazines, including the *Tattler* and *Illustrated News*, and frequently appeared in the major German weeklies. In Paris, where he had married, opened a studio in his apartment, and eventually sired a son, he was commissioned to do numerous advertising projects. One such was the result of a meeting with Alexey Brodovitch, who was art director for the department store Trois Quartiers.

He was also asked to become a member of Alliance Graphique, a loosely knit advertising cooperative that included poster artists A. M. Cassandre, Jean Carlu, and Charles Loupot, for whom Garretto did an Air France campaign.

By the 1930s his friendship with publisher Condé Nast was so close that this corporate chauvinist allowed Garretto to work for the competition. In the meantime the war broke out and Garretto wanted to returned to Paris to be with his wife and child. Being Italian he was not allowed to cross the border, and after various attempts at entry he returned to New York. In 1941 Garretto was interned in the United States with other German, Italian, and Japanese enemy aliens. He was eventually deported, having agreed to an FBI proviso that he not make any anti-American artwork for the duration of the war. This was certainly a little far-fetched and unenforceable, but he did refuse to do caricatures for the Nazis with whom he had no sympathy. Moreover, his stylized but critical caricatures of Mussolini and Hitler did not make him very popular among party officials. In 1944 he was assigned to Budapest to develop a literacy project so that "defeated and conquered peoples" could learn the Italian language through pictures. But when Italy capitulated to the Allies later that year, he was interned as an enemy alien in Hungary for the duration of the war.

After the war he continued to make political and social caricature; he also did fine art in the same style. Paul Rand, who called Garretto a master of illustration, hired him to render the Dubonnet man. He continued to do caricatures well into the 1970s, but he stopped working for American magazines in the 1940s because after the war, he said, the art directors who knew him had changed or died and his kind of design was eclipsed by photography. In 1982 Lloyd Ziff, then design director for the newly revived *Vanity Fair*, located Garretto at his home in Monte Carlo and asked him to do some covers. He did a few, but they were rejected by the editors in favor of a contemporary caricaturist whose drawing was influenced by Garretto's style. Although he was active until his death at the age of eighty-six, Garretto never altered the style that defined his time.

Artone

SEYMOUR CHWAST

The curvilinear style known as art nouveau in France and Jugendstil in Germany was revived by Push Pin Studios during the early 1960s and prefigured the postmodern reappraisal of passé forms by well over a decade. Push Pin, founded in 1955 by Seymour Chwast (b. 1931), Milton Glaser, Edward Sorel, and Reynold Ruffins, was a pioneer of stylistic sampling, known for combining traits of Victorian, arts and crafts, art nouveau, and art deco approaches with contemporary typography and illustration that underscored the influential "Push Pin style." This approach was a model for other American designers interested in decorative form and, as a byproduct, fostered a return of drawing to the design process. The prevailing modern ethos rejected historicism as quaint and unresponsive to contemporary business needs. But Push Pin's eclecticism was based on the idea that historical form could be revitalized and given currency with certain mass media, including book and record covers, advertising, magazines, and package design. There is probably no better example of the appropriateness of this method of historical quotation than Seymour Chwast's 1964 design of the Artone Studio India ink package, the logo of which was the basis for his display typeface called Artone, released that same year by Photolettering Inc.

In 1963 Push Pin Studios was commissioned to repackage the Artone ink carton by the new owner of the art supply company, a Wall Street businessman named Louis Strick. Since his company was small, Strick rejected costly market research and customer profiles. Rather, he left the problem entirely in the hands of Chwast and Glaser (then the two remaining principals of

Push Pin). As was often their procedure, each made sketches independently and only later came together for reaction and critique. "We'd talk about it, do our own ideas, and then talk about it again," Chwast recalled. Glaser's proposals are lost and his ideas forgotten, but Chwast recalled doing a few variants on his best sketch showing a large *a*, which, though not directly copied from an existing alphabet, echoed the fluid art nouveau/Jugendstil lettering he had seen in vintage issues of *Jugend*, the turn-of-the-century German art and satire magazine. In fact, the letterform was based more on the idea that "marks had to be simple and straightforward," than on replicating art nouveau conceits.

The curvilinear *a* was contrasted by a delicate, lightline banknote script used to communicate the other pertinent information. Unlike typical art nouveau/Jugendstil packages known for a preponderance of florid decoration, Chwast favored an unencumbered box, the only decoration was three rows of nine smaller *a*'s—designed with a Zen-like simplicity—on the box top. Chwast insisted that using the *a* by itself was not a radical idea since making a simple, identifiable mark on a package was a proven way of establishing the identity for a product. "I knew it had to be something with graphic impact," he said. "In contrast to Winsor-Newton [a competing brand], which took a different approach by having full color paintings on their packages."

Printed on a white background, the *a* was the most identifiable element. In addition to being the first letter in the alphabet, and therefore memorable in its own right, its curved form was at the same time reminiscent of the Artone ink bottle and a drop of ink. Chwast, however, had acted entirely on blind intuition since he admitted that he did not even realize the strong symbolic relationship until another member of the studio pointed it out to him before the client ever saw it. "Somebody said 'its sort of like an ink drop,' and I thought that was a pretty good way to sell the idea to the client."

Chwast used an existing script as the secondary typeface but realized it would be useful for future advertising and promotional purposes to have a complete alphabet and a set of numerals. So he sketched out the capitals, lower case, and numerals over the course of one week and had a designer in the studio render the finished drawings. Chwast said the *a* was easy, while the idiosyncratic nature of some of the other letters made them more difficult to work out. After the design was resolved, it was offered to Photolettering Inc. as a display face and was immediately accepted. Yet a potential problem having to do with fashion arose in Chwast's mind. "The art nouveau thing had reached its peak [by 1964]," Chwast recalled, "and I thought it might be too late to put this alphabet on the market." He was wrong. Artone became very popular, if not overused. It was so popular that at least two pirated versions were issued by other phototype houses. And the pioneer psychedelic poster artist Victor Moscoso credits Artone specifically, and Chwast generally, as influencing his own distinctive style of design.

Chwast used the upper- and lowercase alphabet on the Artone counter display box and eventually applied it to other projects, including posters and book covers. Strick was not troubled that his logo was being reused as a commercial alphabet because it furthered his product's identity. By the 1970s the popularity of the Artone alphabet was on the wane, but it continues to be emblematic of an era of graphic design when eclecticism was at its peak.

The Lover

LOUISE FILI

According to marketing wisdom, the book jacket designed by Louise Fili (b. 1951) for *The Lover* by Marguerite Duras could never propel the book to the bestseller list. The vignetted portrait of a young woman set against a soft-hued background and titled with delicate typography that casts a gentle shadow was bound to fail the rule that a jacket must strike the viewer's eye from a bookshelf ten feet away.

But *The Lover*, Duras's memoir of being a fifteen-year-old French schoolgirl who becomes the lover of a Chinese financier in prewar Indochina, did become a bestseller. Tales of forbidden sexuality may be commercially appealing, but Duras's story, like its jacket, is subtle and more complicated than it appears. It is filled with contradictions. She recalls the past with knowledge of the future, creating a tableau of memories superimposed one on another like double-exposed film. The prose is spare and unerotic, yet the words trigger imaginative pictures of this girl-woman who at fifteen struggles with sexual awakening amid cultural and familial taboos.

For the jacket, Fili chose a deceptively simple composition that characterized the writer's mix of the intangible and the real. The photograph was of the author at precisely her age in the memoir. Although the head-on pose is direct and engages the viewer, Duras's half-smile is enigmatic and elusive. The jacket's muted tones and feathered background added emotional subjectivity to the photograph's apparent objectivity. The thin-stroke typography complemented the spareness of the composition, but its shadow suggested weight and presence. Published by Pantheon in 1985, *The Lover*'s success was a vindication of Fili's artful style, which marketing people often criticized as too low key to be commercially viable. Readable or not at ten feet, it stood out because of its understated countenance, not in spite of it.

Since the 1960s, consolidations and takeovers in the book publishing industry increased competition for shelf space and put greater emphasis on the marketing and promotion of books. Book jacket and cover design in the 1960s was typified by Paul Bacon's jackets that featured large type for titles and author's names and small, illustrated scenes intended to summarize the book.

In the mid to late 1970s Fili—then art director at Pantheon—and others departed from modernist aesthetics and approached their designs as miniposters with integrated type and image in the spirit of the late nineteenth-century advertising posters. They researched typographic styles of the past and drew inspiration from movements like futurism, Jugendstil, and constructivism, incorporating them into contemporary work. This style, called "retro," was similar to postmodernism in its eclecticism and reliance on past motifs; postmodernism, however, drew more from Greek, Roman, and Renaissance sources. Fili's work was distinguished by a conceptual underpinning and an ability to set a mood appropriate for literature that superseded postmodernism's tendency toward a cut-and-paste pastiche of passé forms.

At Pantheon, a trade division of Random House that published fiction and popular nonfiction titles that leaned toward the academic, Fili was given a comparatively small list of books, which allowed her to design most of the covers herself. Initially little attention was paid to her covers, just like those of the other designers before her. She soon realized what great opportunity for change lay in this environment where no one had high expectations. Fili recalled a comment made to her by an art director colleague, "You're lucky. My editors have bad taste; yours have no taste."

How did she create an environment conducive to innovation and inspired design? "Slowly, very slowly." Fili recalled. "I set out to educate them, albeit very slowly and continuously, with incremental changes and innovations: matte laminations, unusual paper stocks, different types of photography and illustration, and, of course, experimentation with type." She broke new ground graphically but always spent less than any of her colleagues, so no one complained.

By 1985, when *The Lover* was published, Fili had used hundreds of typefaces devised from reinventions or interpretations of existing typefaces that were either outdated, overlooked, or from a different era. In Fili's hands they came alive. Her long-time love of letterforms found a home at Pantheon, where for Fili the best part of designing jackets was that "every day I could use a different typeface." Since college she had frequently traveled to Europe to collect all types of printed ephemera, to photograph signage, and to study poster and type design. She clipped faces from old printing manuals and saved even just a few letters from old books or posters if they caught her eye.

When it came time to design, Fili drew tissue after tissue until just the right letterforms evolved to capture the particular mood or emotional tone of the book. Then, she hunted for a typesetter who carried the typeface. "Usually no one did, so I had to start from scratch and rebuild it, letter by letter, for my needs," Fili told illustrator Dugald Stermer in an article in *Communication Arts* magazine (September/October 1986). With the typeface reconstructed or redesigned, she then hired a professional to render the new letterforms (this was before Fontographer). Occasionally, as was the case with *The Lover*, the title and author's name were rendered exactly as they would appear on the jacket, complete with any special effects like the shadow. She has altered the stress, weight, slant, or width of typefaces to achieve an unusual effect. Her combinations of letterforms and juxtapositions of type styles within a single composition were rarely safe, but the unexpected combinations resulted in work that while respectful of a book's content nevertheless projected a highly intuitive, expressive style.

Considered tame by today's standards, which, thanks to the computer, present custom typography and unexpected visual juxtapositions as the norm, Fili's jackets and covers nevertheless opened the door for further innovation. In the late 1980s art director Carol Carson and designers Barbara de Wilde and Chip Kidd for Alfred A. Knopf, and, later, Michael Ian Kaye for Farrar, Straus, and Giroux in particular have expanded the ways books present themselves in the marketplace. Unusual materials and textures have transformed books into intimate objects. Imagery made of visual fragments, quirky typography, and aggressive compositions have pushed the limits of conceptual interpretation, occasionally providing only tangential clues to the content of the book. Over the eleven years she was at Pantheon, Fili's precisionist covers, with their typographic sensitivity and conceptual illustration, moved beyond mimicking content.

French Paper

CHARLES SPENCER ANDERSON

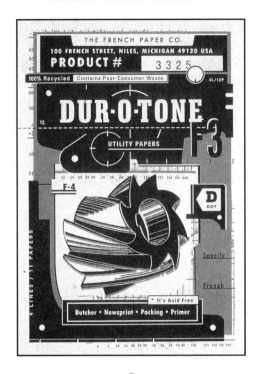

Some call the current trend in revivalist design postmodern, vernacular, or retro; Charles Spencer Anderson (b. 1958) once called it *bonehead*, a word that conjures up goofy cartoon characters and self-mockingly describes a design mannerism that draws heavily on 1930s and 1940s stock commercial art. But Anderson's design is anything but goofy. Sentimental? Maybe. Nostalgic? Possibly. Silly? At times. But *ironic* is more to the point. His is a highly polished graphic style that has evolved into a distinct dialect rooted in American vernacularism. Rather than a trendy trope intended to exploit a popular fashion for quaint pastiche, this is a consistent formal vocabulary, featuring a lexicon of repeatedly used images, typefaces, and dingbats, which signifies both an attitude in contemporary design and this designer's particular obsession with pop visual culture. What began as parody is raised to the level of art, much in the same way that pop artists of the 1960s elevated the artifacts of commercial culture to icon status.

Anderson's long-running campaign for the French Paper Company borrowed the iconography of early commercial printing and incorporated it into witty rebus-like compositions that critiqued the mindless ubiquity of these once anonymous materials by placing them in a comic light. If postmodernism is a reappreciation of passé forms as a critical commentary of modernism, then Anderson's approach is the humorous arm of this graphic design movement. His quotation of common visual advertising clichés and sampling of gothic commercial typography uncovered a lost aesthetic that had been dismissed as artless by the masters of orthodox modern visual communications. By the 1960s the cartoony printer's cuts and trade characters that would later form the corpus of Anderson's work had sunk to the nadir of graphic achievement and were repudiated by modern formalists whose mission was to raise the level of visual beauty and literacy.

Although Anderson did not set out to be a counter-revolutionary, he discovered the graphic integrity woven into the crude innocence of time-worn vernacular images, appreciated them for their nonsensical qualities, and promulgated their use as design imagery. Here the various elements of the French Paper campaign, including paper specimens that were developed as toys, playing cards, and other graphic playthings, exploited the more camp characteristics for the purpose of engaging the viewer in a distinct visual world. Since Anderson was not of a generation that fought the war to make the world safe for universal design, he did not harbor the same aesthetic prejudices as these designers. For him, discovering artifacts in old printing catalogs, type manuals, and other industrial ephemera was like uncovering a Pharaoh's tomb. Yet Anderson did not merely display his archaeological finds, he revived their components by distorting, reshaping, and otherwise transforming vintage iconography into a distinct style that was applied to a range of packages, brochures, books, posters, advertisements, and products.

Anderson's bonehead style began in the mid 1980s when President Ronald Reagan made nostalgia into national policy. It was a time when, as critic Natalia Ilyin writes, "nostalgia twisted truth out of its socket" by forcing the public to accept the false simplification of a vague, mythic past. The earliest iterations of Anderson's design were consistent with retro trends, but it was not the graphic design analog of, say, the nostalgic TV show *Happy Days*. Anderson's was never a totally nostalgic conceit aimed at exploiting that momentary fad. On the contrary, much like the folklorist who discovers lost or forgotten stories that tell grand tales, Anderson's images became the basis for multiple narratives. While the style was used to promote the wares of companies like French Paper, Urban Outfitters, and the Turner Network, among others, it simultaneously told a story of commercial design itself.

Anderson and his design staff position products, establish allure, and attract audiences through precisionist designs. It is noteworthy that such an identifiable design signature succeeded in a field where most graphic designers avoid a single specific stylistic mannerism. But Anderson does not practice monolithic design. Within a proscribed framework there is formal and conceptual range. Over the years much of the vintage advertising sampling has been replaced by original still-life photographs and conceptual illustration, which allows Anderson to communicate with various voices. Still, Anderson's work is governed by an aesthetic that rules the color palette and conceptual thrust. His spirit is equal parts irony, history, and the down and dirty visual effluvia of the twentieth century.

Through the flagship CSA Archive Catalog of Stock Art, Anderson has both reintroduced and laid claim to many of the forgotten artifacts of American commercial printing, and in doing so he has made a ragtag collection of random forms into a regiment of disciplined artworks. Or put another way, he has made a variety of generic visual idioms into an accessible design lexicon. In popularizing these forms Anderson has also contributed to the continuum of design by building on what designer Art Chantry referred to as American commercial folk art—the anonymous artifacts of the commercial era. In the original forms that Anderson draws upon the customer was never aware of the human hand, the images just matter-of-factly materialized in newspapers, "shocards," and flyers. In Anderson's work, however, the presence of the artist/ designer is always apparent, and it is this intervention that makes his appropriation (and ultimate invention) into a commentary of sorts on the state of design, past and present.

Propaganda

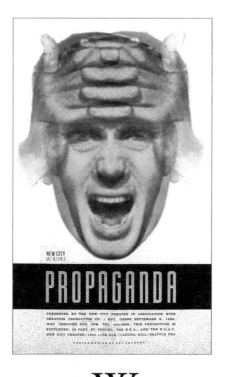

W hen Art Chantry (b. 1954) started designing
posters in the late 1970s, a time when corporate design budgets were high and slickness was the
vogue, he appropriated found art and printed his work on cheap paper. The untutored look was
a preference born of a youthful interest in surfer and hot rod culture, psychedelia, comic books,
and monster magazines. As an adult, Chantry revisited these pop culture influences as the basis
for his personal iconography. Sampling vernacular imagery was an old idea, dating back to 1920s
dada and 1960s psychedelia, but Chantry was not being nostalgic. He distilled the salient points
and developed a cut-and-paste style that reveled in quirky typography, silly lettering, and absurd
collage. "I'm basically an artist masquerading as a graphic designer," he explained. "I have a
degree in painting, though my teacher used to scream because I put type on my paintings."
When he left school in 1978 the punk scene was in full pitch, and scores of posters by seasoned
unprofessionals were plastered everywhere. "I thought, well, here is someplace I can fit in," he
continued.

Chantry defines commercial art as America's true folk art, not so much the work of
individuals as the work of culture itself. "This seems to be kind of an aberrant idea to the design
community, because it rejects the 'great man' theory of history," he said. "Although certain
individuals are great practitioners, the things I tend to champion are subculture design styles that
have been lost or forgotten." He found a fresh vein of vernacular gold in a lost industrial graphic
design style that was prevalent from 1945 to 1955 in tool catalogs and trade journals for the steel,

nuclear, and other heavy industries. He designed advertisements and catalogs for an alternative Seattle arts group by lifting entire pages from old precision machine and tool catalogs and adding only new type. Like the 1960s pop artists, Chantry paid homage to commercial and industrial art, but unlike them he did not merely sanctify these lost artifacts of popular culture; he recycled them as functional graphic designs.

The crude quality achieved by craftsmen isolated from international design movements held great appeal for one who regularly undermined the canon. Years before the vernacular became an official 1980s graphic style, and before the progressive design academies affixed cultural theories to such things, Chantry became a design archaeologist. "I unearthed the work of naïfs and then tried to ape it," he admitted. "Ultimately it became part of my general vocabulary and all of a sudden my language expanded." Other "outlaw" or anti-canonical styles, such as tattoos and "the Hallmark card idea of what hippie stuff looked like in the 1960s" informed his work, too.

A large number of Chantry's posters for alternative theater companies in Seattle were done amidst considerable competition because as he put it, "everyone here seems to be a graphic designer. So it becomes a supply and demand thing; prices are usually low and quality must be high." One of his most memorable projects was the design for a small run of three hundred posters for *Propaganda*, a production of The New City Theatre Company, one of Seattle's most avant-garde independent groups. Although the play opened in 1990 to lukewarm reviews and closed soon afterward, the poster left an indelible image. For this low-budget job, Chantry took a photograph of a man's tormented face from a 1950s clip-art book. It was enlarged and flopped, and printed over itself twice to give the sense of three dimensions. The cheapest way to print it was on a web offset newspaper press, and therefore Chantry produced the original artwork on a smaller scale than the finished, ordering the printer to enlarge it five times to give it an even cruder surface. The poster symbolized the plot of the script but avoided a literal interpretation. "I rejected the billboard school of poster design which says the message should be given and received immediately. I don't think that anyone is going to go to the play based on the poster anyway," Chantry said.

Generally, Chantry comes up with a concept and sells it to the client as an idea. "I became acquainted with the work of the late Robert Brownjohn [Brownjohn Chermayeff Geismar] who during the early 1960s was such a brilliant conceptualist that he could sell ideas to his clients over the telephone. He believed that if it wasn't good enough to talk it out, then it wasn't good enough to take to completion. I try to get so well versed with the client's needs that my concepts fit the problem, and I too can verbalize them before putting them to paper," he explained. If a client demands a more visible interpretation, Chantry sketches things out, but most of his composition is done in the mechanical stage. That's where he does his best work because his art *is* the mechanical. "When I depart from the direct hands-on approach my work gets somewhat rote and sterile, but being that the mechanical is only a step away from reproduction it is closer to fresh than other methods," he said referring to the nineteenth-century method of working directly on the litho stone.

When Chantry began he did not have access to typesetting facilities, so he generated type by photocopying it from books, cutting it out letter by letter, and pasting it into place with glue sticks. Each early project, therefore, had its own personality. Some were image heavy/type light and others were all type, enabling him to learn about the expression of different letterforms. "When I make type decisions that interplay with an image it is usually based on gut reaction. I might scan all my old type books—or comic books and things like that—until I find something that just feels right. I try to avoid type that clashes with my image."

Sooner or later, the immediate advertising function ceases and a poster becomes an artifact. Understanding this, Chantry has designed certain posters, *Propaganda* included, that change over time—inks that fade to reveal other aspects of the work, papers that deteriorate quickly. Sometimes they included thematic ideas that changed with time. "I would love for my posters to have an archaeological function, so that twenty years from now, when people are researching certain aspects of this culture they will be able to refer to my posters for reference to a historical moment."

Commerce

DESIGN AS MARKETING TOOL

Priester Match Poster

LUCIAN BERNHARD

The *Priester Match* poster is so startling that it grabs the viewer's eye in an instant. Of course, the aim of all good advertising is to make the unmemorable memorable by mythologizing the commonplace products of daily life. However, before the *Priester Match* poster first appeared on the Berlin poster hoardings in 1906, most advertising was ornate and wordy. The persuasive simplicity of the Priester poster was rare indeed. Moreover, no one had yet heard the name of its eighteen-year-old creator, Lucian Bernhard (1883–1972), or the genre of advertising he invented, which became known as the *Sachplakat,* or object poster.

Bernhard's early object posters are ubiquitous in poster anthologies. The most striking excel in terms of their graphic eloquence, simplicity, and strength. The method he defined, and the style that ultimately emerged, was predicated on an unadorned, bold-outlined, centered representation of the product being advertised, like a typewriter, spark plug, or piano, placed against a flat color background of forest green, bright purple, or deep orange. The lettering was reduced to a few words, usually the brand name alone. The object in the *Sachplakat,* rendered much like a woodcut, grabbed the attention of passersby as it aesthetically and unambiguously hawked its message. The virtue of this invention was that viewers didn't have to navigate through tedious selling copy, confusing graphics, or other visual distractions. The image was clear, concise, and downright pleasing to the tired eye.

Bernhard's formative years coincided with the explosion of art nouveau in France and

Jugendstil in Germany. Munich was the center of the "radical" German graphic arts, but he decided to settle in Berlin where the wonders of industrial production and commercialism were manifest. Like most turn-of-the-century industrial capitals, Berlin bustled with vehicular traffic, was bathed in electric lights and signs, and exalted in the progress of the industrial age. Berlin businesses routinely sponsored poster competitions as a means of identifying new talent for the expanding advertising industry. When Bernhard was around sixteen he decided to enter a competition sponsored by the Priester Match company and judged by some of the leading promoters of the burgeoning poster movement. Two hundred Marks (about $50) would be awarded to the winner, but more important, the winning entry would be printed and pasted around Berlin. Bernhard jumped at the opportunity, and, with little time to produce his entry, he reportedly made some crucial, instinctive design decisions.

Using paint and brush, he laid down a brown/maroon background—an unusual choice at that time; most posters used either black or bright primaries—on which he rendered an ashtray with a pair of wooden matches along the side. Seeing that the ashtray needed some additional graphic device to balance the composition, he drew in a cigar. Logically, from the cigar wafted smoke, and from the smoke, what else, but a few scantily clad Jugendstil dancing girls. The ashtray needed grounding, so he painted in a checkered tablecloth. At the top of the poster in block letters he rendered the word *Priester.* The original sketch does not exist, but what a mélange it must have been. Nevertheless, proud of his work, he showed it to his mentor at the time, a political caricaturist, who congratulated Bernhard on the wonderful *cigar* poster. Bernhard immediately realized his error and proceeded to remake the poster by painting out the cigar, then the smoke, then the ashtray, then the tablecloth, leaving only a pair of red matches with yellow tips and the brand name, Priester, in gothic lettering. He met the competition deadline without a moment to spare.

Upon seeing it for the first time, the judges, feeling it was too empty, threw it unceremoniously into the garbage can, where it would have remained had not the most important judge arrived late. Burly, bald, and jocular, Ernst Growald was the sales manager for the Hollerbaum and Schmidt lithography firm, which was widely admired as Berlin's leading advertising poster printer—a kind of proto-advertising agency. Growald was a man of unique vision who understood the critical role that advertising could play in Germany's expanding economy. He also had good taste, and, not seeing any other noteworthy entries on the judges table, turned his wayward eyes to the artwork in the trash. Removing it, he hung it on the wall, and was reported to have exclaimed: "This is my first prize. This is genius!" Bernhard won the contest. With Growald as agent and broker, Bernhard never again wanted for paying work.

The Priester poster was a great success for the company, too. In a highly competitive marketplace the message was so simple that it emblazoned the brand in everyone's memory. By chance, Bernhard tapped into the power of simplicity and created a paradigm of modern functionality. Later Bauhaus inventions were hardly more reductive. He modeled much of his subsequent work on that poster, and though many of his designs were good, he never really surpassed Priester for ingenuity. And why should he? The *Sachplakat* was not merely a style, it was a tool for spreading the word. It would become dated over time, but only in the same way that one tool might be superseded by a better tool.

As the one who discovered Bernhard, Growald felt he had the right (and certainly he had Bernhard's permission) to encourage others to work in this manner. He formed a loose-knit "school" of kindred artists known as the Berliner Plakat. Some members followed Bernhard to the letter; others veered off in their own directions, adding a touch of humor or a typographical flourish. As a charter member, indeed the school's foremost innovator, Bernhard became involved with many of what was also known as the *Plakatstil* (poster style).

Bernhard's *Sachplakat* might very well be credited with providing the model of objectivity that was ultimately adopted later by the progressive segments of the advertising industry. In the 1930s dramatic still life photography, responding to the call for a machine art for a machine age, heroicized the industrial product in much the same way that Bernhard celebrated mere matches, spark plugs, and gear shafts. Photographers took Bernhard's notion a step beyond the sentimentality endemic to the drawn or painted image and were therefore even more modern in the formal sense. But Bernhard also prefigured pop art in his popularization of the object. The success of the *Priester Match* poster rested on figuratively rubbing two sticks together that ignited a new methodology. Without Bernhard's pioneering effort, it is possible that objectivity as method and style would have taken much longer to catch on.

Golden Blossom Honey

GUSTAV JENSEN

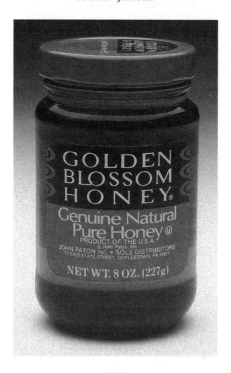

$\mathbf{I}$n promotional advertisements Gustav Jensen (1898–1942?) called himself a "Designer to Industry." He designed some of the most appealing packaging and advertising of the late 1920s and early 1930s. "His peers called him a Designers' Designer," recalled Paul Rand, who, in his early twenties, fruitlessly tried to get a job at Jensen's one-man studio. Rand later borrowed Jensen's *beaux-arts* style before developing his own modern vocabulary. Jensen developed the elegant identity for Charles of the Ritz and other stylish companies, but his most enduring design was the packaging for Golden Blossom Honey, which has kept virtually the same label for some fifty years.

Enigma shrouds Gustav Jensen's life. He is known to have been born in Copenhagen, Denmark, in 1898; his father was a banker and lawyer, and his mother came from a long line of ministers. He studied philosophy at the University of Copenhagen, but with his deep bass voice he wanted instead to become an opera singer. He developed an interest in architecture, however, and architecture somehow led to an absorption in art, and art caused him to pursue aesthetic beauty in typography and printed design. Jensen produced a large body of work for companies like General Motors, Westvaco, Dupont, Edison, American Telephone and Telegraph, Morrel Meats, Gilbert Products, and more. He brought a special elegance to a marketplace obsessed with fashionable conceits. Although making purely functional merchandise was not his primary concern, Jensen believed that the designer had a responsibility to provide the public with appealing products. "The public," he wrote, "is being imposed upon all the time, given stones for bread; the kind of bread we artists can give the public is hard sincere work straight from ourselves. Never mind what the style racketeers say."

Jensen's approach was decorative but not ornate. His work is characterized by economically applied textures derived in part from the Weiner Werkstatte (Vienna Workshop) and the Glasgow School, whose products were imported through Danish retailers. Jensen was a proponent of neither the modern nor the *moderne*: he did not believe in functionalism as an end in itself. Utility is what designers begin with, he said. "The useful tools of civilization come first and then beauty is added. If a thing is to satisfy modern man, it must be beautiful as well as useful." But for Jensen, beauty could be separated from function and simply please the mind and all its mysterious senses. Advertising, he suggested, is only useful when it is beautiful, and Jensen took great pains to see that the many small newspaper ads he designed were eye-catching in the most provocative ways. This aesthetic requirement was apparent in much of his work, even everyday packaging, as exemplified by the Golden Blossom Honey container with its typographic purity and decorative personality.

Jensen based his process on elimination; it was simple but exhaustive. *PM* magazine noted that "he does not make one sketch only, he makes hundreds." Jensen's individuality was expressed as much in the visible style of his wares as in his overall approach. One friend wrote about him this way: "Gustav Jensen has a grand vision. He is a man who has the courage of his own convictions. A lover of everything in nature, he is impatient with fakes, fads, and fashions; he is extremely sensitive to beauty that is noble and poetic; and he is a master of design."

In the 1930s his packaging filled the annuals. But during the war, owing in part to a cessation in the manufacture of nonessential goods, he was underutilized. Nevertheless he continued as a one-man studio, making design and sculpture until he died in the early 1940s.

Advertising Fans

Portable, collapsible, and durable. Before air conditioning, handheld fans were a necessity. In the hotter climes neither man nor woman would be caught without one. During the late nineteenth and early twentieth centuries fans became the ideal vehicle for advertisements. The fan had two sides—perfect for displaying two messages at once—one aimed at the holder and the other, the beholder. It could be argued that the advertising fan prefigured promotional T-shirts and shopping bags.

Advertising fans were used in many commercial cultures. In the United States they were common in the South, promoting social events, local businesses (undertakers were among the most frequent users of advertising fans), and political parties. Certain job printers specialized in fans and offered a variety of standard shapes and stock designs, but none was as widely used as the fattened oval on a wooden stick given out by local merchants for free on unbearably hot summer days. Like all American advertising of the time, however, the typical American advertising fan was essentially utilitarian; devoid of artistic flourish, it conveyed a message clearly and simply.

Compared to French fans of the same period, the American specimens were dreary. Compared to French publicity in general, America appeared to be a backwater rather than a bustling commercial culture and the world's most progressive industrial nation. The French were always ahead of Americans in the marriage of art and commerce, and this was true of its advertising fans, often designed by famous designers to complement their poster campaigns for France's most prestigious industries.

The exact year that advertising was first placed on fans is not known, but the earliest advertising fan has been traced to 1880 when a stylish specimen, like those fashion accessories from the time of Louis XIV, was imprinted with a romantic scene and swash type that announced a French industrial exposition. The French pioneered a variety of formats for advertising fans that ranged from the classic folded and gathered form to a splayed peacock-like version called a "Jenny Lind" and the *coccarda* printed on very thin vellum and glued to two sticks, which when pulled apart and joined in a 360-degree turn revealed a brilliant circle of color. Other classically based formats included the *fontage,* a folded half oval, and the *palmette,* a smallish boxy-shaped pleated type; both were attached to foldable spokes. Conversely, the poor-man's fan was usually either a piece of cardboard pasted on a stick or a single piece of die-cut cardboard that formed a handle and paddle.

In France, fans were the premium of choice for manufacturers and businesses, notably the department store Galleries Lafayette, which complemented each seasonal merchandise campaign with a new fan much the way Bloomingdales does with its thematic shopping bags. Most of the store's fan designs from the 1920s and 1930s were rendered in the elegant *moderne* style popularized in Paris at the 1925 *Exposition Internationale des Arts Décoratifs et Industriels Modernes.* The liquor industry regularly employed advertising fans to complement its various other means of product promotion. Fans for Amer Picon, St. Raphaël, Cognac Sorin, Amourette, and other well-known brands and distilleries were distributed, usually during the summertime, to customers at myriad French cafés. A profusion of colorful fluttering was often seen along the boulevards on the hottest days of the year.

While some mimicked famous posters, notably A. M. Cassandre's well-known Dubonnet sequence, *Dubo, Dobon, Dubonnet,* most fans were custom designed for a specific purpose. Some were quite painterly, showing an elegant vignette or highly stylized characterizations. Usually the fronts had a strong image while the backs were reserved for selling copy; some fans had different images on front and back. Common visual themes included romantic and nostalgic scenes from the eighteenth and nineteenth centuries, but the most common, indeed the most beautiful images were rendered in the contemporary *art moderne* style. The rays of the unfolded fan provided the ideal canvas for *art moderne,* which used radiant lighting patterns borrowed from cubism as the basis for many decorative motifs.

Commercial Modernism

EARNEST ELMO CALKINS

M*odernism* is one of the most slippery terms in our cultural lexicon. It often signifies the revolutionary developments in art and design in Europe during the early twentieth century. As graphic design, modernism was codified in 1925 and called the New Typography, referring to the asymmetric composition, sans-serif letterforms, and abstract images that replaced archaic type design, central axis page layout, and realistic illustration. But back in the 1920s another modernism was also emerging as an alternative to both traditional and radical approaches. This mannerism spread via France throughout Europe and Asia, and, in 1925, made its way to the United States where it was harnessed as an advertising tool. Here modernism was the fuel that ignited the engine of the American consumer boom before the Great Depression. Because this "commercial modernism" was a marriage—though some critics considered it a sordid affair—of art and merchandising, it is overshadowed historically by revolutionary modernism.

The story of commercial modernism began in 1925 at the playground of modernity, in Paris along the banks of the Seine. The *Exposition Internationale des Arts Décoratifs et Industriels Modernes* was laid out in boulevards lined with pavilions decorated with geometric, planar ornament and neoclassical friezes. The world's leading clothing, furniture, and housewares manufacturers, and many grand retail emporia were encouraged to exhibit their latest products and designs. But one player was noticeably absent. The United States, the world's largest industrial nation with the most expansive consumer culture, declined an invitation to participate.

The leaders of American industry believed, as Terry Smith explained in *Making the Modern: Industry, Art, and Design in America* (University of Chicago Press, 1993), "that they could not match the French designers either in making a stripped Arts and Crafts 'modernism' or by boldly countering with a national style."

American products were either nondescript or laden with *beaux-arts* ornament to camouflage a mass-produced look. Although mass production was the foundation on which the modern American economy was built, many cultural critics felt that the items coming off the assembly line lacked good taste. While the Bauhaus and other European avant-garde movements had already embraced the machine and proffered the integration of modern art and industry, American industrialists, who could easily afford to improve their products aesthetically, were usually apathetic, if not resistant to the idea. What they did not resist, however, were marketing strategies that would stimulate greater profits. So following a brief economic downturn in the early 1920s and then a subsequent boom, industry frantically tried to find a new means of increasing sales. It was, therefore, the profit motive, not any transcendent utopian ethic or aesthetic ideal, that paved the way for commercial modernism in the United States.

Commercial modernism was introduced to America in 1925 in no small measure through national advertising by Earnest Elmo Calkins (1868–1964), an advertising pioneer, design reformer, and founder of Calkins and Holden Advertising Company in New York. Like many other American advertising and marketing executives, he visited and was inspired by the *Exposition Internationale des Arts Décoratifs et Industriels Modernes*. After a brief European sojourn he returned to America with a vision of how the American consumer culture could benefit from modernism—or what he interpreted to be modernism.

The difference between what Calkins saw in Paris and most contemporary American advertising art was the total rejection of realism and academic convention in favor of abstraction. Clever abstraction. European illustration was not slavishly or sentimentally representational, but through symbols, metaphors, and allegories it exuded a "magical" atmosphere. Boxes and bottles were not mere utilitarian vessels, but rather represented the essence of what the product should symbolize to the consumer. Years later in his article "The Dividends of Beauty" (*Advertising Arts*, 1933), Calkins summarized the development this way: "Modernism offered the opportunity of expressing the inexpressible, of suggesting not so much a motor car as speed, not so much a gown as style, not so much a compact as beauty." If this had a similar ring to one of F. T. Marinetti's futurist manifestoes, it was because Calkins borrowed his language from the European avant-garde while at the same time ignoring its radicalism. Calkins was not a revolutionary, but rather a tireless advocate of a formalist version of modernity in commercial art and industrial design. Historian Jackson Lears wrote in *Fables of Abundance* (Basic Books, 1994), "what seemed to be a new method for transfiguring commonplace objects became for Calkins a means of disconnecting form and content, thoughts and things." He saw modernism as a tool for creating auras that mythologized products and used "art" as a force to achieve these goals.

No other advertising man was more responsible for spawning the American consumerist revolution than Calkins. He was instrumental in developing such modern marketing concepts as "consumption engineering," "forced obsolescence," and "styling the goods." These buzzwords were the core of an advertising strategy that insinuated modern art and graphic design into a heretofore copy-ruled, devoutly conservative profession whose primary service had been purchasing ad space from magazines and newspapers, and producing lifeless ads to place in those spaces.

Commonplace objects, such as toasters, refrigerators, pencils, shortening, and coffee tins, were presented against novel patterns and at skewed angles; contemporary industrial wares were often shown in surrealistic and futuristic settings accented by contemporary typefaces with names like Cubist Bold, Vulcan, Broadway, and Novel Gothic. Layout, inspired by the European New Typography as codified in A. Tolmer's design handbook *Mise en Page,* also became more dynamic in its asymmetry. Modernism offered what Jackson Lears called the "aura of cosmopolitan culture and avant-garde style" and signaled the spread of an aesthetic coming of age of American advertising. In a retrospective essay titled "Cavalcade" (*Advertising Arts,* 1935), Calkins's art director René Clark enthusiastically recalled the years between 1925 and 1931 as the golden age of advertising, "merchandise sold easily . . . clients spent freely and gave us wide latitude of invention and experiment."

The dichotomy between artistic advertising and humdrum product design sparked the engines of commercial modernism so that by 1926 packages were redesigned and form and color given to old, established, commonplace articles. In Calkins's view, advertising was the high-test octane running the engine of industry. And he was right. "The styling of manufactured goods," he wrote in "Advertising Art in the United States" (*Modern Publicity,* 1931), "is a byproduct of improved advertising design. . . . The technical term for this idea is obsoletism. We no longer wait for things to wear out. We displace them with others that are not more efficient but more attractive." Although clothing manufacturers had long been annually changing styles to increase consumer interest, industry had not adopted this strategy until Calkins made it his mission. "It seemed reasonable that if design and color made advertising more acceptable to the buying public," he wrote, "design and color would add salability of goods." He also noted that the majority of consumers were women, who indeed were accustomed to changes in fashions.

Commercial modernism increased sales, which triggered greater production, which stimulated the economy—or so everyone thought. Manufacturers were happy; shop owners were content, and designers and artists were major contributors to this bounty. An enthusiastic René Clark suggested: "For fifteen years I've seen this styling idea coming closer and closer to the thing that really counts . . . a low priced package . . . a container that millions of hands stretch out to buy because it says something to them that they can't resist!" But at this time business and industry were actually producing *too many* goods to sustain such high levels of continued sales. Calkins's style engineering and obsoletism had become too flagrantly employed. The most trivial items were receiving regular makeovers, which kept designers occupied, factories busy, and retailers ordering more stock until the crash of 1929. Overzealous advertising and product manufacturing in the bull market did not directly cause the catastrophic economic downslide that triggered America's Great Depression, but it was symptomatic of what N. W. Ayer's Harry

Batten described as economic overconfidence, "a sort of gambling fever [which] spread into every level of society." By the mid 1930s, still stinging from the Depression, advertisers and advertising had adopted what was called "shirt-sleeve" advertising, which rejected Calkins's beloved modern art.

In the annals of advertising, Calkins is a pioneer. He elevated illustration, cultivated typography, and introduced behavioral science. He launched commercial modernism in the United States and was its ambassador abroad. While he never designed a page, painted a picture, or spec'd type, he was influential in creating a group of artisans responsible for orchestrating surface effects. In transforming recognizable objects into abstract designs and elevating the commodity to the realm of pure form, he defined what graphic designers would do in the future. Calkins may not have contributed to the formal language of design, like the modern European and American pioneers—indeed many of these pioneers fought against the indulgences that Calkins proffered—but in the 1920s he was the midwife at the birth of modern graphic design.

Since their inception, critics have assailed billboards as a blight on the American landscape. Although legislation has been passed limiting them, outdoor advertising is much too important for business to be outlawed entirely. Moreover, billboard art is the cornerstone of America's poster history. Before radio and television, the billboard—strategically situated on roadways, buildings, and city streets—was the primary mass-advertising vehicle. Although many were produced by anonymous studio artists, leading illustrators and designers such as Lucian Bernhard (Rem Cough Syrup, Amoco Gasoline), N. C. Wyeth (Coca Cola), Otis Shepard (Doublemint Gum), A. M. Cassandre (Ford Motors), and others applied their talents. Today, some of these mammoth images are important artifacts of the material culture.

The earliest recorded leasing of outdoor signboards in the United States occurred in 1870; they were on a fence around a post office under construction in New York City. Noting the increased need for advertising media, in 1872 the printing firm of Kissam and Allen began to lease its own poster panels. Soon poster-stands (as the billboard was first called) dotted the landscape. In 1891 a standard printed sheet (28" × 42") was offered in combinations ranging from one to twenty-four-sheets. And in 1912 the standard twenty-four-sheet poster (8' 10" × 19' 8") was the industry choice as the preferred size for its "Double A" poster panels—the ones still used today. Initially, billboards were sold by solicitors or agents often connected to a printing firm. In the 1920s advertising agencies assumed responsibility. From a handful of independent suppliers grew the Outdoor Advertising Association, which soon became the regulatory group employing inspectors to check on the construction and distribution of panels and the appearance of posters. By 1917, $350,000,000 was spent on outdoor advertising. By the mid 1920s, twice that amount. But according to critics, the quality of the American twenty-four-sheet poster was generally inferior to the smaller yet more innovative English, French, and German posters.

During the 1920s and 1930s, the golden years of American outdoor advertising, artistry was of secondary importance. Both the artist and designer in American advertising (where copywriters were the kings) were less important than in Europe (where the image was dominant). Stark communication, the need to steal viewer's attention for only a split second, dictated the look of billboards. The most successful combined art and message and conformed to historian Hamilton King's dictum that a poster should "seize a moment, exploit a situation with one daring sweep [of line and color] . . . all that can be told of a tale in the passing of an instant. It is dramatic and imaginative, yet it is saliently sincere."

Reeling from the Great Depression, American industry began its uphill drive to repair the damage during the 1930s. The twenty-four-sheet billboard became a symbol of this recovery. Aesthetics improved as some designers became more involved with the creative process. Advertisers accepted the seductive powers of modernistic imagery to sell their wares. And rather than a blight, billboards heralded the new industrial age, fostered a new consumerism, and symbolized a brighter future.

In 1933 Charles Chaplin wrote about the comic strip in society: "In a troubled world such as is the one in which we live, comic strips have become a powerful force to divert the public: to such a degree, in fact, that newspaper circulation depends largely upon their popularity. A comic artist is, therefore, lost if he does not reflect the public mind and appeal to the masses." At the same time cultural critic Gilbert Seldes wrote: "The comic strip is the most despised art form, yet with the exception of the movies it is also the most popular."

The comics offered diversions from daily life. They offered new heroes and antiheroes, spoke new languages and dialects, and fueled the imagination in ways unequaled by any other mass form. "The readership of the comics is one of the amazing phenomena of our contemporary society . . . ," wrote advertising analyst Harvey Zorbaugh. "Readership surveys indicate that every week more than sixty million adult men and women pore over the Sunday comic supplement." Everyone identified with comic characters—kids dressed like Buster Brown and parents named their babies Snookums after the character in *The Newlyweds*. Comic characters were like real people. In the late 1920s and 1930s, as comics became less comical and more dramatic (e.g., *Mary Worth*), they also hit hard and hit home on the basic themes of human nature.

The comic strip has always been a democratic form. Its word/image construction invites easy access and is, therefore, an ideal vehicle for promoting ideas. Not surprisingly, during the 1930s—and lasting well into the 1950s—the comic strip was used to sell products as diverse as vegetable shortening, laundry detergent, acne medicine, breakfast cereal, light bulbs, toothpaste, towels, and automobiles. A few of the ads were penned by the masters themselves, but most were produced by anonymous copyists or acolytes working in advertising bullpens and art-service studios. The quality ranged from primitive comics to highly polished renderings to panels of photographs with speech balloons. Although the majority of the texts were written by hack copywriters, some were entertaining. Who can forget the famous Charles Atlas body-building ads where a weakling is humiliated, loses the girl, eats sand, and ultimately takes the Atlas course and gets revenge?

No one knows who conceived the first comic strip ad, but the comic strip was ignored by advertisers for almost three decades. Only after the pollster George Gallup released a report in 1930, at the height of the Great Depression, that ninety percent of all Americans read the comics and comic pages, did advertisers begin to use the form. In 1935 M. C. Gaines, manager of the color printing department of the McClure Newspaper Syndicate, wrote in *PM* magazine: "As a result of [the] discovery that the comics enjoy the widest appeal of all newspaper features, it is estimated that close to $1 billion worth of space has been filled with advertising of the comic strip type. . . . Color comic advertising has proven so profitable that, in the opinion of one of the country's foremost research authorities, there is a possibility that newspapers will be forced to print comics in color several times a week."

Evidence of the appeal of comic strip advertising was significant. In 1932, six months after initiating a comics advertising campaign to boost failing sales of its Grape Nuts cereal, General Foods announced an unprecedented surge in profits. Soon afterward, J. Walter Thompson's advertising agents requested comic strip ads for all their accounts, regardless of the appropriateness. The 1930s became known in advertising circles as "the balloon talk period." In a contemporary advertising trade journal a columnist wrote: "Psychologically the use of the comic technique is sound. . . . Pictures [are] one of the best attention getting devices. . . . Simple human interest material, based on basic wants, holds interest and the brevity with which the story must be told [says] the reader is not asked to concentrate too long to get the story." Moreover, wrote Roland Marchand in *Advertising the American Dream: Making Way for Modernity 1920–40* (University of California Press, 1985), comic strip formats, like radio commercials, gave print advertisements a time dimension. Viewers also identified with the true story melodramas and real people testimonials so common in strips. No wonder advertisers hopped on the soap opera bandwagon when the *living comic strip* premiered in the mid 1930s.

To introduce the section on comic strip advertising in the *Fourteenth Annual of Advertising Art* (1935) the editor wrote that this new form "has been the complete overthrow of the government of advertising by conventional rule. With the aplomb of Ignatz Mouse tossing a brick at Krazy Kat, continuity and comic strips have impudently tossed aside advertising tradition, become legitimate and frequently astonishingly effective expressions. . . ."

Despite mass appeal and financial success, critics railed against comics, and serious advertising men deplored the comics' frivolity, childish escape, and otherwise degraded standards. Certain advertisers believed that the comic strip craze marked the nadir of an honorable profession, a catering to mindlessness. Despite advancements in advertising media, the Great Depression ultimately caused advertisers to try any scheme to sell their wares. "The cumulative effect of a decade of radio had crushed the vision of advertising as a broad educational force that would lift consumers to higher aesthetic tastes and intellectual pursuits," wrote Roland Marchard.

The critics could not, however, squelch the comics frenzy and were forced into the realization that the American people were not interested in high-brow advertising techniques. The consumer wanted a message that could be quickly and easily understood. The comic strip may have erred on the side of puerility, but until the mid 1950s, when television stole its thunder, comic strip ads were a mainstay of American advertising.

The First Record Album

ALEX STEINWEISS

Alex Steinweiss created the first record albums with original cover art in the late 1930s. What seems commonplace today was revolutionary back then, when heavy shellac seventy-eight rpm records were packaged in unadorned cardboard covers with craft paper sleeves bound inside. The title of the album was usually embossed on the cover's front and spine, and on rare occasions an album might include a reproduction of a famous painting. Steinweiss's art was both original and stylish, conforming to contemporary French and German poster fashions where symbolic forms and metaphors expressed the message. Rather than a portrait of the recording artist, Steinweiss believed, and the management of Columbia Records concurred, that provocative graphic symbols would stimulate the audience's interest in the music. According to a 1939 article in *Newsweek*, sales of the first illustrated album cover rose over eight hundred percent.

"I tried to get into the subject," Steinweiss explained in an interview, "either through the music or the life and times of the artist/composer. For example, for a Bartok piano concerto I took the elements of the piano—the hammers, keys, strings—and composed them in a contemporary setting. Since Bartok is Hungarian, I also put in the suggestion of a peasant figure." For the album *La Conga* Steinweiss painted an enlarged pair of hands playing on a stylized conga drum. For Gershwin's original recording of *Rhapsody in Blue* he placed a piano on a dark blue field illuminated only by the yellow glow of a lone street lamp. The moody scene captured both the music and the city.

Steinweiss's designs maximized the limited image space. All the characteristics of a large poster were brought to the forefront: strong central image, eye-catching typography or lettering, and contrasting colors. At the time the illustrated album cover was first introduced, record stores, which were often sections near the record players in appliance stores, comprised shelf upon shelf of dreary album spines facing outward (they were called *tombstones* in the trade). Steinweiss's albums not only brightened up the surroundings, but the imagery also provided focal points for the consumer. Merchants began to display albums as objects of art, and listeners related the music to this art. Steinweiss inspired other record companies to use evocative covers, but until after World War II his were definitely the most distinctive.

For its formal strength and emotional force the most memorable was his cover for *Songs of Free Men* by Paul Robeson—a slave's chained hand holding a knife resonated as a symbol of freedom and heroism. Other European-inspired, though decidedly original, designs included his constructivist *Eddy Duchin* album and the cubist *Le Sacre du Printemps*. In addition to stylistic sampling, Steinweiss used classical typefaces, though he often complemented (or contrasted) them with a contemporary novelty face. For the cover for *La Bohème* he used an ornamental circus letter because it spoke to the frivolous nature of the opera. By the 1950s, with the advent of Swiss modernism, which proffered economical design, and the increased use of photography, Steinweiss's illustrative work looked dated. But for a moment in design history his invention pushed packaging conventions into an entirely new design genre.

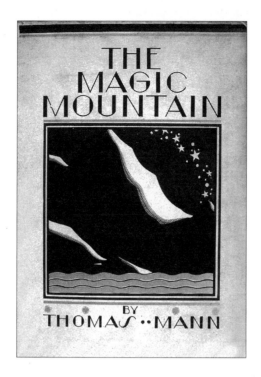

In 1833 the first book jacket was used by Longmans & Co., a British publisher, to protect books from the corrosive effects of dust and light. The heavy paper wrapped around the cloth binding was meant to be discarded after purchase. Such was the ignominious beginning of what in the 1920s and 1930s became a unique artist's medium. For its first fifty years the dust jacket was a plain paper wrapper usually with a window cut out to reveal the title and author's name. The binding of the average trade book (which included the spine and front and back covers) was occasionally stamped or embossed with a modest filigree or vignette for decoration. In the late 1890s decoration was introduced with more regularity. The designs of Aubrey Beardsley, in England, and Will Bradley, in America, were reproduced on book covers as a kind of miniature poster. Soon, in order to increase advertising and eye appeal, publishers also printed on the paper jacket, and by the turn of the century the dust jacket had become the publishing industry's standard promotional tool.

Veteran book designers, however, considered the dust jacket an unwanted appendage. In the classical tradition it was not an intrinsic part of a book's design, which only included the cover, binding, and interior pages. Many esteemed book designers did not design the jackets for their books, but rather passed that dubious assignment on to a "specialist"—usually a layout artist trained in the requisites of commerce. As late as the 1950s the jacket was viewed as the unwanted stepchild. "It could be argued that the jacket is part of the book, [a jury of book critic/practitioners including Herbert Bayer, Merle Armitage, and Sidney Jacobs] feels that this is a temporary and fallacious point of view," wrote Marshall Lee in *Books for Our Times* (Oxford University Press, 1951). "One need only consider the absurdity of having one expensive cover designed that will permanently conceal another! Either the jacket is a temporary protection and sales device meant to be torn from the book the moment it is sold or it is an indispensable cover. If the latter were true, the logical procedure would be to dispense with the costly, unseen binding design. The jacket then becomes the binding, and the function of both binding and jacket will be the same."

Dust jackets were the low end of graphic design practice, tainted by their association to crass advertising departments. As mini billboards, they followed the principles of mass marketing applied to packaging. Dust jackets were ephemera and readers habitually discarded them before books were entombed on the bookshelf. Moreover, during the 1920s and 1930s, trade book jackets were illustrated by taking a key sentence or word and rendering it verbatim as a monumental vignette in either a sentimentally realistic or fashionably stylized (art deco) manner. The lettering was usually done by hand in the *au courant* novelty style of the time. The sole purpose of the jacket was to attract and hook a reader (similar to the movie posters of the era). The pictorial representation often had little to do with the book's essence. Even the classics sometimes acquired contemporary imagery and design motifs in order to eschew any hint of mustiness. It might have been false advertising, but the disparity between the author's intent and the artist's interpretation was accepted for marketing reasons. "This technique of allegory," wrote historian Stephen Greengard in *The Journal of Decorative and Propaganda Art* (No. 7, Winter 1988), "does not require the artist to read the book itself, merely to distill from its pages a high impact visual which may be apprehended at a single glance."

"It seems ironic," wrote Greengard, "so many great, important ideas, the products of the finest minds of humanity, [were] wrapped in pieces of whimsical, brilliantly colored paper." During the 1920s and 1930s, in addition to providing protection, promotion, and genre identification, the design of book jackets made a variety of fiction and nonfiction books appealing and accessible to broad audiences. The old saying "you can't tell a book by its cover," is usually true, but the cover piqued interest. In some cases the cover was the best part of the book.

Common wisdom holds that a poster must lure the eye from a distance of five city blocks (or a quarter of a mile) away and build to a visual crescendo at five feet. This means that a successful poster must not only function in its original size, but also, given the prescribed distance, at the size of a postage stamp.

Between the turn of the century and the late 1920s when the *Sachplakat,* or object poster (a German poster genre that employed minimal lettering and a simple image of a product), was at its peak, the most effective posters were those that could be printed both enlarged and reduced without sacrificing any essential visual information. Lucian Bernhard was the master of this form. His stark, colorful images for Preister Matches, Adler Typewriters, and Osram Lightbulbs were equally suited for mammoth or Lilliputian reproduction. Hollerbaum and Schmidt, Bernhard's selling agent and printer, realized the business potential inherent in this versatile medium and began printing small, adhesive-backed poster stamps as a service to their advertising customers.

Sure, the term *poster stamp* is a contradiction. But semantics aside, what began as a means to earn greater printing revenues, became a popular and—like the poster itself— collectible method of increasing advertising exposure during an epoch when modern advertising was in its infancy. Poster stamps were affixed to all manner of things where posters would not fit. Ultimately the genre became a thriving international industry with thousands of original designs and miniaturized reprises produced annually.

A wide range of products and messages were advertised on these tiny perforated manifestoes.

Insurance agencies, hotels, electric companies, banks, tobacco, food, clothing, and manufacturing companies were among the most prolific users. The aesthetic quality was surprisingly high because many stamps began as larger posters or point-of-purchase displays, and quite a few were designed by well-known artists. But there was another interesting quality: at this scale even the most clichéd image was curiously transformed into a striking miniature. Even trite ideas were made new in this form.

English, French, German, Austrian, and American stamps from between 1910 and 1930 are fragments of commercial history that chronicle as effectively as any official commemorative stamp the burgeoning of free trade and market capitalism. Stamps for light bulbs, lamps, and appliances, for instance, reveal the unrelenting push by industry for electrification of the private home. Stamps for automobiles prefigure the huge budgets later expended on major advertising campaigns.

However, owing to strict postal regulations that legislated what was allowed on mailing envelopes and the rise in high-visibility advertising outlets, by the late 1930s the production of commercial advertising stamps was virtually abandoned. In the postwar years junk mail replaced the advertising stamp as the favored means of invading the consumer's privacy and consciousness. Given the poor quality of these pesky missives, the Lilliputian poster stamps re-emerge from the attic of advertising history as infinitely more appealing.

Atoms for Peace

ERIK NITSCHE

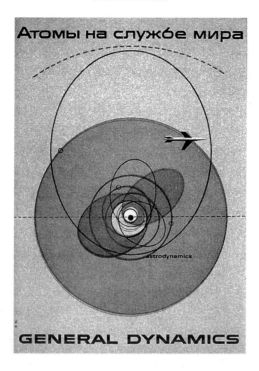

Атомы на служ6е мира

astrodynamics

GENERAL DYNAMICS

Geneneral Dynamics was one of the wellsprings
of design innovation. Formed in 1953 as the parent for a number of manufacturing firms that
catered to the defense needs of the United States, General Dynamics' products included atomic-
powered submarines, electric motors for ships, the B-58 supersonic jet bomber, and the
commercial 880 jet transport. It also sponsored research in electronics, astronautics, aero-
dynamics, hydrodynamics, and nuclear physics. In the mid 1950s nuclear energy was thought to
herald the new age, and General Dynamics' president, John Jay Hopkins, believed that his
company should be positioned in the public's mind as a purveyor of peace. General Dynamics
would benefit all mankind through its scientific research, and communicating this message was
one of the president's primary goals.

Hopkins understood that a skilled graphic designer could successfully forge and promote
General Dynamics' image, and so hired Erik Nitsche (b. 1908), a Swiss who had been working
freelance in the United States since the 1930s, away from the ad agency that originally had the
General Dynamics account. Working from his own studio in New York, Nitsche had been
responsible for some early ads and promotional materials that wed abstract imagery to functional
typography, which gave General Dynamics its progressive image. Hopkins gave Nitsche complete
freedom to build a total graphic identity from scratch. He served as art director between 1955 and
1960 and his identity program—which included posters, advertisements, and annual reports—
was a unique mix of modernism and individualism.

In the spring of 1955 Nitsche was given the first major assignment to design an exhibit that would have far-reaching implications for the company. General Dynamics had agreed to attend the International Conference on the Peaceful Uses of Atomic Energy in Geneva, Switzerland, in August of that year. Hopkins wanted a display that would stand apart from the other mammoth technology firms, including General Electric, Union Carbide, and Westinghouse. As builders of the *Nautilus*, the first atomic submarine, and with contracts to produce the first atomic-powered airplane, General Dynamics had the perfect showpieces. Yet they had nothing to show. The *Nautilus* design was so top secret that Nitsche was only given a vague description of its ultimate design. In the absence of an actual product he had to devise a symbol. Pursuing the idea of "Atoms for Peace" he used graphics to convey the message.

Framing the exhibit, the initial corporate clarion was a series of six multilingual posters with either abstract or symbolic images—in English, Russian, German, French, Hindi, and Japanese—designed specifically for those nations where atomic energy was being used for peaceful purposes. Strongly influenced by Paul Klee since childhood, Nitsche turned to geometric forms and intersecting color planes to symbolize this new energy source. But the principle icon for the most memorable poster was not like Klee at all, but rather a painting of a huge nautilus shell from which shot out a sleek submarine. The *Nautilus*, named after Jules Verne's fictional vessel in *Twenty Thousand Leagues Under the Sea*, was not presented as a missile of war, but as a missive of peace. On some of the posters a text from Isaiah read: "They shall beat swords into plowshares, and their spears into pruning hooks: nation shall not lift up sword against nation, neither shall they learn war anymore." Isaiah's testament was, of course, dramatic, yet ironic in light of the ship's prime mission as a defensive weapon (preserving the peace).

The poster campaign was well received and Nitsche was commissioned to produce what amounted to three different series of twenty-four images. Hopkins wanted to acquaint the public "with the spirit of discovery that motivates the corporation's diverse developments." And so Nitsche's work soon influenced General Dynamics' total corporate style, including the otherwise staid annual reports, which he turned into kinetic displays of visual imagery. Nitsche's crowning achievement, however, was the design of a mammoth book of corporate history entitled *Dynamic America*. With its tip-ins and foldouts *Dynamic America* was an exhibition between boards, a fast paced visual document of the nation's military and industrial history that intersected with the development of General Dynamics Company from its roots in 1880 as Electro Dynamic.

Nitsche's book design was a lesson in economy. Never a superfluous or decorative image, he favored dynamic silhouettes and vignettes of historical artifacts, giving the book a didactic quality. Nitsche somehow knew how to make historical engravings and paintings appear timeless. His typography was clean and crisp, a marriage of classical and modern approaches. A progenitor of information design, he virtually invented the modern time line giving the reader textual and visual information in parallel strips. He further focused on key pieces of visual information through frequent scale changes and juxtapositions. The amazing thing about this book is that if the type were removed it would reveal a perfect visual narrative.

Wolfschmidt

GEORGE LOIS

$\mathcal{G}$eorge Lois (b. 1931), the agent provocateur of advertising's Creative Revolution of the 1960s, didn't force vodka down America's throat, but from 1960 to 1963 he put Wolfschmidt on everyone's lips. The breakthrough ad campaign, which he conceived and art directed, featured a Wolfschmidt bottle bantering with fruits and vegetables. It changed consumers' perceptions and raised the sales of a lackluster brand. Lois had served up the perfect mix of humor with a wit chaser.

Advertising was serious business back in the 1950s. Despite trailblazing ads by Paul Rand in the 1940s and Helmut Krone's VW campaign starting in the late 1950s, real wit was about as common in national ad campaigns as sophisticated typography (which was pretty scarce). Goofy cartoons and comic strips were routinely used, but the humor was usually corny or slapstick. In addition, the design of most ads was dreadful. Liquor advertising was even more dour than most, mainly because tried-and-true conventions were slavishly followed—such as showing a bottle and shot glass set against pictures of men drinking with business associates. By the early 1960s the ubiquitous cocktail party scene appeared and women were added, but they never held drinks.

Anyway, there is nothing inherently funny about liquor. In the 1950s consumers remained loyal to a particular brand either because of perceived prestige or because their cronies preferred it. In liquor advertising a vintage whiskey, its bottle labeled with the heraldic marks of a venerable distillery, had more appeal than some rotgut without heritage. And since it was inappropriate to show guzzlers in advertisements, the bottle became the emblem of consumer allegiance. Even when so-called image advertising did not offer enough of a competitive edge—when, for instance, flavor was emphasized in the copy instead—the bottle icon was always prominent. The goal of all liquor advertising was to get the consumer to identify with the label and, therefore, order the brand by name.

Advertising conventions were ostensibly the same for vodka and the darker liquors, but there was one essential difference: vodka has very little taste. So the advertising challenge was how to distinguish one flavorless drink from another. The solution boiled down to concept, which was also the key distinction between conventional and Creative Revolution advertisements. The latter introduced the so-called Big Idea, which dispelled the notion that advertising was simply hucksterism. The new theory went that advertising was best when it was also entertaining. And one of the earliest campaigns to prove this hypothesis was created in the mid 1950s for Smirnoff vodka, which on the strength of its creative advertising owned seventy percent of the market for almost a decade, far surpassing Wolfschmidt's meager eight to ten percent share.

Smirnoff's clever catch-line "Leaves You Breathless" signaled that it was okay for noontime drinkers to guiltlessly imbibe. Smirnoff vodka, unlike scotch and gin, which caused tell-tale whiskey breath, was touted as tasteless and, therefore, undetectable. Sales soared on the strength of the claim alone, but to further get the message across, the advertising employed smartly elegant, conceptual photography by Irving Penn and Ben Somoroff, who photographed the campaign at different times. Each typically shot against white seamless, adding a modern aura, in which both celebrities and fantasy characters—including Marcel Marceau in one ad and a Minotaur in another—enticed the reader to stop, look, and read the minimal copy below. The requisite Smirnoff bottle was, however, reduced and placed unobtrusively next to the text as a mnemonic device.

Smirnoff's advertising went unsurpassed for many years. Despite the campaign's success, other leading distillers remained conservative in their own advertising. Joseph E. Seagram & Sons, Inc., one of America's foremost distilleries, was resigned to the fact that their own brand, Wolfschmidt vodka, would forever trail behind. But in 1960 Samuel Bronfman, Seagrams' hard-nosed founder and chief executive, turned the failing brand over to his twenty-eight-year-old son, Edgar, as a test of his ability—or one might say, a rite of passage. The younger Bronfman was left on his own to sink or swim. But as fate would have it, he met George Lois, a twenty-eight-year-old former Doyle Dane and Bernbach art director who, confidently, had just opened his own agency, Papert Koenig Lois (Julian Koenig was the writer on the team that conceived the Volkswagen "Think Small" campaign) in the Seagrams building on Park Avenue in New York.

When Bronfman approached him, Lois (with Koenig) had just developed the Allerest brand name and print advertising campaign for Pharmacraft Laboratories, which was partially owned by the Bronfman family, and was hungrily looking for a new project with which to launch his agency and reputation. "It hit me like a shot," Lois recalled, "Smirnoff said it had no taste, so I simply said Wolfschmidt did have taste. Smirnoff's was aimed at the lunch crowd, I aimed Wolfschmidt at the party crowd."

Lois boasted that in one day he devised the entire campaign. He paired a life-size

Wolfschmidt bottle (to both satisfy and satirize conventional wisdom) with an assortment of fruits and vegetables—oranges, tomatoes, celery, etc.—in comic banter. The first ad, however, was a photograph of a bunch of indistinguishable shot glasses with a headline that asked which one was the Wolfschmidt? The answer was "the one with taste," of course. But the now famous second ad that really launched the campaign showed a bottle saying to a ripe tomato, "You're some tomato. . . . We could make a difference. . . ." in a kind of playboy cadence that might seem sexist today but by early 1960s standards was racy, erotic, and unheard of in national advertising. The ad premiered in *Life* magazine and subsequently in other key outlets. And just one week later a third ad was released with the bottle saying: "You sweet doll, I appreciate you. I've got taste. I'll bring out the real orange in you. I'll make you famous. Kiss me." And the orange responded: "Who was that tomato I saw you with last week?" This was the first time that an ad referred back to a previous ad, and it set the serial tone for all future ads. "It was an underground thing to do," continued Lois. "It couldn't be more direct, but it had real style."

The Wolfschmidt campaign was also what Lois called "a purist piece of design." It was not only minimalist layout and typography in the modern tradition, but also, and at the time more importantly, it was storyboarded entirely by Lois himself, which was unheard of in advertising circles. Before the Creative Revolution took hold in the mid 1950s most advertising—with the exception of Paul Rand's work at Weintraub Agency throughout 1940s—was devised by copywriters, who gave precise roughs to art directors, who then supervised the final sketches. Even in the early years of the Creative Revolution, when copywriters and art directors worked more or less together, ads were roughed out by art directors and then precisely painted or comped by bullpen sketch artists. Clients were used to seeing finished paintings. But in one fell swoop Lois changed all that by doing the entire presentation on his own, from sketches to comp. The brash young Lois also broke another taboo: he sold his ideas directly to the client without going through an account executive.

Yet history would be different if young Bronfman had showed his father the first couple of ads before they ran. Lois thinks that "old Sam" probably would have balked or killed them entirely. Luckily, the action in the stores was immediate. "They tickled people," he said. "They were talked about at parties." And since orders came rolling in, the elder Bronfman allowed the rest of the campaign to proceed, even though, according to Lois, "Massa Sam never laughed." In fact, Lois recalled when showing him an ad in the series headlined "Taste my screwdriver" he seemed stunned. "For California," Lois explained.

Decades before Absolut ruled vodka, Wolfschmidt absolutely owned the market. This was not only a testament to the power of smart advertising, it was one hundred percent proof that wit and humor could capture market share. Ultimately, even conservative distilleries began using humor in their ads. Lois notes that the first woman appeared in a primary role in a 1961 Ronrico Rum ad. It featured an eighty-one-year-old "Aunt Agatha," holding a glass of the liquor. "It was a very funny concept," he recalled, "but got the Daughters of the American Revolution up in arms."

The Wolfschmidt campaign continued for three years and included ten different print ads and a couple of posters. However, it abruptly ended, according to Lois, in a dispute when Edgar Bronfman acquired a handful more Seagram brands and did not award any of the new accounts to Papert Koenig Lois. Julian Koenig was furious and summarily pulled the agency off the Wolfschmidt account. It was the end of that relationship, but Lois left behind a remarkable legacy that set the standard, not only for a genre of liquor advertising practiced today, but for helping to inaugurate a period in advertising history when wit and humor were the state of the art.

NYNEX

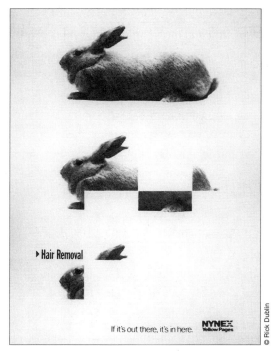

▸ Hair Removal

If it's out there, it's in here.   **NYNEX** Yellow Pages

© Rick Dublin

The average infantry soldier's life expectancy is twelve seconds on a battlefield. New York City's streets might not be as dangerous as a battlefield, but the average life of an advertising poster is certainly comparable. Bills illegally posted on construction scaffolding are routinely defaced within hours. Postings on legal hoardings fare only slightly better; few remain unscathed until the end of their official display periods. This limited life expectancy demands that advertisers often think like military strategists; they must hold as many key positions as possible, accept massive casualties, and reinforce when needed. For a campaign to succeed it must totally capture the hearts, minds, and discretionary income of consumers.

Street posters continue to be the first wave in advertising campaigns for such industries as entertainment, clothing, and consumables. An intensive saturation campaign can be extremely effective in piquing the interest of an often jaded urban public. But what has made the war for consumers and against the vandals and the citigoths a bit easier to win are the protected bus shelters with illuminated display capabilities that have been on New York's streets for nearly two decades. This kind of shelter was developed in Paris decades ago, but until its introduction to New York in the late 1970s, street advertising was limited to large exposed billboards and illegal hoardings. Today more than three thousand shelters throughout New York provide a relatively secure space for more than six thousand posters. And six thousand illuminated posters have had a decisive impact not only on the public's consciousness, but also on advertising designers, as well.

Bus shelters have given certain advertising agencies the impetus to counter mediocre mass-market poster concepts and therefore alter standards. During the past several years shelters have also contributed to a resurgence in the time honored "tease-and-reveal" posters—an image that runs without words for two weeks and then with words for another two, or more. The most innovative example from this renaissance has been NYNEX's 1995 series for the New York Yellow Pages Business Directory, created by Chait/Day/Mojo and based on various riddle/puns of arcane Yellow Page entries.

The fulcrum of this year-long campaign was a series of quirky photographs, such as one of a blue rabbit and another of Barbie and Ken wearing nurse and doctor outfits, originally posted without text (not even the NYNEX logo), then replaced by another poster with the same image and also a caption and the slogan, "If it's out there, it's in here: NYNEX." The caption was a painfully forced pun. For example, the blue hare illustrated "Hair Coloring" and the nurse Barbie and doctor Ken illustrated "Plastic Surgeons."

The degree to which the pun strained was actually the mark of its success. The initial posting of the first billboard displayed a huge blue rabbit in repose; the second posting showed rectangular portions of the same rabbit missing; and the final posting showed all but a small portion of the rabbit's head and ears with the title "Hair Removal." The print campaign, which also appeared as television commercials directed by Godley and Creme, ran in bimonthly cycles with six different concepts presented throughout the year, offering the public a titillating game of wits.

NYNEX's campaign, which echoed the Big Idea advertising concepts of the 1960s was built on a simple premise: when smartly applied, even dumb humor has incalculable appeal, and the more esoteric the better. Although the sport of deducing the riddle could easily have backfired by overwhelming the message itself, the year-long barrage of ubiquitous posters and commercials gave the NYNEX Yellow Pages total recognition among consumers.

The graphic design in this series was transparent. Like masterful serial ads that came before it—Levy's Jewish Rye Bread and Volkswagen—the NYNEX campaign was photographed and filmed for TV against white seamless. The idea was the only focal point. The single line of sans-serif typography echoed a heading in the Yellow Pages and was effectively balanced with the NYNEX logo. The campaign totally dominated the New York streetscape, but its handlers knew when to stop. As delightful and provocative as it was, it ceased before it became trite.

Bibliography

Ades, Dawn. *Photomontage*. London: Thames and Hudson, 1986.

Aldersey-Williams, Hugh. *New American Design*. New York: Rizzoli, 1988.

Anderson, Charles Spencer. *CSA Archive Catalog of Stock Art*. CSA Archive, 1995.

Barron, Stephanie, and Maurice Tuchman, eds. *The Avant-Garde in Russia 1910–1930*. Cambridge and London: The MIT Press, 1980.

Beirut, Michael, William Drenttel, Steven Heller, and DK Holland, eds. *Looking Closer: Critical Writings on Graphic Design*. New York: Allworth Press, 1994.

———. *Looking Closer 2: Critical Writings on Graphic Design*. New York: Allworth Press, 1997.

Berger, John. *Ways of Seeing*. New York: Vintage International, 1985.

Blackwell, Lewis. *20th Century Type*. New York: Rizzoli, 1992.

Blackwell, Lewis, and David Carson. *The End of Print*. San Francisco: Chronicle Books, 1995.

Blauvelt, Andrew. "Desperately Seeking David." *Emigre* #38. 1996.

Broos, Kees, and Paul Hefting. *Dutch Graphic Design: A Century*. Cambridge: The MIT Press, 1993.

Buchanan, Richard and Victor Margolin, eds. *Discovering Design*. Chicago and London: The University of Chicago Press, 1995.

Buchanan, Richard, and Victor Margolin, eds. *The Idea of Design*. Cambridge and London: The MIT Press, 1995.

Burdick, Anne. "Decoding the Monster." *Emigre* #23. 1992.

Celant, Germano, Mildred Constantine, David Revere McFadden, and Joseph Rykwert. *Design: Vignelli*. New York: Rizzoli, 1990.

Chermayeff, Ivan. "Designing in Tongues: What's so Universal about the Visual Language?" *AIGA Journal of Graphic Design*, Vol. 12, No. 2. 1994.

Chwast, Seymour, and Steven Heller, eds. *The Left-Handed Designer*. New York: Harry N. Abrams, 1985.

Cohen, Barbara, Seymour Chwast, and Steven Heller. *Trylon and Perisphere: The 1939 New York World's Fair.* New York: Harry N. Abrams Inc., 1989.

The Book of Oz Cooper. Chicago: The Society of Typographic Arts, 1949.

Cranbrook Design: The New Discourse. New York: Rizzoli International, 1990.

Cullen, Moira. "Tibor Kalman." *Eye*, No. 20, Vol. 5. 1996.

Dooley, Michael. "Defending Joe Camel, Sort of." *Print* L:IV. 1996.

Doordan, Dennis P., ed. *Design History: An Anthology.* Cambridge and London: The MIT Press, 1995.

Ewen, Stuart. *All Consuming Images.* New York: Basic Books, 1988.

Freeman, Judi. *The Dada and Surrealist Word-Image.* Cambridge and London: The MIT Press, 1989.

Friedman, Mildred, ed. *Graphic Design in America: A Visual Language History.* Minneapolis and New York: The Walker Art Center and Harry N. Abrams, 1989.

Glaser, Milton. *Milton Glaser Graphic Design.* Woodstock, New York: The Overlook Press, 1973.

Glauber, Barbara, ed. *Lift and Separate: Graphic Design and the Vernacular.* New York: The Herb Lubalin Study Center of Design and Typography, 1993.

Gottschall, Edward M. *Typographic Communications Today.* Cambridge, Massachusetts, London, England: The MIT Press, 1989.

Greiman, April. *Design Quarterly #133.* Cambridge, Massachusetts, London, England: MIT Press for Walker Art Center, 1986.

———. *Hybrid Imagery.* New York: Watson-Guptill, 1990.

———. "Information Texture." *Octavo* 86.1 1986.

Heller, Steven, and Anne Fink. *Covers and Jackets.* Glen Cove, New York: PBC International Inc., 1993.

Heller, Steven, and Julie Lasky. *Borrowed Design: The Use and Abuse of Historical Form.* New York: Van Nostrand Reinhold, 1993.

Heller, Steven, and Karen Pomeroy. *Designing with Illustration.* New York: Van Nostrand Reinhold, 1990.

Heller, Steven. *Innovators of American Illustration.* New York: Van Nostrand Reinhold, 1986.

———. "Alex Steinweiss: For the Record." *Print* XLVI:II, 1992.

———. "Dr. Leslie's Type Clinic." *Eye*, No. 15, Vol. 4. 1994.

Heller, Steven, and Barbara Kruger. "Smashing the Myths." *AIGA Journal of Graphic Design*, Vol. 9, No. 1. 1991.

Heller, Steven. "Alvin Lustig: Born Modern." *Eye*, No. 10, Vol. 3. 1993.

———. "Big Ideas that Built American Art Direction." *Eye*, No. 22, Vol. 6. 1996.

———. "Oz Cooper: Telling and Selling." *Eye*, No. 7, Vol 2. 1992.

———. "Sutnar." *Eye*, No. 13, Vol. 4. 1994.

———. "Mapbacks: High End of a Low Art." *Print* XLVIII:III. 1994.

———. "Street Theater" *Print* L:III. 1996.

———. "Commercial Modern: American Design Style 1925–1933." *Print* XLIX:V. 1995.

———. "*Life*: Magazine of the Century." *Print* XLVII:III. New York. 1994.

Heller, Steven, and Gail Anderson. *American Typeplay.* New York: PBC International, Inc. 1994.

Heller, Steven, and Seymour Chwast. *Graphic Style: From Victorian to Postmodern.* New York: Harry N. Abrams, Inc. 1988.

Henrion, F. H. K. *Top Graphic Design.* Zurich: ABC Verlag, 1983.

Hollis, Richard. *Graphic Design: A Concise History.* London: Thames and Hudson, 1994.

Homans, Katy. "B. J. Robert Brownjohn: The Ultimate Conceptualist Reassessed." *Eye*, No. 4, Vol 1. 1991.

Jacobs, Karrie. "Barbara Kruger." *Eye*, No. 5, Vol. 2. 1991.

Julier, Guy. *The Thames and Hudson Encyclopaedia of 20th Century Design and Designers.* London: Thames and Hudson, 1993.

E. McKnight Kauffer. New York: The Museum of Modern Art, 1937.

Kazanjian, Dodie and Calvin Tompkins. *Alex: The Life of Alexander Liberman.* New York: Alfred A. Knopf, 1995.

Kinross, Robin. *Modern Typography: An Essay in Critical History.* London: Hyphen Press, 1992.

Kornatzki, Peter Von. "Wolfgang Weingart, A Typographic Rebel," *Graphis*, October 1983.

Kruger, Barbara. *Remote Control*. Cambridge and London: The MIT Press, 1993.

Kruger, Barbara, and Kate Linker. *Love for Sale: The Words and Pictures of Barbara Kruger*. New York: Harry N. Abrams, 1990.

Labuz, Ronald. *Contemporary Graphic Design*. New York: Van Nostrand Reinhold, 1991.

Lawson, Alexander. *Printing Types: An Introduction*. Beacon Press, 1971.

Lears, Jackson. *Fables of Abundance*. New York: Basic Books, 1994.

Livingston, Alan and Isabella. *Dictionary of Graphic Design and Designers*. London: Thames and Hudson, 1992.

Lupton, Ellen. *Mixing Messages*. New York: Princeton Architectural Press, 1996.

———. "The Academy of Deconstructed Design." *Eye*, No. 3, Vol. 1. 1991.

———. "American Dutch/Dutch American: Hands Across the Zee." *Print* XLV:VI. 1991.

Lupton, Ellen, and J. Abbott Miller. "Deconstruction and Graphic Design: History Meets Theory." *Visible Language* 28.4. 1994.

Marchand, Roland. *Advertising the American Dream: Making Way for Modernity 1920–1940*. University of California Press, 1985.

Margolin, Victor, ed. *Design Discourse*. Chicago and London: University of Chicago Press, 1989.

——— "Massimo Vignelli vs. Ed Benguiat." *Print* XLV:V. 1991.

McCoy, Katherine. "American Graphic Design Expression." *Design Quarterly #148*. 1990.

———. "The Evolution of American Typography." *Design Quarterly #148*. Walker Art Center and The MIT Press, 1990.

Meggs, Phil. *A History of Graphic Design*. (Second Edition). New York: Van Nostrand Reinhold, 1992.

———. *Type and Image*. New York: Van Nostrand Reinhold, 1989.

Miller, Abbott J. "Quentin Fiore: Massaging the Message." *Eye*, No. 8, Vol. 2. 1993.

Nöth, Winifred. *Handbook of Semiotics*. Bloomington and Indianapolis: Indiana University Press, 1990.

Pachnicke, Peter, and Klaus Honnef, eds. *John Heartfield*. New York: Harry N. Abrams, Inc., 1992.

Poynor, Rick, and Edward Booth Clibborn. *Typography Now: The Next Wave*. Cincinnati, Ohio: F & W Publications, 1992.

Poynor, Rick. *The Graphic Edge*. London: Booth-Clibborn Editions, 1993.

———. "Pierre Bernard." *Eye*, No. 3, Vol. 1. 1991.

———. "Jon Barnbrook." *Eye*, No. 15, Vol. 4. 1994.

———. "American Gothic." *Eye*, No. 2, Vol. 2. 1992.

———. "Remove Specific and Convert to Ambiguities." *Eye*, No. 20, Vol. 5. 1996.

———. "David Carson Revealed." *I.D.*, November 1995.

———. "Katherine McCoy." *Eye*, No. 16, Vol 4. 1995.

———. "Neville Brody Faces the Future." *I.D.*, September/October 1992.

———. "Neville Brody." *Eye*, No. 6, Vol. 2. 1992.

Rand, Paul. *Paul Rand: A Designer's Art*. New Haven and London: Yale University Press, 1985.

Rea, Peter. "Dan Friedman." *Eye*, No. 14, Vol. 4. 1994.

Remington, R. Roger, and Barbara J. Hodik. *Nine Pioneers in American Graphic Design*. Cambridge and London: The MIT Press, 1989.

Rock, Michael. "Fuse: Beyond Typography." *Eye*, No. 15, Vol. 4. 1994.

Schreuders, Piet. *Paperbacks, U.S.A.: A Graphic History, 1939–1959*. Blue Dolphin Enterprises, 1981.

Schwemer-Scheddin, Yvonne. "Interview with Wolfgang Weingart." *Eye* No.4 Vol. 1. London, 1991.

Scotford, Martha. "Cipe Pineles: The Tenth Pioneer." *Eye*, No. 18, Vol. 5. 1995.

Scott, Douglass. "Bradbury Thompson, Designer and Teacher." *Print* L:III. 1996.

Shapiro, Ellen. "No More War." *Print* L:IV. 1996.

Smith, Terry. *Making the Modern: Industry, Art, and Design in America*. Chicago: University of Chicago Press, 1993.

Snyder, Gertrude, and Alan Peckolick. *Herb Lubalin: Art Director, Graphic Designer and Typographer*. New York: American Showcase Inc., 1985.

Spencer, Herbert, ed. *The Liberated Page.* San Francisco: Bedford Press, 1987.

Stermer, Dugald. "Louise Fili." *Communication Arts,* September/October 1986.

Tufte, Edward R. *Envisioning Information.* Connecticut: Graphics Press, 1990.

Varnedoe, Kirk, and Adam Gopnik. *High and Low: Modern Art Popular Culture.* New York: The Museum of Modern Art, 1990.

Thompson, Bradbury. *Bradbury Thompson: The Art of Graphic Design.* New Haven and London: Yale University Press, 1988.

Thrift, Julia. "Rudy VanderLans." *Eye,* No. 7, Vol 2. 1992.

VanderLans, Rudy. "Second Wind." *Emigre* #24. 1992.

———. "A Telephone Conversation between Rudy VanderLans and David Carson. *Emigre* #27. 1993.

VanderLans, Rudy, and Zuzana Licko with Mary E. Gray. *Emigre: Graphic Design into the Digital Realm.* New York: Van Nostrand Reinhold, 1993.

Weingart, Wolfgang "How Can One Make Swiss Typography? Theoretical and practical typographic results from the teaching period 1968–1973 at the School of Design, Basel." *Octavo 87.4. An International journal of typography.* London: 1987.

———. "Graphic Design in Switzerland." *Emigre* #14. 1990.

Whitford, Frank, ed. *The Bauhaus: Masters & Students by Themselves.* Woodstock, New York: The Overlook Press, 1993.

Wozencroft, Jon. *The Graphic Language of Neville Brody.* New York: Rizzoli, 1988.

Wye, Deborah. *Thinking Print.* New York: The Museum of Modern Art, 1996.

Index

Books from Allworth Press

Looking Closer 2: Critical Writings on Graphic Design
edited by Michael Bierut, William Drenttel, Steven Heller, DK Holland
(softcover, 6¾ × 10, 282 pages, $18.95)

Looking Closer: Critical Writings on Graphic Design
edited by Michael Bierut, William Drenttel, Steven Heller, DK Holland
(softcover, 6¾ × 10, 256 pages, $18.95)

Design Culture: An Anthology of Writing from the AIGA Journal of Graphic Design
edited by Steven Heller and Marie Finamore (softcover, 6¾ × 10, 256 pages, $19.95)

AIGA Professional Practices in Graphic Design
by The American Institute of Graphic Arts (softcover, 6¾ × 10, 320 pages, $24.95)

The New Business of Design
by the International Conference in Aspen (softcover, 6 × 9, 256 pages, $19.95)

Careers by Design: A Headhunter's Secrets for Success and Survival in Graphic Design
Revised Edition by Roz Goldfarb (softcover, 6¾ × 10, 256 pages, $18.95)

Selling Graphic Design
by Don Sparkman (softcover, 6 × 9, 224 pages, $18.95)

Business and Legal Forms for Graphic Designers
Revised Edition by Tad Crawford (softcover, 8½ × 11, 208 pages, $22.95)

The Copyright Guide
by Lee Wilson (softcover, 6 × 9, 192 pages, $18.95)

Electronic Design and Publishing: Business Practices
Second Edition by Liane Sebastian (softcover, 6¾ × 10, 200 pages, $19.95)

The Business of Multimedia
by Nina Schuyler (softcover, 6 × 9, 240 pages, $19.95)

Lectures on Art
by John Ruskin (softcover, 6 × 9, 224 pages, $18.95)

Please write to request our free catalog. If you wish to order a book, send your check or money order to Allworth Press, 10 East 23rd Street, Suite 400, New York, NY 10010. Include $5 for shipping and handling for the first book ordered and $1 for each additional book. Ten dollars plus $1 for each additional book if ordering from Canada. New York State residents must add sales tax.

If you wish to see our catalog on the World Wide Web, you can find us at:
http://www.arts-online.com/allworth/home.html or at **http://www.allworth.com**